Dear Andrea,
I am so proud of you and the hard work you've done here. Keep on choosing healing! One day at a time! Stay true to who you are. You are Amazing!
Blessings—
France

Happy
for the
Rest of Your Life

Dear Andrea,
So glad to have gotten the chance to know you. You have a strong spirit that I know will carry you far! Wishing you many blessings in 2018!
Dr. Ogawa

Andrea,
You have so many gifts. Being strong is one of them that I believe you will grow into even more, as time progresses. Continue to do the hard work and give yourself what you need. Keep rocking those "rain boots"
Lynsey

Andrea —
It was a pleasure
supporting you,
and encouraging
you on your journey.
Keep seeking the
truth and that
choices that
strengthen you!
There is hope
and a future!
Kristen :)

Happy
for the
Rest of Your Life

Gregory L. Jantz, PhD
with Ann McMurray

Andrea - you are delightful in every possible way.
Keep growing and learning more things.
you are valuable in every way possible.

"Neither Height nor ~~god~~ Depth nor
anything else, in all creation will be able
to seperate us from the love of God that is
in Christ Jesus
our lord

SILOAM
A STRANG COMPANY

Romans 8:39
— Victoria (front desk staff.)

Most STRANG COMMUNICATIONS/CHARISMA HOUSE/CHRISTIAN LIFE/EXCEL BOOKS/ FRONTLINE/REALMS/SILOAM products are available at special quantity discounts for bulk purchase for sales promotions, premiums, fund-raising, and educational needs. For details, write Strang Communications Book Group, 600 Rinehart Road, Lake Mary, Florida 32746, or telephone (407) 333-0600.

HAPPY FOR THE REST OF YOUR LIFE by Gregory L. Jantz, PhD, with Ann McMurray
Published by Siloam
A Strang Company
600 Rinehart Road
Lake Mary, Florida 32746
www.strangdirect.com

Unless otherwise noted, all Scripture quotations are from the Holy Bible, New International Version of the Bible. Copyright © 1973, 1978, 1984, International Bible Society. Used by permission.

Scripture quotations marked THE MESSAGE are from *The Message: The Bible in Contemporary English*, copyright © 1993, 1994, 1995, 1996, 2000, 2001, 2002. Used by permission of NavPress Publishing Group.

Scripture quotations marked NAS are from the New American Standard Bible. Copyright © 1960, 1962, 1963, 1968, 1971, 1972, 1973, 1975, 1977 by the Lockman Foundation. Used by permission. (www.Lockman.org)

Design Director: Bill Johnson
Cover design by Judith Wright

Library of Congress Cataloging-in-Publication Data:
Jantz, Gregory L.
  Happy for the rest of your life / Gregory L. Jantz. -- 1st ed.
      p. cm.
  Includes bibliographical references.
  ISBN 978-1-59979-394-8
  1. Happiness--Religious aspects--Christianity. 2. Emotions--Religious aspects--Christianity. I. Title.
  BV4647.J68J36 2009
  248.4--dc22

                              2008043092

First Edition

09 10 11 12 13 — 987654321
Printed in the United States of America

Contents

Acknowledgments

I AM BLESSED TO HAVE TEAMED UP FOR THIS HAPPINESS BOOK WITH someone who is truly an example of living a happy life. For many years now I have had the privilege of working with Ann McMurray on books that carry our organization's theme: helping people change their lives for good with God. Thank you for being a Christlike model of happiness, Ann.

To the reader I dedicate the words in this book to minister hope, healing, encouragement, and joy. May you experience a new measure of happiness from our eternal source of happiness, the love of our Creator.

Andrea,
Although we didn't work together, it was a pleasure having you in lunches. You are kind & sweet. Let your light shine! Best of luck.
Dr. Harding

Dear Andrea,
It has been an honor to be working with you! Keep on choosing healing!
Blessings —
France

Andrea —
Blessings to you as you continue your journey.
♥ Kimmy

ON THE ROAD TRIP TO HAPPINESS, BE CAREFUL WHO YOU ASK FOR DIRECTIONS

WELCOME TO THIS BOOK, *HAPPY FOR THE REST OF Your Life*. Before you start, I'll admit, to some of you, the title might seem a little presumptuous. *(Happiness for life? Right! Who would presume to promise something like that? Especially in this world!)* OK, maybe the title is somewhat presumptuous, but it's intriguing also, isn't it? *(Happiness for life—is that really possible? And is that happiness for all of life or just parts of it? What does he mean by happiness? Gaiety? Giddiness? Contentment? Cheerfulness? Glee? Delight? Those aren't words I normally associate with my life!)* So, presumptuous—a little. Intriguing—mildly, at least enough to pique your interest for you to have picked up the book.

After all, regardless of how you feel about the title, doesn't everyone want to be happy for life? While there may be one or two hiding out somewhere, reveling in despair, most people want to be happy. Deep down they may not think it's possible for them, but it's still a deep-seated desire. A sort of wishful thinking, someday, maybe, if-only kind of desire. So, some of you may feel *Happy for the Rest of Your Life* is a bit presumptuous as a title for a book; others may feel *Happy for the Rest of Your Life*, as a concept, is a bit presumptuous for your own life. If that's you, I'm glad you're joining me on this road trip and would ask you to stick with me just a little while longer.

A Road Trip to Happiness

The *happiness* in the title isn't just some sort of generic happiness for some unnamed person's life; it's meant for you, today, in your own life, right in the midst of whatever circumstances you find yourself in. Over the course of the next so many pages and throughout however long it takes you to get through this book, you're going to take a trip, a road trip to happiness. Of course, this trip isn't literal; it's figurative, but still accurate. Along the way, you and I are going to get to know each other very well. I'm going to let you know about my life and me, and you're going to spend some time really thinking about your own life. There'll probably be times when the two of us won't get along too well, and, on occasion, you may not like me or what I have to say. You may argue with me about who gets to be in the driver's seat and who gets to choose the station on the radio or what CD you listen to. On this road trip, you'll pass through parts of the text that may seem pretty mundane to you and other parts that will be so personal, you'll be looking over your shoulder, sure that I wrote it specifically with you in mind. Even with all that, you're going to take a trip to pursue—and find—the happiness in life that you're looking for.

Whoever said happiness was a pursuit wasn't kidding. (Because you still don't know me very well, yes, that statement was rhetorical. I know it was Thomas Jefferson who wrote about life, liberty, and the pursuit of happiness in the Declaration of Independence.) What was true back in 1776 still resonates today because, for many, happiness can appear to be an object of elusive pursuit. Always searching; never arriving. You always figured *someday* you'd be able to do enough or run fast enough to catch happiness, but someday hasn't arrived yet.

You've surveyed your surroundings, and, according to the world's happiness list, you should be ecstatic by now, with all you've been blessed with; but you're not. Now you're not only unhappy, but you feel guilty about it too.

You've tried just about everything you can think of to obtain happiness, but the only one really happy about all those efforts is your credit card company.

Jefferson said happiness was to be pursued, but in that famous document we're also told that life, liberty, and the pursuit of happiness are unalienable rights. So, happiness isn't just a pursuit; it's a right. If happiness is a right, how come so many people can't seem to get it right? If happiness is a right, then it should be yours for the taking, except you can't seem to find where it is. You search high and low, spend money you may or may not have, engage in all kinds of behaviors for good and ill, and still come up short in the happiness department. Happiness becomes a destination you're supposed to reach, but you never seem to get there. On the road trip to happiness, you seem to spend your life looking up into the heavens and wondering aloud that age-old road trip question: Are we there yet? You look around at your surroundings and the answer is, decidedly, no.

If Happiness Is a Destination, Who Has the Directions?

Do you remember in *The Wizard of Oz* when Dorothy realizes that her heart's desire was really no further than her own backyard? It was right there with her all along, only she didn't see it. Happiness is kind of the same way. You go looking for a Wizard of Oz to give you the secret to happiness when it's really no further than the Bible on your nightstand (or, in some cases, in your nightstand under the latest *PARADE* magazine from last Sunday and the two other books you've been meaning to read). Well, it's time to take that Bible out, dust it off, and jump in. There's no wizard here, just the Word. Using scriptural truths, you're going to journey down a road trip to happiness and discover:

- Misconceptions about what happiness is and where to find it

- How the detours and dead ends of depression, anxiety, worry, and addictions stop you

- How to rev up your whole-person engine

- Why God is really the author of "Don't Worry, Be Happy"

- How to make optimism, hope, and joy your constant companions on the road trip to happiness

At the end of this chapter, and every chapter, you'll find a section called "Rest Stop." I don't know about you, but I can only drive so far before I need to find a place to stop and pull over, get a cup of coffee, use the facilities, and stretch my legs. That's what you'll be doing, again figuratively, in this section, which will feature a series of thoughtful questions and activities, to help you solidify your understanding and engage you in personal reflection and positive action.

Oh, no! You're not more than a few pages into the book and you're already headed for a disagreement! For those of you who sigh and really don't think you want to answer a bunch of questions or, heaven forbid, actually *do* something except just read the pages, I'm going to ask you to withhold judgment for now. I can only tell you that in my personal and professional experience, when people actually take advantage of reflective and active sections like these, they gain insight, understanding, and comprehension so much more quickly. It's kind of like the difference between me telling you how to make lasagna and you actually doing it. (OK, maybe lasagna isn't the best analogy because it's kind of messy. But, then, so is life, so maybe it's not such a bad analogy after all.) There's just a vast difference between someone telling you how to do something and you actually rolling up your sleeves, diving in, getting messy, and doing it yourself. You learn it, experience it, and own it. Then, whatever you're doing becomes *yours*.

I guess that's what I'm really hoping for you to do with the material in this book—make it your own. Do the work, answer the questions, test-drive the concepts, engage the activities, and find out where they lead you. It is my prayer that you'll be led to a greater understanding of how happiness can be an authentic destination for you.

The Problem With Directions

Elusive as happiness might be, it is, nonetheless, still a very popular goal. The problem with pursuing happiness is that people are often misguided in their search for it.

Sometimes pursuing happiness is like getting the wrong directions to your destination. Maybe you've devoted a considerable amount of time trying to find it, thinking that happiness is just over that next hill, so you strain to reach the top, only to find it's still out of sight. It wasn't where you thought it was going to be. It's taking longer than you thought it should take. You're sure you've messed up somewhere but don't have a clue where you took a wrong turn. So, what do you do? You stop and ask for directions. Most of us, in our confusion, will ask just about anybody and go just about anywhere to find happiness. Unfortunately, a lot of people have traveled well off the beaten path because of those directions and ended up in some pretty interesting places, still a long way from their desired destination.

I'm going to tell you a story that happened far from home, which will help illustrate the problem with directions. I was in the maze of freeways, roads, and interchanges better known as Southern California, specifically the megalopolis of Los Angeles. I headed down there to speak and got a car at the airport. I arrived a day early and wanted to drive to the conference site, just to check it out. I also had some books and materials I wanted to drop off early. But before I left my home in Seattle, I'd talked to a good friend who knew the area and asked him how to get from the airport to where I was speaking. He rattled off about four different freeway names and numbers, which I carefully wrote down. Because the directions were so detailed, I felt quite confident when I arrived in Los Angeles as I headed out in my rental car from the airport.

We have plenty of traffic in Seattle; don't get me wrong. But it's nothing compared to the web of roadways in the Los Angeles area. You have to pay close attention to what you're doing and where you're going down there, what lane you're in and where the next interchange is. Nevertheless, my friend's directions were tracking right down the line. I took the next to the last freeway listed on my directions, thinking, "This is a breeze!" I was breezing along for quite some time, noticing that the landscape was gradually turning from cityscape to more rural, with fewer and fewer buildings. I was feeling a bit uneasy but, hey, my friend's directions had proven just great up to this point, so I kept on going. The sun was shining, music playing; I wasn't worried.

Even though I'm not from the LA area, it wasn't too long after that when I realized, "Something's wrong. I'm lost." This was, of course, prior to cell phones, so I got off at the next off-ramp, found a gas station, and ended up calling over to the conference center, telling them where I was. Apparently, my friend had given me directions that were *mostly* right. He'd neglected to mention a little mile-long jog where I picked up one freeway for a short distance in order to transfer to the one that would take me to the conference center. Without that one little detail, I'd gone about twenty-five minutes out of my way. His directions were *almost* correct, which cost me *almost* an hour getting to my destination.

This world is only too happy (pun intended) to point you in the general direction of happiness. *(After all, it's really up to you, and it's over there in that general direction. If you can't find it, then it's really your fault anyway, and I can't be bothered because, frankly, I'm busy with my own issues right now!)* This culture has appointed a spokesperson, a go-to person, for those seeking to find happiness. That person's name is Media. Media is so prevalent in the culture; its messages about happiness and where and how to find it are everywhere. Media's message permeates the culture. So, if the information is so prevalent, why is happiness so elusive? This is because Media's intent is not for you to find happiness. Media's intent is for you to keep looking.

Just as the ad pitches on late-night television, Media has no problem touting any number of surefire, guaranteed roads to happiness. Once this (you fill in the blank) has been obtained, happiness, you're told, is sure to follow. Each of these things, like street directions, is intended to guide you in the general vicinity of happiness. The rest, of course, is left up to you.

The problem with this surefire road to happiness is that it is, in fact, a detour designed to sidetrack you. As you will see in chapter 1, I've outlined some of the most common detours taken on the road to happiness.

Chapter 1

DETOURS ON THE ROAD TO HAPPINESS

O NE DAY I WAS OUT IN MY FRONT YARD, HAVING A FIERCE AND pitched battle between myself and a small green weed that had- -overnight, it seemed—taken over every available inch of my flower beds, when an unfamiliar car pulled up to the curb. A very harried woman got out of the car and came over, as I frantically tried to wipe the dirt off my hands and the knees of my jeans.

"Can you please help me?" she asked in a voice that indicated she thought I could, should, and would.

"Sure," I replied, wondering what I was volunteering for.

"Do you know where this address is?" she asked and handed me a piece of paper with a number and a street written on it.

As I looked over the address, she said, "I think it should be right around here. I've been driving for twenty minutes, and I still can't find it! You're the third person I've asked, and no one seems to know where this is!"

I now felt completely obligated to provide this woman with correct directions. As I looked at the address, it appeared that it should be just down the street around the corner.

As if reading my mind, she said, "I thought it was just down there," pointing down the street, "but I've already been down that way and can't find anything *near* the right number!"

"Hmmm," I said, trying to come up with some way to help her. Then, as I looked again at the number, something hit me. "Do you have the rest of the address?" I asked, for she only had the street number on the piece of paper.

Taking back the piece of paper, she turned it over where the full address was printed. Immediately, I could see what her problem was. The street she was on was correct; however, she was in the wrong town. I don't know what it's like where you live, but around here, we have a bunch of little towns that converge upon one another, without changing street names. She was on the right street but she needed to be in the next town over.

As she was already late and it was probably going to take her at least another fifteen minutes to get to her final destination, she was glad to get my information but not very pleased, if you know what I mean. The other three people she'd asked for help gave it their best shot, but she hadn't given them all the pertinent information, and they hadn't asked. So, she just kept circling around the general area, not finding her destination. The only reason I knew something was wrong was because the number she wanted *should* have been just down the road. The fact it wasn't told me there was something else to the story. As she drove away, I was just hopeful the map I'd drawn on the piece of paper would be clear enough for her to follow. If it wasn't, I didn't envy the next person she stopped to ask directions from.

That's kind of the problem asking directions from other people. Sometimes they don't have all the information, and so they give bad directions. Other times they want to appear helpful, so they'll do their best, which ends up not good enough to get you where you want to go. And still other times they'll leave out just that one little piece of the puzzle that gets you completely off track. If you can get off track and waste time just asking for directions to a co-worker's barbeque, imagine the problem with directions when you're searching for something as important as happiness.

Just as this lady was detoured from her final destination, there are things that will detour you from reaching your final destination—happiness. Although I can name many detours, I'm going to highlight some of the most common ones that seem to trip people:

- Education
- Career
- Love relationships
- Having children

- Philanthropic causes

- Narcissism

- Physical appearance/beauty

- Money/credit cards

"If I Only Had a Brain":
Education as the Road to Happiness

I live in the Seattle area, a part of the country with one of the most educated populations per capita of anywhere in the country. According to the United States Census Bureau, almost half of the residents of Seattle over the age of twenty-five have at least a bachelor's degree, almost double the national average.[1] As the home of Boeing, Microsoft, Nintendo, Amazon, Starbucks, Costco, Paccar, and many more, the Puget Sound region places a significant emphasis on education and academic achievement. People around here are well educated. So am I, with a doctorate degree in clinical psychology. Media will tell you that education is a way to happiness.

If this is so, Seattle and the Puget Sound region should be a happy place to live, with so many of its inhabitants with academic degrees. Think over all the odd bits of trivia you've heard about Seattle over the years. Seattleites have webbed feet because of the rain. People in Seattle have veins that are filled with coffee. People in the Northwest walk around in wool socks and Birkenstocks. Isn't one of them also about Seattle and a high rate of suicide? Some of that has to do with the weather, and a lot has to do with urban myth, but I will tell you, from personal and professional experience, there are some very unhappy people here. I have had many successful, well-educated people in my office who are also absolutely miserable. A bachelor's degree, a master's degree, or even a doctorate are not universal guarantees of happiness in life, no matter what the media ads herald, amidst pictures of smiling students and impressive parchments.

The thought is that an education will give you a purpose, a direction in life. This direction will lead to happiness. But what if you take all that time and spend all that money, only to find out the direction your education is taking you isn't a direction you want to go after all? What if you take all that time and spend all that money and find out, while you think pre-Columbian tribal practices is a fascinating field of study, it's also an incredibly narrow employment path? What if you take all that time and spend all that money only to realize that degree—now that you have it—was really someone else's dream, not yours? What if you take all that time and spend all that money and come to realize that the thrill of academic pursuit doesn't quite prepare you for the mundane realities of the world of work?

"Whistle While You Work": Career as the Road to Happiness

Even with so many people engaged in academic pursuit around here, there is still a sizable segment of the population who foregoes postsecondary education and instead jumps headfirst into the world of work. After that giddy, heady feeling of success and affirmation with the first job offer comes the stark reality for many that you actually have to get up when the alarm clock rings, go in to work when it's a beautiful, sunny day, and spend four hours on your knees stocking boxes, boxes, and more boxes of Fruit Roll-Ups, even when you don't want to. Welcome to adulthood. Nothing gets you there quicker than your first job.

That's a job; what about a career? Doesn't the very word *career* sound so much better, so much happier, than just a job? *Merriam-Webster's Collegiate Dictionary* highlights the difference. A *job* is defined as "a piece of work; especially a small, miscellaneous piece of work undertaken on order at a stated rate."[2] A job, then, is a piece of work, small and miscellaneous. Doesn't sound very impressive, does it? Career, on the other hand, is something different. *Career* is defined as "a field for or pursuit of consecutive progressive achievement especially in public, professional, or business life."[3] Now, that's more like it. Career even has the word *pursuit* in its definition. Surely you're getting closer to happiness when you have a career.

I wish I could agree with Media and say that a career is a surefire path to happiness. Unfortunately, in my experience, it's no guarantee. Imagine the difficulty a person faces who, after four years of college, decides their academic path isn't leading to happiness. Then imagine the difficulty a person faces who, after twenty-five years in a career, decides their career path isn't leading to happiness. Careers take time, energy, and resources to build, often in greater proportion even to education. The disappointment, then, when a career doesn't lead to happiness can be devastating. Often it comes at a time when the person has greater obligations and responsibilities than they did while in school.

Jobs, even careers, often come with a "what-have-you-done-for-me-lately" component. It's all about what's happening right now. Supervisors come and go, expectations change, technology changes, and responsibilities change. I have known far too many people who became so comfortable in their job that they chose to derive their happiness from their careers, only to find, after twenty years with the same company, they wound up with a crystal clock with their name on it, a hearty handshake of thanks, and a pink slip during the next round of downsizing.

With all the changes that take place on a job or in a career, the one change I didn't mention above is the fact that often people change. As individuals mature and age, they may one day find they have changed slowly over time so that they no longer "fit" the career they've chosen. I heard of one man who spent over twenty years as a social worker, dealing with difficult, troubled, and in-trouble teenagers moving through the criminal justice system. He took up this career right after college and devoted considerable time and energy to it. There came a point, however, when he decided he just couldn't do it anymore. Criminal justice was his career, but he gave it up because it wasn't bringing him happiness. Instead, it had become a source of discouragement and despair. The job was the same, but he wasn't. The demands of the job, which used to excite and motivate him, were now dragging him down, and he found he had to leave that career. Careers promise a lot, and when they don't deliver, the results can be anything but happy.

"I Only Have Eyes for You": Love as the Road to Happiness

This is one of Media's favorite paths to happiness. If you can only find love, true love, you'll find happiness. Of course, Media is also filled with the abject misery that falling in love can bring, as represented in big-screen films, newspaper stories, reality shows, magazine articles, and weekly sitcoms. Love and its promises are a huge media business. Media promises love conquers all and then makes sure you are aware of love's colossal failures. Sensitive to your confusion and natural apprehension, Media then produces reams of information on how to find love, how to be in love, how to maintain love, how to avoid the wrong kinds of love, how to get over broken love, and how to find love again.

Relationships and the love they bring are a source of great happiness. I can say this wholeheartedly as a husband and father. The false promise, however, comes when just being in love or just being in a relationship is sold as the road to happiness. The unspoken threat is that you cannot be happy unless you are in love and in a relationship. The pressure, then, to get on with it, to fall in love and be in a relationship, is huge.

This pressure, of course, is also right alongside the pressure and promise of happiness in education and career. So, according to Media, in order to hedge your happiness bets, you should be simultaneously pursuing education, career, *and* relationship. I'm not sure about the happiness part, but this looks like a recipe for stress! (I speak from personal experience, having simultaneously got married, started The Center, and pursued my doctorate all within two years. I have a vague recollection of those twenty-four months, but you'd have to ask my wife, LaFon, if you want to know any specifics!)

Relationships, just taken on their own, are often stressful enough. When you add the unspoken expectation that this person, this relationship, is supposed to make you truly happy, it's an invitation for failure and disappointment. If you thought your career was a "what-have-you-done-for-me-lately" proposition, it's nothing compared to being in a relationship where your partner looks to you to bring him or her happiness all the time. I don't know of anyone who can pull off that kind of miracle.

The Pitter-Patter of Tiny Feet: Children as the Road to Happiness

I'm not sure if this is universal, but, in my experience, this particular road to happiness is often traveled by women. These women are loving and well intentioned. They put a great deal of energy and time into their relationships, with their primary focus being their role as a mother. At the beginning, the thought of having children means this woman will have meaning, purpose, and significance in her life. Often, the bumps along that road occur at the beginning, middle, and end of her child-rearing journey.

Here are a couple of composite examples of what I mean, taken from years of working with women at The Center:

A young mother will come in. She's been married for around five to seven years and has two children. Right off the bat she'll express her deep love and devotion for her family. She says she loves being a mother but then immediately goes into all of the negatives this has brought into her life: lack of sleep, impact on career, excess weight, loss of intimacy with her husband, and guilt over competing demands of family and job. She feels there's something terribly wrong with her for even thinking this way. She's angry and upset at how stretched she is, and angry and upset that she's even angry and upset. Tears are a predictable event, as she agonizes over how the pitter-patter of little feet has become a thunderous din of demands and pressures she feels inadequate to address. Being a mother was supposed to make her happy, and she's anything but happy.

A woman around forty years old will come in. The problem isn't her, she'll inform me; it's her kids. They're stuck in some teenage phase of utter selfishness, ingratitude, and defiance. She's done her part, all right, to love and nurture them, and look where it's gotten her. She's in a constant battle over every little thing, including their clothes, homework, household chores, friends, and their lousy attitude toward school. There's never a cease-fire in the conflict, and she's exhausted and disillusioned. She doesn't feel inadequate; she's angry. Being a mother was supposed to make her happy, and she's anything but happy.

In this next example, the woman is in her fifties. For more than twenty years, she's devoted her entire being to being a mother. Now her kids are grown and have left the house for education, career, or another relationship (see above). They have flown the coop, and she's left with an empty nest. The house is quiet, uninteresting, and unnaturally clean. It's sterile, and she feels the same way, kind of bleached of feeling and purpose. Being a mother did make her happy, but what's she supposed to do now?

Children aren't like puppies and kittens. When they grow up, they aren't going to stay small and close to home. Children are supposed to grow up, mature, and live out on their own. If you bundle your happiness too tightly around your children, they're apt to take it with them when they leave out the front door, along with all your hand-me-down furniture and dishes.

"The Impossible Dream": Cause as the Road to Happiness

I don't see this one as much as the others mentioned because, frankly, the amount of time and energy it takes to pull off the others doesn't leave a tremendous amount of resources for this one. However, I have seen this from time to time and so feel compelled to discuss it here. It seems that if a person eschews the others talked about so far, it often is so they can pursue a cause as their road to happiness. This could be a religious cause, a political cause, or a social cause. Often, it's a very good thing in and of itself.

The danger comes when working for the cause is no longer sufficient to bring about happiness. Instead, happiness is measured by the person's definition of progress in the cause. In other words, because you're putting in so much time and energy, because you've sacrificed relationships and career in order to pursue this cause, it had better start producing results. Causes are notoriously slow movers. Fighting world hunger, promoting peaceful coexistence, winning the world for Christ, ending poverty, exposing oppression, convincing the other side of how right you are—none of these are movie-of-the-week kind of endeavors. They take time and, often, progress is glacial. If after time the results are not what the person perceives they should be, years of happiness can dissipate, leaving only disappointment and disillusionment in their wake.

Causes are also notoriously enmeshed with charismatic, persuasive individuals. The leaders can be political, cultural, or religious. Larger than life, these figures are often found to have feet of clay (to use a biblical expression out of the Old Testament Book of Daniel, chapter 2. See, I put some Bible in here. Don't worry, though, there's going to be more. It's the world's turn at the moment.). These clay feet cause the strong and imperious leader to crumple. When they come crashing down, their followers can get crushed underneath. When the leader falls, the followers tend to blend back into the crowd, angry, weary, and hardened. One thing they seldom are is happy about it.

"I Feel Pretty":
Narcissism as the Road to Happiness

I love the first sentence of the first chapter of Rick Warren's *The Purpose-Driven Life*. It says simply, "It's not about you."[4] This sentence is in complete contradiction to Media's rather strident assertion to the contrary. In order to find happiness, Media claims that it is *all about you*—your needs, your desires, your wants, and your rights. Media explains that all of these things must be fulfilled—needs, desires, wants, rights—in order for you to be truly happy. It obligingly communicates what you have to do to get your needs, desires, wants, and rights filled and how to battle against all those forces arrayed against you achieving them. Life, then, and happiness are not so much a pursuit as they are a struggle. People in your life are either for or against you in your struggle. For a narcissist, people are either friend or foe.

Media's message is extremely subtle and ubiquitous. (I recognize not everyone will know what the word *ubiquitous* means. I use it anyway because it's become one of my favorite words and a gift, really, from my good friend and colleague, Mike Weiford, at The Center. He is also enamored of the word *ubiquitous* and finds a way to use it about twice a year. It means existing or being everywhere at the same time.[5]) This narcissism promoted by Media is just saturated into the fabric of our culture.

Media is the opposite of Rick Warren. Media tells us, "It is all about you. You have a right to have every need, desire, and wish granted. Whatever you must do, whatever you must sacrifice, whoever you must coerce and cajole, is open season and justifiable. After all, it (fill in the blank) is your right. Happiness is an unalienable right promised to you in the Declaration of Independence as a part of your birthright as an American and as a human being, so whatever you need to do to get it is reasonable and understandable. Put yourself first in order to be happy, and don't take a backseat to anyone until you've attained the happiness you seek. It's your right. You deserve it. Nobody else is going to do it for you."

The single-minded focus of the narcissist is very much akin to the single-minded focus of many I work with at The Center, the anorexic. Both are absolutely absorbed with forcing the shape of the world into their own box. For the anorexic, it's irrelevant that drinking diet sodas and eating only a banana a day will cause irreparable physical and psychological damage. That reality doesn't fit into the controlled world they seek. Reality is irrelevant; intent is everything. For the narcissist, it's irrelevant that a total focus on self-seeking behaviors will cause irreparable social and relational damage. That reality doesn't fit into the comfortable world they seek. Again, reality is irrelevant; intent is everything. For both, everything that happens around them, to them, for them, about them is only ever about them. And I can tell you, tragically, happiness doesn't enter this picture.

The Young and the Restless: Physicality as the Road to Happiness

As a culture, the population is getting older and fatter. (I encourage you to check out the resource list at the end of this book to take a look at the many books I've written on this subject, designed to help people in this area.) It's a huge topic, but the part I want to talk about here is the message Media broadcasts on a daily basis about the part physical attractiveness and youth have in achieving happiness. This message of discontent is crafted across the age spectrum, from the types of clothing hawked to preteens (to look youthful instead of childish) to vitamin supplements advertised to seniors (to look youthful instead of old). Happiness, you're told, is found in being youthful in appearance (no matter what end of the spectrum you're on) and physically attractive. Fat is not attractive. Age is not attractive. Therefore, if you are aging and fat, you can't be happy. Again, the country is getting older and fatter, so people should be desperate to find out how to regain their youth and lose weight. In truth, the culture is desperate.

People are desperate to somehow regain their youth, to "turn back the effects of aging" as the commercials say and to lose weight. Think about the vast majority of content in popular magazines, the kind you see at the checkout counter at the grocery store. What do the majority of the headlines trumpet? Looking younger and losing weight.

This is what Media does best—concentrate on the superficial. Highlight those the culture has decreed as the most physically perfect. Showcase the genetic lottery winners whose physical characteristics win the perfection jackpot and then pressure everyone else to look the same. Of course, the

Media will explain to you exactly how to do that—what pill to take, what machine to buy, what cream to use, what food to eat or not eat, what style of clothing to wear, what makeup to use, what hair dye to use…the list is endless.

If the only way to be happy is to be young and thin, why is it I see so many young and thin people at The Center who are anything but happy? I can tell you unequivocally that being young and thin doesn't buy you happiness, no matter what Media says. The reason is that no matter what age you are, the age you are isn't quite right, and, if it is right, it won't be that way for long. (You've heard about everyone's fifteen minutes of fame. The time for physical perfection in this culture is about half that.) It is actually possible to be too thin, and even those whose bodies have been starved into bone-popping, skeletal thinness can still be consumed with any number of perceived physical imperfections.

The same culture that promotes the instant gratification of fast food and the feel-good emptiness of packaged foods also punishes excess weight and the inevitable signs of age. This, to me, is the cruelty of the culture, designed to send a person into an endless loop of desire and despair.

"Pick a Card, Any (Credit) Card": Materialism as the Road to Happiness

I don't know about you, but I am really tired of going through my mail. Every day it seems I get at least one offer from some company for a credit card. It used to be, back in the days before identity theft, I would just pitch the offer into the trash. Of course, that was also before recycling, which is one of those "good-news-bad-news" kind of deals. The good news about recycling is it saves trees; the bad news is it provides personal debris that can be picked through by more than your garbage hauler. Now, with all the credit card offers, I go through and open up the envelope. I take out the preprinted "application" inside. I throw out the plastic fake credit card, recycle the disclosure form and return envelope, and shred the actual application that comes preprinted with an acceptance "code" and some of my personal information.

Why do I go to all this trouble? Because I have enough credit cards as it is, let alone having credit cards with my name on them floating around and being used by other people. If I wanted to, I could be in debt up to my eyeballs. All I'd have to do is say "yes" to every offer and then charge up each card to its limit. Granted, I could buy some really great stuff. I just love electronic gadgets, so Best Buy and Circuit City could come to know me by my first name if I was so inclined.

Of course, I'm not so inclined. I've worked hard to build up my business and my good credit, and I am not going to do anything to jeopardize that. However, I've known quite a few people who don't have that same reticence. For them, another credit card means more things; more things mean more things to make them happy. Happiness, for them, is not a pursuit but a purchase, even if they don't have the money.

On the other hand, I've known a few people who actually do have the money. So, they use that money to buy and spend and consume, with each purchase hoping they'll feel better about life, about themselves. These people have a hole, a rather large, expensive hole, being filled with things. Happiness isn't so much a destination as it is a filling up of that void in their lives. Cram enough furnishings, cars, trips, jewelry, gadgets, toys, and clothing into the hole, and certainly someday it will be all filled up. There's just one problem: the hole isn't sealed at the bottom. Instead, whatever is packed in eventually seeps out the bottom through use, disappointment, or disinterest. Luckily, however, through Media, they're kept up to date on the next great thing that will, surely this time, pack in the hole.

All of these roads promise to bring you to happiness but can fail to deliver miserably. Again, Media, as the spokesperson for this world, is not interested in your finding happiness. Rather, Media is interested in you continuing to look for it. Because far too many people look for happiness through the world and Media, they cede control over their lives and their happiness to the world.

You might be saying, "For a book on happiness, this is really quite depressing." Actually, this chapter is a setup for the next one. It is necessary for you to give up the siren song of Media and all its promises about happiness so you'll actually start listening to the truth about what real happiness is and where it comes from.

Before you go there, I'd like to take just a moment to talk about another way the world complicates the search for happiness. It not only sends up false signals, but it also attempts to keep you from venturing down roads that might actually take you to where you want to go.

"Proceed With Caution" and Other Signs Along the Way

In case you're in suspense, the way that leads to true happiness is through a belief in God and a relationship with Jesus Christ. The next chapter will discuss Scripture more in depth, but because the focus here is about the world and Media, it must be said that neither of these is exactly friendly toward religion in general and Christianity in particular. The world and Media is much more comfortable with vague, spiritual proclamations that assert nothing, offend no one, and effect zilch. Therefore, if you actually stand up for your faith, assert biblical truth, risk offending evil, and are effective against sin in the world, you become an enemy of the world. Media will tell you that you are bigoted, small minded, a zealot, irrational, illogical, puritanical, phobic, insecure, uneducated, and dangerous. These are huge signs in the culture, designed to detour you from your faith in general, from expressing your faith in particular, and especially from exercising your faith in a public arena. You are told that your faith must be kept private (*shhhhhhhh*)—head and arms inside the car at all times with the windows rolled up. You are told that you are not allowed to be offended by the sin of others because your faith is offensive to them and their feelings are more enlightened than yours.

Now, everybody wants to fit in and is influenced every day by the culture. When the culture itself is hostile to your faith and you see your faith daily disparaged, you can become discouraged and disheartened. When you become discouraged and disheartened in your faith, you become more susceptible to what the world says you need to do to be happy. You become confused about what happiness is and where it comes from and can end up picking from one of the pathways talked about in this chapter. The pathway to the world's idea of happiness is a huge superhighway of choices. God's way, however, is a little smaller and can be harder to find, especially when the world really has no interest in you finding it.

Time to take a break and stop for just a minute. Before you head into the next chapter and look at what God has to say on this subject, I want you to take some time and evaluate just how deeply the world and its values have colored your concepts of happiness and how to achieve it.

To review, here are the ways we talked about:

- Education as the road to happiness

- Career as the road to happiness

- Love as the road to happiness

- Children as the road to happiness

- Cause as the road to happiness

- Narcissism as the road to happiness

- Physicality as the road to happiness

- Materialism as the road to happiness

1. Take a look at each of these and indicate on a scale of 1 to 5, with 5 being the highest, how much you rely on each for your personal happiness.

2. Next, beside each, I'd like you to assign at least one other adjective for how these things make you feel. With an arrow pointing either up or down, indicate whether these feelings are a negative or a positive for you.

3. If you had to give one of these up tomorrow—if it was no longer a part of your life—which one would you choose, and why?

4. If you had to give them all up but one, which one would you hang on to, and why?

5. Is there any one thing on the list that began for you as a way to be happy and has turned into something else? Which one, and what has it turned into for you?

6. On a happiness scale of 1 to 10, with 10 being happy on a continual basis, where would you rate yourself right now in your life?

7. Have there been other times in your life when this score was significantly different? Were you more or less happy? What were those times, and why did you feel differently?

8. If there were times in your life when you were happier, can you identify areas that you would be able to duplicate today?

9. If there were times in your life when you were not happier than today, can you identify reasons? What positive steps have you taken to reclaim some of your personal happiness?

10. Name three specific ways happiness has been promised to you that were false. Who told you each, and why did you believe that person?

Only by examining what you believe and why can you come to understand the beginnings of your beliefs and the basis upon which those beliefs rest. That's why it's important for you to be alert to the effect that culture has upon your personal understanding of happiness. As you continue on, you will need to jettison anything that's based upon the world's wisdom and follow a spiritual road map that helps guide you to a different path.

Chapter 2

MAKE SURE TO
USE MAPQUEST

A NYONE WHO HAS TRAVELED WITH A SPECIFIC DESTINA-
tion in mind knows that before you head out on the road, it helps
to map out your route. If you're not lucky enough to own a GPS
(Global Positioning System), then you at least need to use a road atlas or go
online and map out your route using MapQuest.

As many people travel down life's highway in search of happiness, they
figure they'll run into it somewhere, someday. They head off in a general
direction, assuming happiness will pop up on the way like a highway sign
directing them which way to turn, how many miles to go, and what exit to
take to get there. Happiness, however, isn't like a tourist attraction, an all-
you-can-eat buffet, or a new theme park.

Some people aren't even sure what they're looking for. Take, for example,
Gordon. Gordon is thirty-eight years old, on his second marriage, with
three kids—two from his first marriage and one from his second, which
means he's doing the whole day care drop-off/pick-up routine again. He
was just promoted at work to a lead position. While he appreciates the
extra money, with the promotion comes longer hours, so he had to quit
the men's softball league he's been a part of for over ten years. His children
from his first marriage visit every other weekend and on Wednesdays, so
the house he's living in with his second wife and their new baby is cramped
when all the kids are there. It seems like his life is now dictated by a rigid
schedule he has no real control over. Ever since the birth of his new baby,
his first wife's mood has been chancy at best, which makes the handoff of

the kids an emotional gamble. It's adding stress to his life. Gordon tells me he's just not happy.

Julie hit fifty years old this year. A week after her birthday, with all the prerequisite "humorous" age cards, geriatric gifts, and black balloons, her twenty-three-year-old son got his second DUI. With the first one, they'd been able to get him off with just an eight-hour "information" class on a Saturday. He promised it wouldn't happen again, that he was really serious this time about finishing up his last two semesters at school and getting a real job. Now, with another DUI, there is no way he's going to get off, which means thousands of dollars for attorneys, thousands more for treatment, and the loss of his driver's license, which complicates everything. Fifty wasn't supposed to be like this. She was supposed to have her kids raised and out of the house, out of her hair. She wasn't supposed to still be worried about them. Her son's situation is adding stress to her life. Julie tells me she's just not happy.

Paul is thirty-one. He's been married for five years with no kids yet. He's been far too busy buying and building up his dental practice. It's going well, but he has the debt on the business along with paying off the last of his school loans. There's no way he wants to add the burden of kids right now. His wife, however, doesn't agree, so they're having some issues in their marriage. He's explained his reasoning and rationale over and over again to Brittany, but she refuses to drop the kid thing. She wants to start a family, even though the timing is obviously not right, right now. Whether or not to have kids is adding stress to his life. Paul tells me he's just not happy.

Kelli is nineteen. She's a freshman at an out-of-state college, home for a midyear break. School has been tough so far. She went from a graduating senior class of about four hundred to a freshman class of about four thousand. A member of the drill team in high school, she didn't even bother trying out in college. She saw what those other girls looked like and knew there was just no way, so she talked herself out of it and didn't even try. Besides, she's probably put on almost ten pounds since beginning school. Her clothes don't fit right; every time she looks in the mirror, she looks fat. She really has no idea what she wants to do or be in school now that drill isn't a part of her life. Trying to figure it all out is stressful, and when she's stressed, she eats. Kelli tells me she's just not happy.

Yes, some people aren't even sure what they're looking for. They say "Happiness," but they think, "No problems." They say, "Happiness," but they think, "Perfect family." They say, "Happiness," but think, "Financial freedom." They say, "Happiness," but think, "Physical attractiveness." If only they could find their way to the latter, the former is guaranteed.

In each of these instances, Gordon, Julie, Paul, and Kelli decided what would make them happy. They, in essence, wrote the script of their own happiness by defining first the source of their unhappiness at the present moment. Gordon identified the complications of his life as the source of his unhappiness. His conclusion: a life with no problems is a happy life. Julie identified the foibles of her offspring as the source of her unhappiness. Her conclusion: a proper family means a happy life. Paul identified debt obligations as the source of his unhappiness. His conclusion: financial freedom means a happy life. Kelli identified her body as the source of her unhappiness. Her conclusion: an attractive body means a happy life.

Even the world can look at these people and immediately pick out misconceptions and fallacies in their conclusions.

Gordon, call me up when you have no more problems! And I won't sit by the phone waiting.

Julie, there's been no such family since the sitcoms of the fifties, which weren't real to begin with! Time to move on—there is no perfect family.

Paul, what are you whining about? You're doing better than I am and better than most of the people I know!

Kelli, grow up! At nineteen, you're as good as you're gonna get. Didn't anybody tell you it's all downhill from there?

The world is not known for its empathy or compassion. Of course, the world says nothing about the fact that it is responsible for many of those same misconceptions and fallacies. This, once again, reinforces the theme that *on the road to happiness, you should be careful who you ask for directions.*

The world is lousy in the empathy and compassion department. It's lousy at giving directions. Thankfully, the world is not the only place to look for direction in life. (You know where this is going, don't you?) There is a kind of MapQuest for life that's readily available to those who have the insight and ability to go "online" to get it.

Spiritual MapQuest

I love MapQuest. Granted, I was pretty good at finding my way around before, but with MapQuest, I can get where I'm going in the most efficient way possible. No more wandering around streets in the general direction. Now I know not only where I'm going but also how far away it is, how long it should take me to get there, and explicit, step-by-step directions on how to go each leg of the trip. If I want to, I can ask it to find the shortest trip possible or the quickest trip possible. I can choose to avoid highways, toll roads, even roads that are closed seasonally. I can see the traffic conditions associated with my route, real time, to be alerted to congestion and traffic bottlenecks (a real plus in and around Seattle). I can even print up a visual map, along with text instructions. Whoever thought of this was a genius.

This is what Gordon, Julie, Paul, and Kelli really wanted me to be. They wanted me to be able to type in "life problems" or "family problems" or "financial problems" or "body problems" as the beginning point, push a button, and—*voilà!*—have a step-by-step, individualized map created for them with "happiness" as the ending point. They wanted a personalized printout of how to get from their place of problems and arrive at that elusive destination of happiness.

It's a tall order, but, yes, I can do that. Not that I'm such a genius myself. I just happen to know the Genius who created a different kind of MapQuest, a spiritual MapQuest. Like the earthbound MapQuest, access to it is free for the asking. All you need is to be connected. The spiritual MapQuest is called Scripture, and the Creator is God Himself. Eventually, Gordon, Julie, Paul, and Kelli each received a personalized plan to move them from their place of problem to a point of personal happiness. First, however, each had a bit of work to do, determining just what their beginning point really was. Next, they needed to uncover the difference between what they thought would make them happy and where happiness really comes from.

After all, if you don't know where were you really are or where you're really going, how can you expect to get anywhere?

Let's Start at the Very Beginning

If Gordon had been able to use his own life MapQuest in the pursuit of happiness, he probably would have typed in his starting location as "too many problems" with "blended families, job stress, time pressures, money pressures, a daily juggling act, and a mad ex-wife" as the street address, city, state, and zip code with four-digit extension. Left up to Gordon, he would have put in a wrong starting address, which would have fouled up his ability to achieve his desired destination. What Gordon should have put down instead of "too many problems" was "unacknowledged consequences." I supposed he could have put down "unrealistic expectations," but I think he would have gotten the big red explanation point that told him he wasn't being specific enough to obtain correct directions. (That always happens to me on MapQuest when I hit the "Enter" key instead of the "Tab" key while putting in the address. I can't believe I do it again every time I do it.)

Gordon's true starting place was really unacknowledged consequences. With two families—an ex-wife, a current wife, and two sets of kids—come consequences. It means juggling schedules and adhering to parenting plans. It means money earned today still needs to go to the children conceived yesterday, with the other woman in that other life. A promotion and more money at work generally mean more responsibility and more time on the job. With more job responsibilities and additions to the family, there's less time to invest in other activities, such as recreational activities. These aren't problems; they're consequences that must be acknowledged and adjusted for.

Julie wanted to put down "problem child" as her starting location, with all her complaints about her son's current predicament. If only her son would stop acting foolish, straighten up, and become an adult, then all of her problems would vanish. She'd given him everything he needed to make the right choices, do the right thing, and act the right way. One of these days, it was supposed to kick in and take hold. Things had been going better, and now he got a second DUI. To Julie, this was a one-time, just-fix-it kind of problem—that kept happening over and over and over again.

The true starting point for Julie wasn't with her son; it was with herself. Julie was an enabler, overlooking, excusing, and attempting to fix his problems for years. Each difficulty, each incident, each occurrence was viewed as an aberration instead of as a pattern. Julie didn't want to see the pattern that had developed over the years with her son. He was her baby, the one in the family who seemed to understand her the best, the one who seemed to need her the most. Above all, Julie wanted to be needed, so she had carefully woven the umbilical cord tighter and tighter around their relationship until her son felt he was being strangled, and Julie was being dragged into places she no longer wished to go. Her true starting location wasn't "problem child." It was "overinvolved mother."

Paul wanted to put down "debt obligations" as his starting point to find his way to happiness. For Paul, everything came down to money—his choice of a career, when to get married, how to acquire a business, and, finally, when to start a family. The sooner he could discharge his debt obligations, the happier he'd be, and a better life would begin. He saw it all in the form of a mathematical equation. If he could just add up all the requisite parts in the correct order, it was bound to equal peace, security, and happiness at the end. There was just one problem: the cofactors in the equation kept changing as his life changed. He never felt like he could get a handle on the left side of the equation in order to achieve the right side.

For Paul, happiness wasn't really about money. Money was a symptom of Paul's deep insecurity. His true starting point was "need for control." Having grown up in a very materialistic household, money was the way the behavior of family members was controlled. If you wanted your allowance, you had to hit a moving target of requirements as a kid. If you wanted a car as a teen, you had to live up to the family standards academically. If you wanted to have your college education paid for, you had to go to the school chosen for you. Paul, of course, rebelled, choosing his own path and own school, even with the dire warnings about the potential for failure. He worked almost full time, while also going to dental school. Summers weren't play time; they were full of cheaper summer-school offerings and night jobs. Focused and highly disciplined, Paul, at thirty-one, was well on his way to achieving his goals.

There was just one problem with Paul's goals; they were Paul's goals. Paul was no longer just Paul. Now he was Paul and Brittany. Brittany brought different goals and priorities into the marriage. She brought a different attitude, having been raised in a much more laid-back household where things were just allowed to happen without much foresight or planning, for good or for bad. That's what attracted her to Paul, his discipline and organization. Brittany's spontaneity and turn-on-a-dime personality were part of what had first attracted Paul. What had first attracted them to each other was now forcing them apart and driving them further and further from happiness.

Even from the relatively young age of nineteen, Kelli was quite sure what would make her happy. After all, when she was involved and popular in high school, she was happy. Of course, she still worried about her weight and how she looked and who her boyfriend was and what he thought of her, but, overall, Kelli had life figured out. If you were a girl, being cute and thin meant things went better for you. You got more attention, more invitations, more opportunities. She always thought college would be like a supercharged high school experience, with all of that admiration, attention, status, and more. It never dawned on her that college would be worse than high school. She never dreamed she wouldn't be cute enough to succeed or thin enough to be popular in a larger setting. If high school was full of pressure, college was ten times worse, with all of the competition and without the support of her parents or friends. Without the constant busyness of the social life she'd had in high school, Kelli found she had more time on her hands. Time to think, to fret, to worry, and to eat. Kelli would have said "body problems" was her starting location and could have easily written in "mouth too big, hair too thin, chest too small, thighs too big, and just too fat in general" on the address line.

In truth, there was nothing wrong with Kelli's body. "Body problems" wasn't her true starting place. Instead, it was "body image," Kelli's internal image of her own body and its perceived myriad of imperfections. There was absolutely no way for Kelli to arrive at happiness using "body problems" as a starting point. Because Kelli was unable to truthfully see herself, it didn't matter what she did to her body; Kelli would always see her body as a problem. And since it was always a problem, there was no way for her to achieve the happiness she sought.

Gordon, Julie, Paul, and Kelli are just like people everywhere, just like you. You often have a problem figuring out your true starting point on the road to happiness. It's no wonder, then, when you can't seem to find it. Until you know where you really are, you'll constantly go off in random directions, following a formula that's flawed in the first place. This is further complicated, of course, because you also have difficulty accurately inputting the "ending location" of happiness. What you think is the end-all and be-all of happiness too often comes from the world's definition. Blithely, you type in where you think you are in the first place and where you ought to end up at the end and find yourself hopeless, lost, and utterly miserable.

Destination Happiness

Our destination of happiness and God's are a little different. As much as I hate to admit it, my destination of happiness often reminds me of my son, Benjamin's. For him, happiness is arrived at when everything around him is going his way and all the adults in the general vicinity are in sync with his needs. He's five, after all. I'm a bit older than that, but I still fight against a childish view of happiness that's more akin to the excitement and self-satisfaction of a five-year-old. This destination of happiness is about the "woohoo" rush of exhilaration and the "that's what I'm talkin' 'bout" pumped fist of fulfillment. It's a great place to be, but it isn't a place you stay very long.

If that's not it, then what is? The dictionary definition of *happiness* is interesting. *Merriam-Webster's Collegiate Dictionary* has three definitions.[1] The first is considered obsolete and equates happiness with good fortune and prosperity, tying happiness in with wealth. I'm not sure why it's considered obsolete because I know a large number of people who still, deep down, feel this way, including Paul. The second definition is "a state of well-being and contentment." I like this one at first glance, although who determines if you're in a state of well-being? *Well-being* is defined as being happy, healthy, or prosperous,[2] which is kind of a circular argument and reminds me very much of that verse out of *Poor Richard's Almanac* by Benjamin Franklin: "Early to bed and early to rise, makes a man healthy, wealthy, and wise."[3] So, in order to be happy, you need to be healthy, wealthy, and go to bed early. Well, that was Julie; she was in good health, was financially secure, and went to bed every night by 9:30 p.m., even on the weekends. The third definition of happiness is very much in tune with this age and this culture when it says happiness is a pleasurable or satisfying experience. Of the three, I think this would have been Gordon's choice. I think its inverse would have been Kelli's: happiness as a life devoid of any unpleasant or unsatisfying experiences. I personally think this third one probably comes the closest to most people's definition of happiness.

As it happens, this definition of happiness, as a result of pleasurable or satisfying experiences, is very different from God's. All three of them are actually in contrast to God's definition of what it is to be happy. As followers of Christ, we want to go with God's definition, not the world's. God says that happiness is found in being poor, in mourning, in meekness, and in hunger and thirst. He says that happy people aren't those who get even but those who get walked on. He says happy people aren't those who satisfy their desires but those who control them. He says happy people aren't those who fight for what they're due but those who make peace. He says happiness is found in persecution. This really isn't what the world says! Deep down, I have to admit a part of me likes the dictionary's definition better. It just seems those definitions sound more like where I want to go in my life. A big part of me wants to have good fortune, be prosperous, and live in a state of well-being and contentment, with a life of pleasurable and satisfying experiences. The question I have to ask myself is, Do I really want to end up at God's destination of happiness?

God's definition is not the world's definition, not even close. God's definition appears to go against the culture and what you've been taught on almost every level. Frankly, you like the world's definition. It seems to be more what you're looking for. God's definition seems rather harsh, actually. There doesn't seem to be much room in there for "woohoo" and "that's what I'm talkin' 'bout!" There appears to be a stark divide between where you want to go and what God has in mind. This dichotomy is the truth of the garden, bluntly stated in Isaiah 55:8, "'For my thoughts are not your thoughts, neither are your ways my ways,' declares the LORD." The unspoken conclusion, of course, is because your thoughts and your ways are not God's, you end up drawing the wrong conclusions and go off in the wrong direction.

Happy Are They

It seems perfectly logical to me that God would use an unlikely candidate to explain His definition of happiness. After all, 1 Corinthians 1:27 says,

"God chose the foolish things of the world to shame the wise; God chose the weak things of the world to shame the strong." It would be completely true to form for Him to use the following individual to explain happiness: "He was despised and rejected by men, a man of sorrows, and familiar with suffering. Like one from whom men hide their faces he was despised, and we esteemed him not" (Isaiah 53:3). Who is this despised, rejected, sorrowful, and suffering man who was decidedly unpopular? The answer, of course, is Jesus. The Isaiah passage is a prophecy concerning the Christ and, as history and Scripture recount, a completely accurate rendition. The Man of sorrows is the One God chose to teach us how to be happy. (Already I'm feeling a little uneasy about what this is going to mean for all my "woohoos.")

The happiness teachings are from one of the most compelling passages in Scripture, a sermon of Jesus, called the Sermon on the Mount. It's found starting in Matthew 5 and ending in Matthew 7. It's an amazing sermon, full of paradox and contradiction with the world. It is in this context that Jesus starts out His sermon by explaining who the happy people are in the world. Now, this is valuable information. If happiness itself is hard to arrive at as a destination, it makes sense to study the happy people, because they have the destination figured out. If you can figure out why they are happy, maybe you can find out how to be happy too. Following are Jesus's words on the subject, from Matthew 5:3–12:

- Blessed are the poor in spirit, for theirs is the kingdom of heaven.

- Blessed are those who mourn, for they will be comforted.

- Blessed are the meek, for they will inherit the earth.

- Blessed are those who hunger and thirst for righteousness, for they will be filled.

- Blessed are the merciful, for they will be shown mercy.

- Blessed are the pure in heart, for they will see God.

- Blessed are the peacemakers, for they will be called sons of God.

- Blessed are those who are persecuted because of righteousness, for theirs is the kingdom of heaven.

- Blessed are you when people insult you, persecute you and falsely say all kinds of evil against you because of me. Rejoice and be glad, because great is your reward in heaven, for in the same way they persecuted the prophets who were before you.

I can already hear the protests from the passenger seats. For some of you, this isn't a road you want to go down. "But wait," you say, "this says *blessed* not *happy*! This is talking about the superrighteous people, like nuns and monks who live a life of sacrifice and service and deprivation for God. They're not supposed to be happy. They're supposed to be serious and committed and dedicated. They go into that life knowing what it's going to be about, and God blesses them for it. This passage is for those types of people; it really doesn't apply to everyday people like me. It's about being *blessed*, not about being *happy*."

Of course, I respectfully beg to differ. The word used here, translated *blessed*, can also be translated *happy*.[4] They're kind of interchangeable, so this does, in fact, speak specifically about happy people and not just the superrighteous but everyday, you-and-me kind of people; the kind of people that followed Jesus around during His public ministry. So, you are going to go down this road, not from the point of view of a religious scholar, which I'm not, but from the point of view of a therapist and counselor, which I am. Oh, and I'm going to translate the word as *happy*.

Happy are the poor in spirit, for theirs is the kingdom of heaven.

You probably look at this verse and cringe at the term "poor." Who wants to be poor? Conventional wisdom says happiness comes through prosperity and wealth. How can you be happy when you're poor? If you read again, you see the entire phrase is "poor in spirit." But doesn't that still seem to indicate a deficit, a lack of something? Why should you want to be poor if it means lacking anything, from money to spiritual things? Shouldn't you be happy when you're "rich in spirit"?

Welcome to the paradox of Scripture. I have seen grown men, learned, religious men of high position, weep because of their spiritual poverty. Their sorrow comes not from being poor in spirit, rather their sorrow comes from realizing their arrogance in thinking they were spiritually rich because of their education, their church affiliation, their community position, or their congregational power. They thought all of these things would be a bulwark against spiritual poverty, which they perceived to be a negative, only to realize after ten, twenty, or thirty years, after a divorce, an affair, a breakdown, or a time of depression, the reality of their true spiritual poverty.

Their tears of sorrow and the recognition of their spiritual poverty were like taking a U-turn and going the opposite direction on the road to happiness. Instead of trying desperately to cover up and compensate for their spiritual poverty, they learned to embrace it. After all, compared to God, everyone is spiritually poor. This is the condition of human beings. If you were able to create or work toward and achieve spiritual richness on your own, you would not have such a deep-seated, fundamental need for God. When people truly understand the deficit, the poverty of their spiritual condition, and look to God instead of themselves to fill it, they find happiness because God is ready, willing, and able to provide it. Everyone is poor in spirit; the happy people are those who understand this and rely not on their own works but on God's mercy and grace.

Happy are those who mourn, for they shall be comforted.

I cannot tell you the number of times people have wept in my office, profusely apologizing for it, even as the tears flow down their faces. In my line of work, tears are generally a good thing; they're considered a breakthrough. Too often, people come up with all kinds of ingenious and destructive ways to forestall tears and emotion. These strategies have a tendency to take over a person's life and provide chilling numbness. As an exchange for no tears, they'll give up any feelings at all. This is a terrible way to live, and those caught within its web are truly some of the most unhappy.

Numbing out pain and denying emotion isn't healthy. It is natural to grieve and to mourn, to work through your disappointments and heartaches, the pain you feel just living this life. When you succumb to this grief and mourn, you are able to be comforted. If you hide your pain, gloss it over, work it away, cover it up with destructive behaviors, you never get to the core of the issue. You never put yourself in a position to be comforted, either by

God or by others. The source of all comfort, of course, is God and, through God, other people. Second Corinthians 1:3–4 says, "Praise be to the God and Father of our Lord Jesus Christ, the Father of compassion and the God of all comfort, who comforts us in all our troubles, so that we can comfort those in any trouble with the comfort we ourselves have received from God."

When you open yourself up to mourning, you accept the world and its pain as it is. You don't try to deny it or avoid it or pretend it doesn't exist. There is pain and suffering in this world and in your own life. When you acknowledge it, you open yourself up to God, who promises to comfort you if you'll trust Him enough to mourn. You find purpose through your mourning as you take the comfort you have received and reflect it back onto others in similar situations. Many people in my line of work have done this very thing. Through difficult life circumstances and situations, they found a life direction of helping other people, taking the comfort they received from God and pouring it back onto others. It's sort of like spiritual recycling and a way many people have found in their own lives to exchange "beauty for ashes" (Isaiah 61:3).

Happy are the meek, for they will inherit the earth.

This hardly seems like a bargain. In order to inherit the earth someday, you have to get walked on today? In this culture, meekness is not considered a virtue. You are taught to stand up, to take charge, to take a stand, to not back down. The dictionary definition of *meek* pretty much sums this up: "enduring injury with patience and without resentment; deficient in spirit and courage; not violent or strong."[5] Why in the world would you endure injury with patience and without resentment? In this culture, you endure injury with litigation and without dollar limit. Of course, the second definition sounds right; it seems right to consider a meek person to be deficient. After all, the expression goes, "Fool me once, shame on you; fool me twice, shame on me." If I get walked on the first time, it's your fault; if I get walked on the second time, it's my fault for letting you do it. Now, what about the third definition? No one wants to be considered violent, but most people do want to be considered strong. How many people wore the yellow wristband with just that admonition? With all of this, why would meek people be considered happy people?

Meek people are considered by this world to be those who cede control of their lives to others. After all, they patiently endure injury and wouldn't think to resent it. They are timid and weak. Another word for meek is *humble*. Again, from Scripture, here are the words of a humble person: "Take my yoke upon you and learn from me, for I am gentle and humble in heart, and you will find rest for your souls" (Matthew 11:29). Again, the speaker of these words is Jesus, the Son of God, who, in 1 Corinthians 1:24, is called "the power of God." Someone with the power of God identifies himself as humble or meek, as in the old King James Version. How can someone who is all-powerful also be meek, and why would that make you happy?

Meekness is an attitude, not a condition. A condition is something that happens to you, over which you have little or no control. An attitude is an intentional response to what happens to you. I've known strong people with some pretty lousy attitudes, and I've known meek people who approach life with some of the best attitudes I've ever seen. These meek people have servant's hearts. They overlook the faults of others; they are slow to anger and to speak but quick to listen; they consider others better than themselves; they exhibit extraordinary patience and perseverance in the face of suffering; they look out for the interests of others. They are some of the happiest people I know. Take a minute and think about the attributes of meek people. Then, go over in your mind the classic definition of love, found in 1 Corinthians 13: "Love is patient, love is kind. It does not envy, it does not boast, it is not proud. It is not rude, it is not self-seeking, it is not easily angered, and it keeps no record of wrongs. Love does not delight in evil but rejoices with the truth. It always protects, always trusts, always hopes, and always perseveres" (vv. 4–7). Can you see the parallels? No wonder meek people are happy people—they're in love! And who are they in love with? They're in love with other people, with you and me. This is why Christ, all powerful, gave up that power and became humble and obedient to death, because of His love for us. In this way, He rewrites our flawed understanding of meekness and shows it to be an attitude of great power, with love as its great purpose.

Happy are those who hunger and thirst for righteousness, for they will be filled.

I must admit this verse haunts me quite a bit, as I work with people who have eating disorders. I have seen young people emaciated and skeletal, whose bodies are literally starving and thirsting to death. They grant themselves mere bites of food and sips of water each day in an attempt to substitute control of the body for pain of the heart. I have seen people so filled with an unquenchable hunger and thirst they will consume vast quantities of food and drink. They uncontrollably binge in a desperate attempt to fill up all the empty places in their lives. I have seen people so obese that walking or moving is a physical act of exertion. Through their outer surplus, they herald an inner need. It is the heart's desire of each of these, across the spectrum, to be filled. Confused, they have substituted food for righteousness and wonder why the emptiness never goes away.

Feelings of hunger and thirst, of want, are simply a part of this world. Desire to be filled is a strong, visceral motivation. Our materialistic, consumer-driven culture should listen to this warning from the prophet Haggai: "You have planted much, but have harvested little. You eat, but never have enough. You drink, but never have your fill. You put on clothes, but are not warm. You earn wages, only to put them in a purse with holes in it" (Haggai 1:6). When you hunger and thirst for the wrong things, you will never find satisfaction or happiness. Deep down, each person knows this feeling of confusion, frustration, and dissatisfaction. You did what you were supposed to do, what you were told would fill you up, and it hasn't worked. This kind of life is a rodent-on-a-wheel life, always running, always working, always striving but going nowhere, never filled.

Perhaps you resonate with the hunger and thirst part, but how can you be filled? Listen to Jesus a little further down in Matthew:

> Therefore I tell you, do not worry about your life, what you will eat or drink; or about your body, what you will wear. Is not life more important than food, and the body more important than clothes? Look at the birds of the air; they do not sow or reap or store away in barns, and yet your heavenly Father feeds them. Are you not much more valuable than they? Who of you by worrying can add a single hour to his

life?...So do not worry, saying, "What shall we eat" or "What shall we drink?" or "What shall we wear?" For the pagans run after all these things, and your heavenly Father knows that you need them. But seek first his kingdom and his righteousness, and all these things will be given to you as well.

—MATTHEW 6:25–27, 31–33

Your focus is on being filled physically to alleviate your feelings of hunger and thirst when the true emptiness that you need filled is emotional and spiritual. You need to turn your priorities around; again, make a U-turn on the road to happiness. You need to make your starting location a hunger and thirst for righteousness. Along the way, God Himself fills you spiritually, emotionally, and physically. When you are filled, you are happy.

Happy are the merciful, for they will be shown mercy.

A little earlier, I talked about seeing the tears of others in my line of work. I have also wept tears myself and some of the most amazing people who have brought me to tears are the merciful. I have seen people battered and abused by parents who found a way through their pain to forgive. I have seen spouses who were betrayed in every manner find a way through their anger and bitterness to accept remorse and repentance and to be merciful in response. Every time I am privileged to witness such a miracle, I am quite literally moved to tears. The older I get, the more of a miracle it seems and the more it moves me.

One of the first scriptures I memorized as a child was the Lord's Prayer. It is found, interestingly enough, within this Sermon on the Mount, as Jesus was teaching His disciples and the crowd of people: "This, then, is how you should pray: 'Our Father in heaven, hallowed be your name, your kingdom come, your will be done on earth as it is in heaven. Give us today our daily bread. Forgive us our debts, as we also have forgiven our debtors. And lead us not into temptation, but deliver us from the evil one'" (Matthew 6:9–13).

In some ways, I was better at forgiveness when I was a child. Children rarely hold grudges. It is in their nature to forgive and move on. It is only as we grow older that this becomes a harder feat to pull off. Adults both hold grudges and withhold forgiveness. Mercy becomes an unused implement in an adult relational toolbox, pressed down into a forgotten corner, with assertiveness, empowerment, retribution, restitution, justice, and fairness piled on top.

Not that these other tools don't have their proper place and use, but there are some times, some situations, when they simply will not work to bring about reconciliation and restoration. The only way to bring healing is to be merciful. This is a tall order for the merciful who are emulating God.

Zechariah, the father of John the Baptist, sings this beautiful song upon his son's birth. Through the Spirit, Zechariah says, "And you, my child, will be called prophet of the Most High; for you will go on before the Lord to prepare the way for him, to give his people the knowledge of salvation through the forgiveness of their sins, because of the tender mercy of our God, by which the rising sun will come to us from heaven to shine on those living in darkness and in the shadow of death, to guide our feet into the path of peace" (Luke 1:76–79).

God is a God of tender mercy. Mercy, in my opinion, takes divine effort. It is not easy to be merciful. It goes against the grain. It requires a great deal of love, faith, and trust. Perhaps, because it is so difficult, God has coupled it with a kind of two-way characteristic, a powerful motivation to go ahead and give mercy a try even though it's hard to do. In both the Matthew 5:7 beatitude and the Lord's Prayer, the mercy and forgiveness you show to others is the measure by which God says He will bestow His mercy and forgiveness upon you. If you want God to forgive us your debts, you need to forgive the debts of others. If you are merciful to others, God is merciful to you. This mercy of God is not a blank check; there is a quid pro quo involved. If you want mercy for yourself, you need to be merciful to others.

The mercy extended to others, I have found, comes with some pretty amazing dividends. When you are merciful, God shines the light of His mercy upon your life; this is a cause for joy and happiness. When you are merciful, not only is your relationship with God kept strong, but your relationship with others is also. This is a cause for joy and happiness. When you are merciful, you provide redemption for other people, often those you love very much. This is a cause for joy and happiness.

Happy are the pure in heart, for they will see God.

This beatitude is self-explanatory, and you can readily see how the pure in heart would be happy because they are able to see God. I get in my mind the picture of small, trusting children, whose innocence and purity allow them to comprehend God at a fundamental level. It becomes a little harder to see yourself, however, as that pure and trusting child. You'd love to be that child, but you left purity behind in your search for happiness awhile back. In fact, you exchanged some of your purity for a map to happiness that left you stuck in a decidedly unhappy place.

Children don't make it into adulthood and retain their spiritual purity because of our sinful nature. When you read Scripture, it's hard for you to miss the point that sin has dire consequences. Occasionally, in your own life, I imagine you've deluded yourself into thinking you can skate above these consequences. But this delusion that the consequences of sin won't surface to interfere with your life eventually cracks. When you live a life of active sin, you are skating on thin ice, which will break, plunging you into frigid and sometimes life-threatening circumstances.

People don't generally come to see a person in my line of work (therapy) when all is going well. Instead, something is going wrong, and they want help to fix it. Now, please don't misunderstand me here; there are plenty of people who come to me for help who are in a difficult situation through no fault of their own. However, sin may still be an issue if their difficulties arise not from their own sin but from the sin of others: the sin of abandonment, neglect, abuse, selfishness, pride, favoritism, stubbornness, apathy, oppression, or evil intent. The sins of others have poisoned their lives and hearts, and they need help to detoxify, to heal and recover.

Now, there are some people who just seem to be naturally pure in heart. They are generous, forgiving, long-suffering, and patient, and they run far, far away from even the appearance of evil. You may look at them and think, "How can I be like that?" The apostle Paul, in a letter to Timothy, provides an answer: "Flee the evil desires of youth, and pursue righteousness, faith, love and peace, along with those who call on the Lord out of a pure heart" (2 Timothy 2:22). You're back at the word *pursue* again, aren't you? It all depends on what you're pursing and how you conduct your pursuit.

In my line of work, I've also seen a great many people who wind up in the pit of despair by jumping in feetfirst themselves. No one pushed them in; they climbed down willingly, often on a misguided quest for happiness. Covered with the muck and stink of their current situation, they find themselves well removed from any sort of purity. They need help to extricate themselves from their pit. They want to leave their pit, but a small part of them doesn't. They got into their pit for a reason in the first place, and leaving it is hard, even though they are tired of being trapped inside. I've seen so many people struggle to get out of some pretty horrific pits, only to become fearful and dive right back in.

This pit leaving is a process. It requires a refocused life, a life dedicated to pursuing righteousness, faith, love, and peace. This is how you get your purity back. Deep down, don't you long to be that little child again, the one who was trusting and innocent, the one who was able to see God? You cry out, as David did in Psalm 51:10, "Create in me a pure heart, O God, and renew a steadfast spirit within me." David cried out this prayer after digging his own deep pit of adultery. God granted David's prayer and renewed his heart once David repented and acknowledged his sin.

Sin has consequences, and it stains you. If you give in to it, it blinds your ability to see God. If you give in to it, you will be unhappy, guaranteed. Sin needs to be called out for what it is, for the destructive force it is in your life, whether it is your own sin or the sin of others that has adversely affected you. When you reject and turn away from that sin and instead pursue God, you are cleansed and returned to your childlike state of being pure in heart. Your lives are redeemed from the pit (Psalm 103:4), and that's a cause for happiness!

Happy are the peacemakers, for they will be called sons of God.

As part of our intensive recovery programs at The Center, we encourage families to participate at therapeutically appropriate times in treatment. Because so often family dynamics are at the heart of the issue (e.g., depression, anxiety, substance abuse, eating disorders), families need to be part of the healing process. We have had spouses, parents, siblings, and extended family members participate. Not only do you need a larger office, but you also need a greater dose of intestinal fortitude for these kinds of family interactions. They carry with them the potential for great healing and the possibility of additional harm. They need to be managed well, with a great deal of foresight and, frankly, prayer. These situations don't just happen; they are made. When I read the term "peacemakers," I think of the clinicians who facilitate these meetings. Peace must be made with effort, foresight, and prayer.

Why would anyone, trained or not, enter into such a situation fraught with potential disaster? And why would anyone expect to be happy about doing it? Speaking from my own personal experience with these types of situations, I facilitate them despite the problems because the depth of healing and reconciliation that can happen is truly breathtaking. I often find myself in a room with a group of people who have legitimate issues with and against each other. Some of them want to be there, and some of them really do not. Truths that have been left hidden, secret, and unacknowledged need to come out for the sake of the person in treatment. Even speaking the truth can act as the key to a Pandora's box of other issues and resentments.

And then a miracle happens. One person from the group, who could or maybe even should act in a certain way, reacts differently. Instead of being defensive, he allows himself to be vulnerable. Instead of making excuses, he accepts responsibility. Instead of reacting in anger, he shows humility. Instead of placing blame, he extends forgiveness. This sacrificial act sets the tone for the rest of the family and the rest of the meeting. This person is a peacemaker. He determines he will act in such a way that peace is made out of a difficult situation. He will take the materials he has and find a way to forge a peaceful solution. His intentionality provides an example for the rest of the group to follow. His decision to act lovingly, even in the face of tremendous temptation to do otherwise, sets the tone for what follows, long after the actual meeting has ended. Is it any wonder such a courageous person is called a child of God?

In each of these instances, the peacemakers do the right thing, they say the right thing, and they act in the right way. Even when the responses are not all they hope for, they still have the knowledge that they had the courage, the strength, and the faith to step out and do the right thing, to make peace, as far as it depended upon them. This can become their source of happiness in the situation.

Happy are those who are persecuted because of righteousness, for theirs is the kingdom of heaven.

Over and over again, I have heard the anguished cry of someone saying to me, "But it's not fair!" Often I cannot offer them anything more than agreement; their situation and what happened to them is not fair. This world is not fair. The good die young while the wicked prosper and live to a ripe, old age. The proud make millions while the humble scrape to get by. The flatterer gets promoted while the hard worker is taken for granted. Perversion is rewarded while righteousness is persecuted. Welcome to the world; life is not fair.

It has pretty much always been this way. Back in the days of Job, he asked, "Why do the wicked live on, growing old and increasing in power?" (Job 21:7) This treatment is not a recent phenomenon. Back in the time of King David, the psalmist wrote, "We have endured much ridicule from the proud, much contempt from the arrogant" (Psalm 123:4). The fact that life is unfair is an age-old theme. Jude writes, "These men are grumblers and faultfinders; they follow their own evil desires; they boast about themselves and flatter others for their own advantage" (Jude 1:16). As King Solomon wrote thousands of years ago, "There is nothing new under the sun" (Ecclesiastes 1:9). Life has pretty much always been unfair, with bad things happening to good people.

How can you be happy in this topsy-turvy, unfair world? The only way this is possible is if your happiness is based upon an inner gyroscope that seeks out the equilibrium of righteousness, regardless of the pressure put on it by the hostile vortexes of this world.

A happy person is a person who is centered on God's values and not the world's. It is natural, therefore, that this type of happy person will experience persecution. This is especially true if the person seeking after righteousness lives in close proximity to those who do not.

If you are living a righteous life, it will stand in stark contrast to the unrighteous lives lived by those around you. Your goodness highlights their not-so-goodness, and they will tend to retaliate against you, to get you to pipe down, sit down, or turn your light down. John puts it this way: "If you belonged to the world, it would love you as its own. As it is, you do not belong to the world, but I have chosen you out of the world. That is why the world hates you" (John 15:19). This world is not fair, and you will not always be treated fairly. On the contrary, you will be persecuted. This can be a lonely place to take a stand. You seek the approval of others and you want people to like you, especially if you grew up in an environment where more value was placed on the opinions of others than on yours. In order to be happy, you need to bind your happiness to God's approval and divorce it from the approval of others. In the paradoxical way of Scripture, what this means in real life is that it is possible to be happy when you're persecuted because you know you're on the right track; you've ticked off the world by choosing to align yourself with God, and it's throwing a temper tantrum your way. You can duck, but you can't always avoid getting hit with persecution.

Happy are you when...

"...people insult you, persecute you and falsely say all kinds of evil against you because of me. Rejoice and be glad, because great is your reward in heaven, for in the same way they persecuted the prophets who were before you" (Matthew 5:11–12). This one goes hand in hand with the previous one. To me, it is the amplification of what sort of persecution you're bound to receive for aligning yourself with God and Christ. When people insult you, persecute you, and lie about you, you join a sort of club, made up of the people of God over the years who had the same done to them and worse.

Do you remember I said earlier that taking a stand can be lonely? What this means is that you're really not alone. You join a much larger group of happy, persecuted people, sort of a "persecuted club." It can be easier to take a stand when you realize others have done so before you and will do so after you.

There are some perks associated with this persecuted club. You're told you have a great reward in heaven. So even if you're persecuted today, you have something pretty special in line for you tomorrow. Even though you're persecuted today, you know you'll be vindicated in the end. What this means is that there really is someone keeping score and noticing all the times you've been persecuted and ridiculed, insulted and lied about. You'll be rewarded, and those who persecute you will be punished (Deuteronomy 32:35). So, while life may be unfair, God is not, and He's the One keeping score. So, be happy; it'll all come out in the wash.

Inner vs. Outer

You've just looked at this apparent contradiction between what the world says brings happiness and where God says happiness can be found. The differences are pretty significant. Using the world's definition, you've chased after happiness, only to find you didn't end up where you wanted to be. Looking at God's definition, you've found happiness isn't so easy to find as the latest relationship or jump in salary. Instead, God's definition of "good times" looks like anything but good times.

I think what it all boils down to is that the world says happiness comes about through the correct alignment of outward circumstances such as no problems, good looks, wealth, health, and pleasant and satisfying experiences. The world says just line up enough of these circumstances on the left side of the equation and it's guaranteed to equal happiness on the right side. The huge disclaimer, of course, is that if your right side doesn't add up correctly, then it's because you didn't appropriately line up the things on the left side. The world is perfectly happy for you to just keep at it, rearranging the deck chairs on the Titanic while your boat to happiness sinks.

The world says to control your outer circumstances, and if you don't, keep trying endlessly. God says happiness comes about through the correct alignment of inner qualities of love, faith, righteousness, peace, and self-control. And the beautiful thing about God is that He doesn't expect you to find and fine-tune these qualities on your own. Instead, He gives them to you as a gift of His Spirit. Galatians 5:22–23 lists these spiritual dividends from God: "But the fruit of the Spirit is love, joy, peace, patience, kindness, goodness, faithfulness, gentleness and self-control. Against such things there is no law." Aligning yourself with God brings you closer in line with the qualities of the Spirit. When you live a life full of love, joy, peace, patience, kindness, goodness, faithfulness, gentleness, and self-control, you live a happy life.

God wrote the map of your life. He knows every step of the way before you do. He knows what works and what doesn't. He knows how this world works and how to work around how this world works. He knows what will make you truly happy because He made you—mind, body, and soul. He knows the best path for you to happiness through following the directions in His spiritual MapQuest.

There are just a couple of complications, of course. You have to follow the directions. Sometimes you don't like the way the directions are written and think you know a better way. And, sometimes, you allow yourself to be detoured along the way. You're going to take a look at those situations in the next section. So, keep going; you aren't, as they say, there yet.

This was a pretty long chapter, with a lot to think about. Before we head down the next junction, I want you to take a moment to pause and reflect on how you really feel about God's definition of what it takes to be happy. I want you to realize where you're out of alignment with what God has to say. Then you're going to look at steps you can take to begin to move back into alignment. This will be like a spiritual chiropractic appointment. You've gotten off-kilter; you need to see how far so you can begin a process of realignment.

I'd like you to think about and project yourself in two different scenarios. I'd like you to be as detailed and imaginative as you can be. Here's the first one:

Imagine you've won the lottery. It's a lot of money—say, $85 million. Needless to say, if you didn't want to, you wouldn't have to work another day in your life. You could pay off your bills. OK, keep going. I want you to write out all of the things you would do with the money. There are no "right" answers here. I want you to think about how your life would be different and what you would do with the money. Be really specific. Would you pay off your mortgage? Put your kids through college? Buy a new house? Start a business? What would you do?

Now, write it down.

_____

_____

_____

That was pretty fun, wasn't it? Wasn't it fun to think about all you would do with the money? Wasn't it fun to dream and think about all of the stresses you'd get yourself out from under—from financial to job to family? Wasn't that fun? While listening to the radio or reading the paper about other people who have won large amounts of money, haven't you found yourself thinking about what you'd do? It's called daydreaming and most people would say it was fun.

Now, how did it make you feel to think about all of these things? Could you imagine yourself happy or at least happier than you are now? Deep down, doesn't part of you think that this kind of lightning-out-of-the-sky financial windfall would solve a great deal of your problems and make you a happier person?

Now finish this sentence: if I won the lottery, I'd be a happier person because... (go ahead, be honest about this!).

This kind of thinking is daydreaming and wishful and wistful thinking. The reason I had you engage in it is because, even though you've read all about what God says about happiness, most of us still harbor some of the Merriam-Webster definition of *wealth* and *prosperity*, no matter how "obsolete" it supposedly is.

Now, let's go one step further. For some of you, prosperity may not be the "trigger" for you for this kind of wishful, wistful thinking of what happiness is. It could be restoration of a relationship, losing a certain amount of weight, fixing a chronic physical condition, or attaining professional or personal prestige. Whatever it is for you, I want you to take a moment and write down what life would be like for you if whatever that is came true for your life.

Now describe how you felt while you were "living" within that daydream. Were you happy, relieved, vindicated, refreshed, excited, encouraged? How did you feel?

Coming back down to earth. How do you feel now that you're back to reality, where this is not the circumstance of your current life? Do you feel disappointed, frustrated, melancholy, angry, or sad? Whatever you feel, write it down.

_____

_____

_____

_____

Put that on hold for a moment, and let's go into our next scenario: someone has accused you of something you didn't do. No one seems to believe that you didn't do it. Even your friends, or those you thought were your friends, believe you're guilty. Even if they don't believe you're guilty, they've withdrawn their friendship from you because of all the controversy. You've lost your job because of all the legal problems and are having to spend savings for attorneys. Your spouse is now holding down two jobs because of this and your kids are humiliated every time they go out in public. The prosecutor has taken an innocent situation and turned it into something terrible. The description of what you've done is so compelling, you're starting to believe it yourself, or at least doubt your own motives.

How do you feel? Where do you turn? What is your source of solace and strength?

You know what the "right" answer is, but what else are you tempted to do to alleviate your suffering?

For some of you, this won't be just an intellectual exercise. You've lived out a scenario with some of these aspects in your own life. You can extrapolate how you'd feel in a situation like this because you've undergone something akin to it, even in a small way.

Thinking about it isn't fun, is it? Living it sure wasn't either.

Not knowing everyone who will read this book, I set up this situation so you would feel what is normal to feel in these disparate situations. One that is supposed to make you happy and one that is supposed to make you sad.

I want you to realize how it is possible for you to know in your head how you're supposed to feel but still feel a different way in your heart.

This U-turn we're making on the road to happiness, turning away from what the world says and turning toward what God says, is going to take time and practice. It's not going to happen overnight. You can find a reason to be happy in the first scenario because money means power and privilege in this society. Money doesn't buy happiness, but it does buy physical comfort. It can make you happy to think about. But winning the lottery is at best unlikely and at worst impossible. If you wait to be happy until you win life's lottery, you're going to be waiting awhile.

On the other hand, persecution and problems are pretty much a given in this world. You don't have to wait long for them to show up. Remember, life isn't fair, and you are promised you will have problems in this life. If you wait to be happy until you have no problems, you're going to be waiting awhile.

God does not want you to wait to be happy. He wants to give you happiness and joy right now. His happiness is not contingent upon outside circumstances. It is instead contingent upon the willingness of your heart to accept it. Is it logical to be happy while persecuted? No, but it is possible with God. Is it logical to be happy in the midst of grief? No, but it is possible with God. Is it logical to be happy in the midst of pain? No, but it is possible with God.

There are certain situations in life that are just natural sources of joy. Each of these is a gift from God. For the rest of life, there is a happiness that has its basis in God's goodness and mercy, apart from circumstances. This is the happiness the Beatitudes speak of and the type of happiness we're all working toward.

Chapter 3

THE DETOUR
OF DEPRESSION

OST PEOPLE DON'T START OUT IN LIFE INTENTIONALLY headed toward depression. Life just takes you down that detour sometimes, for a whole host of reasons. Sometimes it's a traumatic event that shakes your world and shatters your confidence. Sometimes it's the cumulative effect of anxiety and fear about yourself and your future. Sometimes it's the sheer weariness of never seeming to get on the right road to happiness. Sometimes it's the constant criticism and negativity of the people you travel with. Sometimes it's because no matter how fast you go, you can't seem to outrun your past. Sometimes it's because no matter how far you go, it's still your face you see in the rearview mirror.

It's like when you're traveling along without a care in the world, and then something unexpected happens in front of you. You get caught up in it, and, before you know it, you're off track. You've taken a detour on the road to happiness. Now you have to follow a jury-rigged, less convenient, less comfortable, less efficient track. The trip seems interminable. You're tired of being in the car, tired of hearing the same songs over and over again. You're tired of the people sitting next to you. (In fact, the next time one of them opens their mouth, you're going to scream out loud, just to drown out whatever inane thing they were planning to say. Call it a survival strategy.) You're tired of not really knowing how you're going to get where you're going. You're tired of not really knowing where you are. You're tired of just about everything at this point in the trip. This trip, which started out so sunny, has turned into a gloomy, dreary, unending trudge. Just turning on the engine each day and heading out onto the road of life seems just too much work to bother.

But how do you know when you're depressed? How do you know if what you're feeling is the normal consequence of your current circumstances in life? How do you know if it's more than just having a string of lousy days? Depression isn't like a sprained ankle. With a sprained ankle, you are very much aware the moment it happens. People see you limping and ask you what's wrong, and you think, "Isn't it obvious? I sprained my ankle."

Depression isn't generally that obvious. People ask, "What's wrong with you?" and you have trouble giving them a definitive answer. You can't point down at your ankle askew and say, "There—that's what's wrong with me!" You ask yourself what's wrong, and all you can come up with is a vague excuse of not feeling well or not feeling like yourself. Now, it's true that sudden, traumatic events can trigger a depressive episode, such as the death of a loved one, a major health crisis, a financial catastrophe, or an unexpected move. These are events that can knock us off our bearings, resulting in a period of depression.

Depression isn't even one thing, like spraining your ankle. You could be in the midst of a major depressive episode, during which you have trouble working, sleeping, and eating. You're so focused on just getting through the day that you've stopped focusing on how you feel. All the activities you used to really get a kick out of have now gone flat, or maybe you've gone flat, but what does it really matter, because it's all just flat. You could be in the midst of long-term dysthymia, which to me is like a kind of low-grade depressive fever. You're still marginally functional but nothing seems to go right, and you sure don't feel right most of the time. You could be in the midst of seasonal affective disorder, aptly named S.A.D., where the drab and dreary days of winter precisely mirror your drab and dreary outlook and feelings.

It would be nice if depression were like a sprained ankle. Fixing a sprained ankle is pretty straightforward—bind it up to support it, and stay off of it until it heals. But what do you do with depression when it's hard for you to pinpoint where it really hurts and your life isn't really something you can "stay off" of until you feel better? Most people who experience symptoms of depression but keep powering on anyway get used to the feeling of walking around with the weight of the world on their shoulders. I mean, it's not the end of the world. The sun still comes up every morning, and so do they, in a manner of speaking. They're still walking around, functioning at some level, even though walking feels like it's through really thick sand that clings to their feet and makes each step an effort. They get used to thinking, "This is just the way life is." They stopped looking for happiness a long time ago. They're just trying to make it through the detour of depression; who cares about the destination?

I've seen it over and over again. Depression can get you so off track that you spend a good portion of your life on the off-ramp of depression, circling round and round, thinking that as long as you're moving, you're actually getting somewhere. In actuality, you're going in circles and not making any forward progress. But before you can get back on the road to happiness, you need to be able to watch the signs and recognize when you've taken a detour of depression.

Look for the Flashing Yellow Light

Let's take a look at some, what I call, "yellow indicators" of depression. These are symptoms or conditions you may have been living with for quite a long time, maybe even years. They're like the smell from that spill in the backseat from a while back. When you first get in the car, you smell it, but, after a while, you just don't notice it anymore. It's just so much a part of your experience that you stop noticing it. However, if anyone new gets in the car, the first thing they do is crinkle their nose and exclaim, "What *died* back there?" So often when your depressive behaviors are called into question, your responses can be pretty similar. "Oh, *that*? You get used to it after a while," or "That's just the way I am." Take a look at the yellow indicators, and see if they are present in your own life.

No thanks; not today. One of the yellow indicators of depression is *a loss of enjoyment in established activities*. These are things you used to do that you really enjoyed doing. However, now, nothing seems to really float your boat anymore, and the energy and time it takes to do those activities just don't seem worth it for the payout you feel. Things are sort of grayed out; it's not that you really love or hate doing them anymore, you just don't feel that strong one way or the other.

Teacher, I need to go to the bathroom. Do you ever remember being in an elementary school class and just feeling antsy? There was no legitimate way of leaving, so you used the tried and true method of school-age kids across the ages; in order to get out of class, you faked a full bladder. If the teacher had asked you what was really wrong, you wouldn't have known what to say, just that you were bored and slightly discontent for no apparent reason. Another of the yellow indicators of depression is kind of like that—*a feeling of restlessness or a lack of motivation.* It's as if your life is the classroom and you're just antsy to leave it, to do something to change where you are but have no idea what or why.

Don't bother me right now! Any one of us can have a bad day; I know I've certainly had my share. My day will get off-kilter, and the next thing you know, I'm short-tempered and frustrated and not caring if the world knows it. One day is one thing, but if this grouchiness continues, it's a problem. One way to spot depression is through *an increase in irritability or impatience.* Sometimes you need to let off a little steam, vent your feelings of anger and frustration at the world around you. This venting should reduce the pressure and allow you to put those bulging eyes back in their sockets and pulsing veins back in your neck. Venting situations should be few and far between. Depression, however, keeps the pressure building all the time. It just builds and builds until a casual remark, a reasonable setback, an understandable action trips the switch and the other person gets blasted with the hot steam of your discontent. Instead of relieving the pressure, this just causes more resentment to boil under the surface until others around you, for safety's sake, consider you someone always in the red zone and tiptoe around you accordingly.

A camel just waiting for a straw. Another way to know if you've detoured off into depression is experiencing *a sense of being weighed down, overburdened with life and its activities.* Just like the proverbial camel, you're waiting for the last straw that's going to tip you over the edge. Everything about your life seems burdensome. You're sure you're not going to make it and dread waking up each day, fearful today will be the day you don't. Some days, it's all too much and you'd rather just bury your head in the pillows and stay in bed all day.

Where are you, God? As Christians, we rely on a sense of God's presence in our lives. Depression has a way, however, of creating spiritual interference, and you experience *a lack of spiritual peace or well-being.* The source of your greatest comfort and connection instead feels like nobody's home. You're not sure if it's God or if it's you, but there's a disconnect somewhere. You keep crying out to God for help, but all you hear is silence.

You can't eat just one. You're depressed; you want to feel better. As an adult, you're used to taking care of yourself and finding a way to get by. As a Christian, you're aware of the spiritual and ethical problems of drug and alcohol, some of the most common ways the rest of the world self-medicates their depression. Those options are out, so, instead, you substitute another yellow indicator: *turning to food for personal comfort and relief.* You may not realize it, but sitting down in the evening and consuming a bag of chips and a pint of ice cream is a way to self-medicate your feelings of depression.

Waiting for the other shoe to drop. I recognize that, for some of you, this phrase may seem a bit obscure. I'm not sure where it comes from or where I first heard it, but here's the explanation from Michael Quinion (it's remarkable what you can Google nowadays).

> Its source would seem to be the following story. A man comes in late at night to a lodging house, rather the worse for wear. He sits on his bed, drags one shoe off and drops it on the floor. Guiltily remembering everyone around him trying to sleep, he takes the other one off much more carefully and quietly puts in on the floor. He then finishes undressing and gets into bed. Just as he is drifting off to sleep, a shout comes from the man in the room below: "Well, drop the other one then! I can't sleep, waiting for you to drop the other shoe!"[1]

I realize I'm that way sometimes. When I'm anxious or fearful about what is going to happen, or what I think is going to happen, I stay on alert, waiting for any sign that the something bad I'm waiting for is about to happen. Therein lies another yellow indicator of depression—*anxiety or fear about the future.* When you're in a depressed state, you're hypersensitive to things like shoes dropping on the floor above you. Instead of just rolling over and going back to sleep, you sit up, worrying and straining for the next "bad thing" to happen. Every little sound causes a panic or fear reaction. You're jumpy, you're fearful, you're tired from living each moment waiting for the other "shoe" to drop.

The Cinderella syndrome. Perception is a funny thing. It isn't necessarily reality but rather what is perceived to be the truth. Depression can skew the truth and warp your perceptions. It can lead to you believing that the world is against you, that you're being taken advantage of. Because you're so tired and stressed all of the time, any additional task, no matter how small or insignificant, can feel like a tremendous weight. You remember every favor you've been asked to do and have a tendency to forget or minimize when you've been helped by others. You begin to see yourself as a present-day Cinderella, always being put upon to do the work of others, unappreciated, taken advantage of, with your true worth hidden under a load of care. This constant sense of "poor me" leads straight to another yellow indicator of depression: *a sense of being unappreciated by others, of martyrdom, as if constantly asked to do others' work.*

Eat, drink, and be merry, for tomorrow we die. Circling around and around on your detour of depression, you can get pretty tired of the scenery. This may cause you to make unwise choices about how to get yourself out of the depression cycle. All of a sudden, leaving your spouse and starting over may sound like a really great idea. All of a sudden, quitting your job and taking up astral projections may seem like an appropriate career move. All of a sudden, spending the rent check at the casino looks like a wise investment. Another yellow indicator of depression is *a pattern of impulsivity or rash judgments.* This isn't the same thing as going to the store to buy a shirt and coming back with a suit instead. These are decisions that are not thought through and carried out regardless of obvious negative consequences. They are not spontaneous as much as they are desperate. They're meant to catapult you out of the pit of despair but end up just digging you in deeper.

Sorry—I'm busy. Granted, in our peculiar culture of online communities and neighbors not knowing neighbors, social cohesion has taken a real hit. People simply don't spend as much time around other people as they used to. This is even true in the Christian community. It seems as if nowadays you need to put out effort to go to church and social functions, to know your neighbors and get out of your home at the end of the day. Depression does nothing to help with this societal schism by bringing on *increased social isolation*. When you feel like something the cat dragged in, who wants to be around other people? You're sure you have nothing to offer, and their laughter and cheerfulness just present an unbearable contrast to how you're feeling inside. It's less effort, less work, less pain to just curl up inside your house and stay there.

Not tonight; I have a headache. One of the pleasures to be grayed out in depression is sexual arousal and performance. Because of this, *sexual difficulties or a loss of interest in sexual activities* is a yellow indicator. Part of this comes from a sense of being unlovable, and part of this comes from the social isolation. As your world gets smaller and smaller, you eventually shut out your family and your spouse. You couldn't begin to see yourself as attractive enough, as desirable enough, for sexual activity. Besides, it's frankly too much effort. And when things don't go right, it's too humiliating.

No way out. Everyone has aspects of their lives that they're not thrilled about. You put up with little things because there's not too much you can do about them. For example, I really don't like driving to work. I don't live that far away, and it always seems to me it should take less time than it does. When I get up and am ready to go, I want to *be there*. Instead, I have to put up the garage door, get in my car, back out of the garage, put down the door, turn the car around, get out of my driveway, drive in to work, and then back up at least twice to park. All of this seems like a distraction. If it were up to me, I'd have a matter transporter (you know, from *Star Trek*, where you could instantly be transported from place to place with the twinkling of some lights). As long as transporter technology is relegated to science fiction, I'll always resent, just a little, the time it takes to get from home to work. I do it, but I'm not happy about it. Imagine how it is for someone who is depressed. That feeling of being trapped in an activity you can't change is all-consuming. It isn't just about a small thing, like driving to work; it's about everything you do. This is the yellow indicator that is typified by *a sense of being trapped by the day's activities*. You're not just mildly annoyed; you feel like you're suffocating. Every action requires effort, which wouldn't be so bad if you enjoyed what you do, but you don't. You do it because you *have* to, not because you *want* to. If there was a way to get out of it, you would; but there's no way out.

The glass is half empty. Have you ever known anyone who was consistently negative—who viewed the world and what happened to them in the worst possible light? Have you known someone who was able to find the dark cloud in every silver lining? Often, these people are so ingrained in this way of thinking that they see it as normal. They are unable to see it as pessimistic, negative, or critical. They think they're being honest, realistic, and pragmatic. These people are toxic. Their view of life is so polluted that they contaminate those around them with their *pattern of pessimistic or critical comments and/or behaviors*. Given this propensity, these people don't really need to socially isolate themselves, as most people will eventually give them a wide berth. They're abrasive and negative. This is a yellow indicator of depression, and, like it or not, this person could be you.

The golden days of yesteryear. A depressive attitude contains the yellow indicator *belief that your best days are behind you and the future holds little promise.* Sometimes this comes about due to the death of a dream. Sometimes this comes about because of aging and a realization that the time you've lived is longer than the time you have left. Sometimes this comes about because of a negative change in your circumstances, as if your future and all it holds was tied to what you lost, not what you have left. Whatever the reason, once this mind-set takes hold, it has a way of becoming a self-fulfilling prophecy.

Pass the pain pill. Sometimes, the psychological pain of depression finds a physical outlet. This yellow indicator occurs with *a recurrent pattern of headaches, muscle aches, and body aches*. You hurt, so you go to the doctor, who can find nothing wrong with you. Your tests come back "normal" but you still hurt. So, you get a pill to ease the pain, to help you sleep. After a while, though, it doesn't work so well, so you get another, and another, and another. Now you're so overmedicated that you can't even think straight, and you still hurt. You're too tired to do anything, and you're blowing up like a balloon with excess weight. You feel worse than ever, so you go back to the doctor for another pill.

An old shoe. Take all of the above and combine them and you can end up with a *perception of being overweight, unattractive, discarded, or without value*, another yellow indicator. At this point, despair sets in, and it becomes difficult to find the motivation to reach outside yourself and seek help.

Yellow indicators tend to be behaviors and feelings you can exist with for quite a length of time. They are ways to cope and vent and get through the day when you're depressed. Some people I've worked with were stunned to realize these negative behaviors and patterns had depression as their root cause. These were often successful, self-sufficient people who stubbornly refused to read the yellow indicators for months, even years. Usually it was family and friends who put their collective foot down and demanded the person get help.

Red Light Means *Stop*!

I've also worked with people who continued to ignore the mounting number of yellow indicators in their lives and cycled further and further into deep depression. There comes a point at which something shifts in the status quo and yellow indicators switch to red indicators. I call them red indicators because when one of these shows up in your life or in the life of a loved one, something has shifted and it's time to take immediate action.

The following are serious, debilitating conditions that need to be addressed immediately, especially the last two dealing with suicidal thoughts and plans. These aren't just a detour where you are able to maintain a certain level of functioning; these can literally stop you in your tracks.

A significant change in appetite, lasting longer than two weeks.

Ask yourself why the drastic change in eating habits. This isn't trying to take off weight in May for summer. It's not the seven pounds you gained over the holidays. The components to look for here are *intensity* and *duration* without a reasonable explanation. And it goes both way—overeating or starving yourself.

Recurring disturbances in sleep patterns, lasting longer than two weeks.

You'll read in a later chapter about the physiological reasons why depression and sleep disturbances go hand-in-hand. This isn't being unable to sleep the night before a big presentation or inexplicably needing a nap on a sunny Saturday afternoon. Look for erratic sleep patterns, such as waking up at 2:00 a.m. and being unable to go back to sleep. Sleep is one of the most basic human needs, and not getting it or having it disturbed for any length of time has serious consequences.

Increased agitation or inability to relax, for an extended period of time.

Just like sleep, our bodies need time to relax, to rejuvenate, and to recoup from the stresses of life. This isn't feeling anxious before a planned surgery or a couple of days being keyed up before a major event. Those things are understandable, and people tend to work through them. Once the stressor is over, so is the stress. Instead, this is the stress dial cranked up to full without any upcoming event to flick it off. This is being angry and upset and keyed up for days, weeks, even months. A state of such agitation is unhealthy and why this is a red indicator.

Fatigue, lethargy, or loss of energy for an extended period of time.

This isn't just feeling a little more tired than usual. It isn't tied to intense physical activity, late nights, or a busy lifestyle, such as a mother of young children. It isn't deciding you'll run two miles instead of four or skip the gym today. Again, this must be filtered through the lenses of *intensity* and *duration*. It's when you're barely able to get up, get out, and function for several weeks without a respite. Even the smallest task leaves you physically drained.

Sadness, despondency, despair, loneliness, or feelings of worthlessness for an extended period of time.

Life is hard and it takes its toll on us emotionally and physically. You get knocked down, and it can be difficult to bounce back. But you should bounce back at some point. If that point doesn't ever seem to arrive, it's time to pay attention. These are intense feelings of negativity and despair, and they lead down a dark path where hope is hidden. This is not a path anyone should stay on for any length of time without seeking help.

Inability to concentrate, to focus, or to make decisions, recurring over more than a two-week period of time.

This isn't having trouble deciding what color to paint your living room or daydreaming in the middle of the day. This is about a debilitating condition where you are unable to make the decision you need to. It's about being unable to bring yourself to focus or concentrate on a task, something you need or want to do. You're not putting off a decision; you literally cannot bring yourself to make one. And this happens with frightening regularity, adversely affecting your ability to function in your life.

Recurring thoughts of death or suicide.

I am amazed at how many depressed people don't consider this red indicator to be all that significant. After all, they reason, it seems pretty reasonable, given their life and their circumstances. If their life is unbearable, they think about an end to the pain. Instead of being alarmed at these thoughts, they can instead feel a sense of relief, as they contemplate a cessation of suffering. This thinking is based on a false assumption that life is unbearable and the pain is unending. Again, this is a product of perception and not reality. If you have or are entertaining thoughts of this kind, I'll be plain: *you're not thinking clearly. Life is worth living; your life is worth living today, tomorrow, and beyond.* If you've lost sight of hope, recognize that it's due to your blindness, not because it isn't there. You need to find professional help to bring back your vision.

A plan for suicide or an attempt at suicide.

This isn't just a red indicator; it's a glaring, flashing, hands-waving, voice-bellowing "Look out!" red indicator. If you've sunk to the depths of creating a plan, you are more likely to carry it out. If you've made an attempt to end your life, you are more likely to try it again. This is your life we're talking about here—not just your circumstances in life, but your life itself—your eyes-opening, lungs-filling, hands-touching, ears-hearing, nose-smelling life. If you've gotten to this point in your depression, you need to seek professional help immediately—not tomorrow, but today…right now.

These red indicators are definite warning signs to get off the path you're on and seek out professional help. However, don't run into the trap of thinking that the yellow indicators are just the way life is, or just the way you are, or surely things that will work themselves out in time. This is not the life God intends for you. These are serious issues and must not be minimized or overlooked. This isn't the way life should be. Depression is not a road you must travel indefinitely. Did you note the words "longer than two weeks" and "extended period of time"? Depression is a serious mental and physical issue that needs to be addressed, just like any significant health crisis.

The detour of depression can be navigated, and you can get back on the road to happiness. The first thing you need to do is recognize when you've veered off the path. The second thing is to turn over the navigation to professionals who can get you on the right course. You'll still be at the wheel, but you need professional help and direction. There is no shame in asking for and accepting help. After all, if you sprained your ankle, you'd go to a doctor for help. Depression isn't a sprained ankle, but there is still plenty of help available.

When you're depressed, asking for help is the most reasonable thing you can do. When you've lost your way, it does no good to keep driving around aimlessly, hoping you'll find something that looks familiar. Depression alters your perception to the point you wouldn't recognize an exit even if you came upon it by accident. Instead, you need help to interpret correctly what's happening, and you need help to assist you in finding your way back.

It's time to take inventory of how you're feeling. Often serious, intentional consideration of where you are in your life gets put on the back burner. You're so busy just getting through the day that you have little time to think about tomorrow and rarely about a month, a year, or several years down the road. But it's time for you to stop and take stock.

Reading through this, you may already have identified several depressive behaviors and attitudes in your life. This may merely be verification of what you've suspected or been told by others. Or, for the first time you may be considering whether or not some of these patterns are being played out in your own life in negative ways. You've never given serious thought to depression as a factor in your life but recognize you suffer from some of the yellow, even red, indicators. For others of you, please recognize you don't have to be clinically depressed to have your life adversely affected by some of these indicators. Before you can devise a plan to deal with your own personal detours and find a way out of the depression spiral, you need to know where you're most susceptible.

I recognize that those of you reading this book will come from a full spectrum of experience. Some of you will recognize some negative patterns in your life that you've stubbornly clung to as being depressive in nature. If this is you, it's time to really identify what those patterns are so you can be aware of them and look for specific information in this book that addresses your issues. Some of you are aware that you have a tendency toward depression but have been dealing with it yourself, without any professional help. My hope is, through this exercise and through the information presented throughout this book, you'll fine-tune your understanding of what is keeping you from the happiness you seek and determine whether or not it's time to utilize professional assistance. Some of you will be actively working with a health-care professional to recover. I heartily encourage you to continue working through this chapter and the entire book, sharing with your doctor, therapist, or health-care team what resonates with you in order for you to actively participate in your own recovery.

Let's take some time right now to go over the yellow indicators in order to help you begin to identify areas of detour on your road to happiness. Take a look at each set of questions, and search deep inside yourself for the most truthful answer. Be brave and honest with yourself. This isn't a test to project what you want to be; it's a way to determine how you are right now.

1. As I think about my life, have I stopped enjoying things I always liked doing before? If my world and activities are shrinking, what have I stopped doing, and what reason did I give when I stopped?

2. As I look at the list of things I wrote above, are there any activities I realize I'd like to start doing again? If so, which ones? If I'm still not interested, why is that?

3. Can I see myself as being more listless these days? If I find it hard to be excited or motivated about much of anything these days, can I identify any reasons why I might feel that way?

4. I really have been barking at people lately. Little things seem to really set me off. What are the things that really have been bothering me? Are those really the reasons, or is there something else that makes me angry? If so, what is the real reason I'm so irritable?

5. Is it hard for me to get motivated to even get up and get going in the morning? Do I feel like I'm walking around with a weight on my shoulders, making everything I do more difficult? What am I having the most trouble doing? What do I think is standing in my way?

6. As I look at my life and all the tasks and responsibilities I have, do I find it difficult to get done everything I need to

do? Do I find myself always behind, never being able to get ahead of my day? Why do I have such trouble? If there was one thing that could help me manage better, what would that one thing be?

7. How connected do I feel to God? Do I pray? If I do, does it seem like no one is listening? How does God feel about me?

8. If I'm honest, what is my relationship with food? Is eating and drinking a major source of pleasure in my life? Do I eat when I'm full? Do I eat things I know aren't good for me because it feels good to eat them? Is food a reward for the stress in my life?

9. Am I the kind of person who, even when things are good, still looks over my shoulder, not really trusting it's going to stay good for very long? Do I believe that I'm just one of those people who bad things happen to? If so, why do I feel that way?

10. Is my job driving me nuts? Do I feel that no one appreciates how hard I work? Do people at work keep asking me to do more and more things without caring about how it affects

me? Am I angry about the way I'm treated? Is my work a source of stress and negativity in my life?

11. Sometimes do I just want to throw caution to the wind and do something crazy? Am I tired of always being the good person and playing by the rules? When I dream about doing something crazy, what is it? How do I feel about myself when I do that?

12. Do I find myself regularly at the end of the day just wanting to go home and close out the world? Have I stopped participating in social activities? Do I spend less time on the phone, talking with friends? Do I get angry or resent it when people intrude upon my personal time? Why have I stopped wanting to be around people?

13. Have I stopped considering myself an attractive person? Did I ever consider myself an attractive person? Is it difficult for me to initiate or engage in sexual intimacy? If I could name three things that stand in the way of allowing myself to be intimate, what would they be?

14. Do I ever dream about winning the lottery as a way to escape from the worries of my life? If I won the lottery, what changes would I make in my life, and why?

15. As I think about my recent decisions, are there any I've made that I didn't think through very well? What were they, and what did I hope would happen? What really did happen?

16. Am I a negative person? As I sit back and listen to myself talk, are my comments positive, or do I always find a way to think of the negative in any person or situation? Has anyone ever mentioned my negativity? What reasons do I give for these negative comments? Do I think I'm being helpful? Am I worried that if I don't mention the bad things that could happen, it will be my fault when they do?

17. How do I feel about myself today compared with five years ago, ten years ago, twenty years ago, or more? Do I think I have less value now than I did then? What are the things I've lost? What are the things I've gained? What do I think about tomorrow? Will it be better or worse?

18. How am I doing physically? Do I hurt all the time or have chronic conditions? If so, what are they? What am I doing to make them better? Are there things I've been told to do that would make them better that I'm not willing to do at this time? If so, what are they? Why don't I want to do them, even though I'd feel better?

_____

_____

19. Am I afraid to go to the doctor for fear of what he or she will find out about me physically? Am I worried about my health? Why?

_____

_____

My hope is that, through this exercise, you'll see just how much these statements can be firmly entrenched in the negative thinking, pessimism, and despair of depression. If even one of them has a toehold in your life and you're thinking it is hindering your ability to experience happiness, then the more of these reflected in your life, the harder it will be for you to have a joyful attitude. Each one is an anchor, weighing you down, and each takes precious energy to compensate for. For right now, I want you to be aware of the patterns that have built up and begin to accept the truth that you need to rid them from your life. As we continue, you'll learn how to do just that. This first step, though, was to help you identify your own personal challenges of yellow indicators.

For those of you in the yellow zone, here are the yellow indicators again.

- A loss of enjoyment in established activities

- A feeling of restlessness or a lack of motivation

- An increase in irritability or impatience

- A sense of being weighed down, overburdened with life and its activities

- A lack of spiritual peace or well-being

- Turning to food for personal comfort and relief

- Anxiety or fear about the future

- A sense of being unappreciated by others, of martyrdom, as if constantly asked to do others' work

- A pattern of impulsivity or rash judgments

- Increased social isolation

- Sexual difficulties or a loss of interest in sexual activities

- A sense of being trapped by the day's activities

- A pattern of pessimistic or critical comments and/or behaviors

- A belief that your best days are behind you and the future holds little promise

- A recurrent pattern of headaches, muscle aches, or body aches

- A perception of being overweight, unattractive, discarded, or without value

I want you to circle those that most reflect how you're feeling right now. Now, interrogate each of them with the following questions:

- Is this truly the way I feel?

- How often do I feel this way?

- Is this truly the way things are?

- Is it possible I'm focusing too much on the negative?

- As I look at each statement and each scenario, what can I begin to identify as just too extreme a statement?

- Could I substitute the word *sometimes* for *always*? Could I substitute the word *rarely* for *sometimes*?

- If I showed my family these statements, how would they react?

- Have I spoken to anyone about feeling this way?

- Does the person I've spoken to just accept what I say, or do they ask questions to determine if what I'm feeling is really true?

We've talked about the yellow indicators, but you may be asking, "What about the red indicators?" Let's take a look at those again:

- A significant change in appetite, lasting longer than two weeks

- Recurring disturbances in sleep patterns, lasting longer than two weeks

- Increased agitation or inability to relax for an extended period of time

- Fatigue, lethargy, or loss of energy for an extended period of time

- Sadness, despondency, despair, loneliness, or feelings of worthlessness for an extended period of time

- Inability to concentrate, to focus, or to make decisions, recurring over more than a two-week period of time

- Recurring thoughts of death or suicide

- A plan for suicide or an attempt at suicide

If you have identified any of the red indicators present in your life, you need to obtain professional help right now. These are warning signs that you need to pay attention to. They cannot be put off any longer, and they are not going to go away by themselves. I urge you to get on our Web site at www.aplaceofhope.com, where you'll find detailed information about our whole-person recovery programs, including healing from depression. If you need to seek treatment locally, don't put it off another day. Find a qualified therapist, preferably a Christian, who can work with you. This isn't something you can do alone.

Actually, working through any of these indicators isn't something you can or should do alone. Even if you only have a couple of yellow indicators present in your life, they carry a level of debilitation and need to be addressed. Those of you with three or more yellow indicators or any one of the red indicators need to seek professional help from a mental-health and/or health-care professional. Remember, if you sprained your ankle, you wouldn't hesitate to see a doctor, so don't hesitate to get the help you need here. If depression has detoured you from your happiness in life, turn around, get the help you need, and head in a different direction!

Having said that, I recognize that many people find comfort and strength through talking things over with their friends or family. Hopefully, that person will echo my sentiments about getting professional help if you have three or more yellow indicators or any one of the red indicators. The help you need is more than they can give. They know it, you know it, and it's not fair to ask them to constantly provide what they simply are not able to give.

But if you have recognized one or two yellow indicators that are causing interference in someone else's life, I want you to do something for me. I want you to look over the yellow indicators and answer how many of them are true for that person, as best you can, knowing what you know about them.

Here's what I'm getting at: Scripture says that if a blind person leads a blind person, they'll both end up in a pit. If you want to get out of a detour of depression, you need to associate yourself with people who are positive and will build you up, not bring you down even further. If the person you spend time with and talk to is a generally positive person, congratulations! Now, thank God for bringing this person into your life. This person is truly a blessing for you, and you'll want to take full advantage of this blessing. The next time the two of you talk about life and how it's going, why don't you spend more time listening and less time talking? It may be this person has been placed in your life expressly to speak words of encouragement and hope into you. If you spend all your time together complaining, there won't be very much time left for uplifting. This person's positive nature can provide balance and a counter to negative perceptions and patterns. You want to spend your time being influenced by this positive person instead of dragging him or her down.

But what if you realize this other person has as many or more yellow indicators as you do? If the two of you are peas in a pod, begin to search outside of this relationship for the positive affirmation and relationship you need. Until you find that person, you may need to begin to be that positive person for yourself, even if you don't really feel like it at first. If that's too difficult for you right now, why not imagine you're talking about your life to Jesus? As you think about your life and process what you've learned about yourself in this chapter, why not turn it into a *What would Jesus say?*

If you've discovered seeds of depression choking out the joy in your life, take heart and keep going. Soon you will take a detailed look at how the whole-person approach to life can produce amazing results in healing and recovery.

In the next chapter, we'll take a look at two other issues—worry and anxiety—that often detour people from the road to happiness. And sometimes, because they are so often a part of our "normal" life, we don't even recognize them.

Chapter 4

THE DETOUR OF WORRY AND ANXIETY

THERE'S SOMETHING FUNNY ABOUT THE DETOUR OF WORRY AND anxiety that makes it different. When you're on this detour, you're fooled into thinking you're onto something really important, when, in fact, it's really just a whole lotta nothin'. Like an internal announcer who took lessons from late-night infomercials and county fair hucksters, incessantly presenting every potential as proven disaster, this detour is filled with hyperbole. Just when you think you can relax and get a handle on your problems, this irritating announcer menacingly proclaims, "But wait…there's more!" You're looping around a backwater, going nowhere, but every twist and turn in the road is presented as fraught with catastrophe. This detour isn't an easy ride; it's a white-knuckled, heart-pounding, sweat-drenching, adrenaline-producing ride called fear.

Worry + Anxiety = Fear

When you're on the detour of worry and anxiety, you're smack-dab in the middle of fear, no matter where else you think you're going. I've known far too many people who have lived a life of fear, and fear can be a crippling, debilitating straitjacket that limits movement, induces panic, and strangles peace.

Fear has the enviable position of forcing you to prove the impossible. How can you prove, for example, that you're not going to fail in business two years from today, or that your kid won't end up doing drugs as a teenager, or you won't come down with an incurable disease when you're fifty? Knowing definitively those things won't happen requires a greater ability than yours to predict the future.

So, you start worrying about your business, even in the midst of a record year. You start intensely watching your child for signs of problems, even though he's only seven. Every ache and pain is filtered through the latest medical condition headline. None of these fit your particular situation? Fear has an endless array of possible scenarios in its arsenal, ready to exploit your personal worries and defeat any stray thought of *surely not*. Worry and anxiety double-team to shout in response, "Surely so, and sooner rather than later!"

This is tyranny. When you are circling in the clutches of worry, anxiety, and fear, happiness is, at best, glimpsed—never permanent, never complete.

Worry and anxiety are a "which came first—the chicken or the egg?" proposition. They're a packaged deal. Although in the alphabet the letter *a* comes before the letter *w*, worry actually comes before anxiety. Of course, some people are anxious about their worrying and worry about their anxiety, so they are a bit circular.

Are you a worrywart?

A cartoonist by the name of J. R. Williams invented a character named Worry Wart for his *Out Our Way With the Worry Wart* cartoon.[1] From this cartoon, we derive the term *worrywart*, which means "a person who is inclined to worry unduly."[2]

In reality, worry is a whole lot more problematic than a wart. It's a pernicious pattern of negative thinking that takes a stranglehold on your life and can lead to serious and debilitating anxiety disorders, which are like worry on steroids.

Before we go much further, let's see what the secular definitions are for *worry* and *anxiety* from *Merriam-Webster's Dictionary*:

- *Worry*—1: a: mental distress or agitation resulting from concern usually for something impending or anticipated; anxiety; b: an instance or occurrence of such distress or agitation.[3]

- *Anxiety*—1: a: painful or apprehensive uneasiness of mind usually over an impending or anticipated ill; b: fearful concern or interest; c: a cause of anxiety; 2: an abnormal and overwhelming sense of apprehension and fear often marked by physiological signs (as sweating, tension, and increased pulse), by doubt concerning the reality and nature of the threat, and by self-doubt about one's capacity to cope with it.[4]

Let's take a look at worry first, since I believe it is the seed from which anxiety grows. Worry, it seems, can literally grab you by the throat. I heard of a woman who found herself in this very predicament; she was worrying herself to death. She lived a stressful life, with a great deal to worry about. She found it harder and harder to catch her breath. Naturally, she went to the doctor, believing she was suffering from a physical condition. His conclusion, however, was unexpected. Her physical reaction to the stresses and worries in her life were being played out in the muscles around her throat, which were constricting tighter and tighter over time. The doctor explained she was slowly suffocating herself due to her stressful life. I have known many people who felt that way, metaphorically.

It makes sense, though, doesn't it? Worries literally choke us off from living a full and happy life. Jesus uses this analogy Himself during the parable of the seeds found in Matthew 13. It's the story of a farmer who goes out to plant seeds. Some of the seeds fell on a footpath, and the birds ate them. Some of the seeds fell on the rocky soil, where they took root but quickly died for lack of water. Other seed fell among the thorns, where it started to grow but got choked out. The rest of the seed was planted in good soil, where it produced a bountiful harvest.

Jesus had just finished telling this story to the crowds when the disciples came up and asked Him about it. He said that the seed is the Word of God in our lives. This is a great story with multiple applications, but I want to focus on the third kind of seed, the seed that fell and started to grow among the thorns. Jesus said:

> The one who received the seed that fell among the thorns is the man
> who hears the word, but the worries of this life and the deceitfulness
> of wealth choke it, making it unfruitful.
>
> —MATTHEW 13:22

Worries become like thorns around you, ever growing, crowding out the good things in your life, including God's Word. Worries consume your energy and resources, only to entangle your very life, thoughts, and hopes. Like being caught up among thorns, you need to find a way out.

How worry makes its way in

I believe a negative pattern of worry is established in childhood, based upon life circumstances, experiences, and perceptions. (I further believe this pattern of worry can be exacerbated by physical realities and predispositions, but that's something you'll read about later. Since you're in the worry chapter, I'll just say—*but wait, there's more!*) So, in order to find a way out, you need to be able to backtrack along your way in, to where worry started in the first place. When you find your entry point, you're that much closer to rediscovering the world outside of worry.

A place of worry can come from a lack of security. Your feelings of security are formed in childhood. When you're a child, you learn to feel secure in your surroundings, your family, yourself, and your abilities. This sense of security provides a stable, strong foundation on which to venture forth into life. When this doesn't happen, you develop a foundation of insecurity, which substitutes a rickety, weakened foundation, ill-suited for adulthood and its challenges, risks, and dilemmas.

A child with a sense of security looks out across the gulf to adulthood and sees a broadly supported expanse with plenty of room to move and solid railings. There's no need to focus on the abyss below because there is no fear of falling. Instead, the child has a wide-open view of the wonders that await. A child with a sense of insecurity looks out across the gulf to adulthood and sees a gap-filled, narrow track hemmed in on all sides by frayed, untrustworthy ropes. Forget looking up and out; there's an absolute need to focus on the abyss below because each fearful step forward contains the potential for falling. What starts out in childhood translates into adulthood. There are a variety of situations and conditions that can lead to this kind of insecurity growing up.

- *Death of a parent.* A child is utterly dependent upon the care and protection of a parent. When a parent dies, that shield is ripped from the child. Even within a family with a surviving parent or other supportive adults, children experience psychological shock when a parent dies. The world irrevocably changes for a child, even an adult child, when a parent is no longer there. *A child learns that the worst can happen.*

- *Abandonment by a parent.* In our culture of throwaway children and families, I wish this wasn't as prevalent as it is. When a parent basically discards a child through abandonment, damage occurs. In a death, a child learns all is not right with the world. In abandonment, a child assumes all is not right with him or her. *A child learns how much one person can hurt another.*

- *Rejection by a parent.* This is different from abandonment and is when a parent intentionally chooses to reject a child, whether or not there is a physical leaving. *A child learns that no matter what, they just aren't good enough.*

- *Divorce.* Volumes have been written on the effects of divorce on children. Overwhelmingly, divorce not only sunders the relationship of the spouses but also rips apart the world of the children. *A child learns it is possible for someone you love to stop loving you.*

- *Frequent moves.* This is a transient society, so moving from place to place is just a part of what this culture is. Often, parents view a move as a positive change, due to a new house or new job. Children, however, have different priorities, and the one thing they cherish, such as a friend, a teacher, a school, an activity, or even a pet can be sacrificed in the decision to relocate. *A child learns favorite things can be taken away by those who love them.*

- *Learning disabilities.* Imagine what it would be like to go to school every day, apprehensive that you won't be able to meet expectations. Imagine living a life where each new experience was a challenge to identify, cope, sort, assimilate, and learn from. Imagine new situations as a frustrating confrontation, highlighting your inabilities. *A child learns to become resigned to failure.*

- *Difficulties in school.* Children often worry about their work in school but they also worry about other issues, such as social interactions. A child who is unpopular, bullied, unsuccessful, or simply unnoticed learns to distrust what could happen tomorrow. *A child learns what it feels like on the outside.*

- *Excessive criticism or negativity by a parent or significant adult.* Adults are supposed to be a child's biggest teacher and cheerleader. Sadly, too often what they teach isn't very cheery. The child then lives with a critical, negative adult who specializes in blame. This pattern is then internalized by the child and often emulated. *A child learns they are the problem.*

- *Family alcoholism or drug abuse.* When alcohol or drug abuse is present in the home, it becomes a home of calm and crisis. There are lulls between violent storms, whose appearance is not so much a matter of *if* but *when.* A child learns to survive within the chaos of crisis and to never take anything for granted. A calm sky only means a storm is coming. *A child learns up is down and down is up.*

- *Significant legal issues surrounding family members.* Legal issues, though rarely life threatening, nonetheless can be disruptive to family life. Domestic violence, evictions, and short-term incarcerations are all traumatic events because they strip away the stability of the family. *A child learns a home is not a refuge.*

- *A fearful or insecure parent or significant adult.* Some parents communicate hostility and negativity that damage the self-esteem of their children. Other parents or adults can be more passively damaging through a pattern of constant doubt, fear, worry, and anxiety. *A child learns the world is a scary place not to be trusted.*

- *Chronic medical conditions.* Imagine the concern of a child who never knows if a parent is going to have some sort of medical issue, from diabetic shock to an epileptic episode. Children, of course, can be instructed on how to cope with these health challenges in a loved one and even in themselves, but the potential exists for the child to develop an excessive concern about an event reoccurring. *A child learns how quickly things can change.*

- *Perfectionism in the family.* This is one of the most pervasive ways a child is taught to worry. No one can be perfect all the time, so every task, every expectation has a built-in guarantee of failure. Even if the child believes something is right, it's not his or her opinion that counts. *A child learns it's never good enough.*

- *Overinvolved parenting.* When a child is smothered by a parent, he or she is not allowed to experience the world outside of the parental cocoon. Negative consequences are immediately treated as crises and whisked away by the parent. Instead of being strengthened by learning to deal with natural consequences and adversity, a coddled child is weakened and unprepared for the realities of a life detached from the parent. *A child learns the thoughts of others are more important than their own.*

- *Emotional abuse.* I wrote an entire book on this subject (check the resource list for more details), so this is a large issue, but suffice it to say that emotional abuse undermines a child's last stand against worry—their sense of self. If they are told over and over they are not good enough, they'll believe it and be fearful of venturing out much as an adult. *A child learns the lesson of inadequacy.*

- *Physical abuse, including sexual abuse.* The devastation of physical and sexual abuse is so vast that it permeates all aspects of a child's life. This includes the concept of secrecy and holding on to family truths in secret. Bad things, then, are not dealt with out in the open; they are hidden away behind closed doors. *A child learns to wrap their pain in shame and hide it away.*

- *Trauma.* While all abuse is traumatic, there are traumatic events that do not stem from abuse, such as catastrophic accidents. A child's world simply does not contain the possibility for such devastation—until, of course, it happens. Then, all bets are off, and a child may become confused about what is a legitimate concern and what is an improbability. The worry dial has been reset, as it were, by the trauma. *A child learns to fear it could happen again.*

I'd like to take a look again at the "a child learns" statements:

- A child learns that the worst can happen.
- A child learns how much one person can hurt another.
- A child learns that no matter what, they just aren't good enough.
- A child learns it is possible for someone you love to stop loving you.
- A child learns favorite things can be taken away by those who love them.
- A child learns to become resigned to failure.
- A child learns what it feels like on the outside.
- A child learns they are the problem.
- A child learns up is down and down is up.

- A child learns a home is not a refuge.

- A child learns the world is a scary place, not to be trusted.

- A child learns how quickly things can change.

- A child learns it's never good enough.

- A child learns the thoughts of others are more important than their own.

- A child learns the lesson of inadequacy.

- A child learns to wrap their pain in shame and hide it away.

- A child learns to fear it could happen again.

All grown up

Is it any wonder, if you grew up with any of these, that you'd be a little more suspicious about life? Is it any wonder you might have developed a survival strategy of worry? If life taught you that you needed to be prepared for anything at any time, is it any wonder now as an adult you're constantly evaluating potential scenarios to tease out possible disasters just so you can be prepared? If life continually has thrown you a curve ball, you're going to go around crouched in a defensive stance, bat at the ready, tense, and on alert. After all, *fool me once, shame on you—fool me twice, shame on me.* You won't get fooled again. This time, you're going to be ready.

The pattern of worry is like gambling. Every time a worry "pays off," the appropriateness of worry itself is enhanced. Why do people spend money on lotteries, even when they know the odds of winning are astronomical? Because the rewards are also astronomical. Why do people spend time worrying about every little thing even when they know the odds of something happening are minute? The pay-off for a worry isn't money or a trip or anything positive; the pay-off for worry is pain. Worry is all about finding a way to avoid anticipated pain. When you've been hurt so much in the past, worry seems to be a prudent approach to life.

Some people are very attached to their pattern of worry. It's so ingrained that they erroneously assume their worry is just like an innocuous music track, running with little effort or energy in the background. Sure, they can tell what it says if they really listen to it, but most of the time, they say, they don't; they're able to ignore it. Sure, they worry, but it's not a big deal.

This is a fallacy. Look at the verbs associated with worry from our definition: choke, strangle, harass, tear, bite, snap, shake, pull, touch, disturb, change, adjust, push, haul, assail, attack, subject, afflict. Is there anything there that looks easy to ignore?

Worry, even a constant buzz of background worry, is busy causing damage. Worry is like termites, eating away at the foundation of your life. All termites need to thrive is something to feed on and hidden places. Worries thrive by feeding on the insecurities and traumas of life and staying hidden away in your heart and mind. A little worry is like the small dusting of wood particles left on the floor by termites. Those small little worries on the surface can reveal extensive damage going on underneath. Eventually, that damage is going to become evident. When worry goes on unabated too long, anxiety results.

Anxiety—an Outward Sign of an Inward Fear

Anxiety is worry taken one step further. If worry is the inward dialogue of fear, anxiety is its outward broadcast. You may be able to keep your worry hidden but anxiety has a way of announcing its presence. According to the National Institutes of Mental Health, which is a division of the National Institutes of Health (www.nimh.nih.gov), there are several profound conditions arising from anxiety. We will look at four common anxiety disorders—generalized anxiety disorder, obsessive-compulsive disorder, panic disorder, and social anxiety disorder.

Generalized anxiety disorder

Dale, a man in his midforties, came in to see me. He was overwhelmed by the stress in his life—his marriage, his job, his finances, his health, and his kids. A good night's sleep was something he couldn't buy, not even through a little pill. His primary-care doctor suggested becoming dependent on sleep medication wasn't the answer and recommended Dale see a therapist. It took him almost half a year continuing to suffer silently before Dale decided to take him up on his advice.

It became clear after just a few visits that Dale worried about everything. I kept gently probing to see if any of the dire predictions he was sure to come to pass actually had. Apart from his inability to sleep and a very frustrated spouse, as far as I could see, Dale's life was not beset with an overabundance of problems. His life was beset with an overabundance of worries. Dale was struggling with GAD—generalized anxiety disorder.

This is a sort of free-floating condition of anxiety that isn't attached to any specific reason or event. It's a negative pattern of living in a what-if world instead of a what-is world. This disorder is characterized by worry about everyday type of issues—health, family, money, and work. This isn't a worry about the end of the world; it's a worry about the end of life as you know it. GAD is "a mountain out of a molehill" way of looking at life: indigestion is an ulcer; a twinge in the chest is a heart attack; a fight with a spouse spells divorce; a late teenager is in a traffic accident; an unexpected bill is bankruptcy; a bobble in the stock market is a crash; a mess-up at work is a pink slip; an off-hand comment means no promotion.

Another way I've used to illustrate this mind-set is the Chicken Little syndrome. Do you remember that children's story? It's where Chicken Little is out walking one day and is hit in the head with an acorn. As a folk tale, there are about a hundred different versions of this story, but it is usually typified by Chicken Little's cry, "The sky is falling! The sky is falling!" Of course, the sky isn't falling; she was just hit on the head with an acorn. It's an amusing little story for children with a very grown-up application. For people with an overanxious response to life, any normal occurrence, like an acorn falling, translates into, "The sky is falling!"

The anxiety that is produced by this out-of-proportion worry is anything but amusing. The real-life symptoms of generalized anxiety disorder are a pretty serious list: fatigue, headaches, muscle tension, muscle aches, difficulty swallowing, trembling, twitching, irritability, sweating, nausea, lightheadedness, having to go to the bathroom frequently, feeling out of breath, and hot flashes.[5] All of this for an acorn.

Obsessive-compulsive disorder

Sometimes people will take their feelings of dread and impending disaster and concentrate it into a single area of concern.

Pamela was terrified of germs, of unclean things harming her body and making her sick. It was not unusual for Pamela to wash her hands twenty times a day. Public restrooms, stair railings, door handles, telephones, and computer keyboards all presented huge challenges to be hurtled. She kept antibacterial liquid and wipes in her purse at all times. Her day at work could not start until she'd thoroughly disinfected all her personal surfaces. Because crowds were a potential threat of airborne illness, she scrupulously avoided them. She never ate a leftover or took food home from a restaurant. Any cooking was done with great suspicion and extensive precautions against salmonella or other contaminants. She never ate raw egg or raw fish. Pamela's health was her treasure, and she scrupulously worked to protect it against any and all attacks. Pamela had taken her anxiety of sickness and death and laser-focused it into an OCD—obsessive-compulsive disorder.

The first part of OCD is similar to GAD, in that there is an obsessive focus on the negative, a mental barrage of persistent thoughts of potential disaster. Because of the anxiety generated by this thought pattern, a person then develops elaborate rituals and behaviors in order to control the fear. Pamela was concerned about her health and developed compulsivity around hand-washing and avoidance of germs. However, the rituals involved with OCD are varied and can include things like having to go back into your house multiple times to make sure all the appliances are off, or never walking on a crack in a sidewalk. Some people develop a need to count, to find numerical patterns in their surroundings. These compulsions provide a temporary relief from anxiety but are extremely disruptive to your life. Some people who suffer from OCD have unwanted, recurrent thoughts of harming loved ones or engaging in acts the person considers perverted or religiously unacceptable. To me, OCD is anxiety distilled, a potent onslaught of negative thoughts coupled with crippling ritual, disrupting a person's ability to function.

Panic disorder

Jeff remembers vividly the first time it hit. He was on his way to work, to a new job he'd just landed. While riding the bus into downtown, he suddenly felt hot and nauseous, with his heart racing a mile a minute. Everything felt disconnected, and he remembers looking around at the other riders with a feeling of total isolation. Even though it wasn't his destination, he stumbled out at the next stop, compelled to get away, to move. Too embarrassed to ask for help, he found an empty corner of a fast-food restaurant and waited until the feeling passed, sweating and praying and trying to act normal. The feeling passed, but his fear of ever feeling that way again hadn't. It seemed even thinking about having another attack would eventually bring one on. He worried it was the beginnings of a heart attack. It wasn't; Jeff had a panic attack.

When this level of anxiety hits a person, it truly is an attack. Panic attacks are sudden, overwhelming, and often mistaken for a heart attack. The symptoms of a panic attack are pounding heart, sweats, weakness, feeling faint or dizzy, nausea, chest pain, feeling smothered, experiencing a sense of doom, a fear of losing control, feeling flushed or chilled, and tingling or numbness in hands or feet.[6] Because of these symptoms, it's pretty easy to understand why you would think you were having a heart attack. Many people with a panic attack wind up in the emergency room, where someone deals with what they are feeling but usually not with why they are feeling it. It may take several late-night trips to the ER to figure out that it's not a heart attack. Panic disorder is anxiety on an aggressive attack, demanding the front-and-center attention of a physical crisis.

Social anxiety disorder

Shirley rarely left the house, except to go to church on Sunday, where she sat near the back door and left right as services were ending. She shopped late at night, when few people were around. Her family was resigned to picking up take-out and bringing it home because Shirley refused to go to a restaurant. She found excuses not to attend extended family functions and was hardly ever seen around the holidays. She was missing at every band concert and school play, every soccer game and awards banquet. The kids just got used to telling their friends their mom was sick all the time and didn't get out of the house much. That seemed to satisfy their curiosity. Although Shirley was fine at home, she was fine *only* at home. Terrified of being out of her safety zone, Shirley suffered from social anxiety disorder.

If you suffer from this anxiety disorder, your danger zone is anywhere other people are. It may be limited to an especially stressful social situation like speaking in public or in front of a group of people. For others, just being around people is stressful because of the persistent dread of doing something embarrassing or fear of being watched and observed, especially around eating. You assume if others pay attention to you, they'll come away with an unfavorable impression. Deep down, you know you don't belong in the group; you're not good enough to be there and are terrified you'll somehow be found out and asked to leave or booted out in humiliation. There is no safety in numbers for those with social anxiety disorder; the only acceptable number is one and possibly a small group of either friends or family who have proven to be safe over the years. This social phobia is anxiety as self-incarceration.

Agoraphobia

With all of these types of anxiety disorders, there can come a time when your world shrinks. Perhaps you've heard the expression "his home is his castle." For someone with an anxiety disorder, the home can become a fortress, the lone defensible position in a hostile, anxiety-ridden world. When the list of safe places and safe people contracts, it is possible for a person to develop *agoraphobia*. Agoraphobia is a combination of two Greek words: *agora*, meaning "marketplace," and *phobia*, meaning "fear." Fear of the marketplace translates to fear of being outside, around people, in social situations. At The Center, we have had people who called multiple times and literally took months to gather up the courage to leave their homes and come to our offices for help. We've taken phone calls from people in full panic mode at the side of the road, terrified of driving to an appointment. The psychological impact and physical toll of these anxiety disorders is real and debilitating. When anxiety reaches this level, it's not a detour; it's a dead stop on the road to happiness with terror and fear as your unwelcome companions.

Next, you're going to take a look at how to get a hold on these persistent, negative thoughts and patterns, so, please be patient! Right now, your job in this Rest Stop is to uncover the worries you're riding around with. Worry, like white noise, can be so pervasive in your thought patterns that it's hard to pick it out as such.

To help you identify your patterns of worry and what activities or thoughts they are most associated with, you need to answer the following questions. Space is provided for you to write down your answers. I urge you to take time with these questions and really think about your answers. Write down anything that immediately pops into your mind as soon as you read the question. These are the answers that lie on the surface of your mind but I don't want you to stop there.

I want you to continue to sift through the conditions of your life as you answer the questions. This isn't a time to try to smooth over or sugarcoat your answers. You need to understand how deeply these patterns of worry and anxiety are present in your life so you can begin a systematic way to overcome them, which we'll deal with from a whole-person perspective. For right now, your job is to be alert to that little pile of sawdust in the corner of your mind and determine what sort of activity is going on underneath. It's time to get a little exposure into those dark corners.

1. Think back over what your school-age childhood was like. What did you worry about then?

_____

_____

2. How did those worries make you feel?

_____

3. When you were a child, before you became a teenager, did your parent(s) worry about things? What did they worry about?

4. How did your parents' response to worrying about things affect you?

5. Do you remember worrying about the things your parent(s) worried about? If so, why?

6. As a teenager or young adult, what did you worry about? How did you cope with those things that worried you? Did your coping mechanisms help you control your worries? Why or why not?

7. Today, what situations cause you the most stress? Why?

8. When you feel stressed, what sort of things do you do to try to relieve the stress?

9. Look back at the answers you wrote for question 8; evaluate whether or not those are really effective or good for you. Mark the ones that are positive and beneficial with an up-pointing arrow. Mark the ones that are negative and harmful with a down-pointing arrow. Now that you've had another chance to think about question 8, are there any more you'd like to add? If so, mark them with the appropriate arrows also.

10. If you read or hear about something bad happening, like an accident or a new caution about disease, do you worry it could happen to you? How long do you think about it?

11. If you asked five of your family members, friends, or acquaintances, would they categorize you as a positive or a negative person? Why do you think that is?

12. When presented with a new situation or opportunity, what is your first reaction? Are you ready to jump right in, or do you evaluate it to see what the potential downsides are? Why do you think you choose that way to react?

13. Name three things you fear happening to you.

14. Of the three things you listed above, place a percentage amount of how likely you think each is to happen to you immediately, within five years, within ten years, within your lifetime.

Before you go on to the next chapter, I'd like you to think also about what physical symptoms of anxiety you may be experiencing, from generalized anxiety disorder to social phobia. Here they are again, for review:

Generalized anxiety disorder: A free-floating general feeling of anxiety not attached to any known or probable event. Symptoms include fatigue, headaches, muscle tension, muscle aches, difficulty swallowing, trembling, twitching, irritability, sweating, nausea, lightheadedness, having to go to the bathroom frequently, feeling out of breath, and hot flashes.

Obsessive-compulsive disorder: Unwanted, intrusive thoughts of doom and disaster concentrated around a specific fear, such as fear of germs or fear of losing something or fear of not doing something important. This is coupled with compulsive rituals or behavior patterns meant to hold the fear at bay, such as hand-washing, going back numerous times to check the same thing, and establishing patterns involving numbers.

Panic disorder: Also known as panic attacks, this disorder is identified by a sudden, overwhelming sense of dread or doom, and attacks can be mistaken for a heart attack. The symptoms of a panic attack are pounding heart, sweats, weakness, feeling faint or dizzy, nausea, chest pain, feeling smothered, experiencing a sense of doom, a fear of losing control, feeling flushed or chilled, and tingling or numbness in the hands or feet.

Social anxiety disorder: Unwarranted fear of people or social situations, being convinced that people are watching and judging you. Social phobias can center around a single, dreaded activity such as public speaking or large social gatherings or having other people view you eating. Symptoms of social phobia can include blushing, profuse sweating, trembling, nausea, and difficulty talking.[7]

Agoraphobia: Agoraphobia is "fear of the marketplace" and translates to fear of being outside, around people, and in social situations. Agoraphobia results in a person becoming more and more tied to their home or residence, fearful of venturing outside, even for significant and positive reasons.

As you read back over how debilitating anxiety can be, I want you to be honest about any of the situations above that sound like what you are experiencing. Below, write down patterns in your life that contain any of the above components:

_____

_____

If you are experiencing symptoms of anxiety, I urge you to seek out professional help. There are effective treatments available for all of these anxiety disorders, and caring, competent professionals able to help. (More information about The Center's Intensive Recovery Programs for anxiety and depression, as well as other issues, is available at www.aplaceofhope.com.)

Worry and anxiety choke out your ability to grow in a whole person way—emotionally, intellectually, relationally, physically, and spiritually. Such a stranglehold on your life, your happiness, may lead you to numb your pain through a variety of addictive behaviors. In the next chapter, I'll help explain why so many of these addictive behaviors lead to dead ends.

Chapter 5

THE DEAD END
OF ADDICTIONS

I T CAN TAKE AWHILE TO FIND HAPPINESS. SOMETIMES, IT JUST doesn't seem worth the wait. When you're tired of waiting, you can fall prey to big, bright, colorful signposts along the way. These promise a shortcut to happiness and just a couple of exits away! All you have to do is stop going the way you're going to happiness and take an alternate route instead.

These alternate routes, however, do not lead you on a shortcut to happiness. Instead, they deposit you on a dead end—the dead end of addictions. Some addictions are pretty familiar, like alcoholism and illegal drug use. Others are less obvious as dead ends but ultimately lead to the same place, such as prescription drug abuse, gambling, workaholism, Internet addictions, compulsive shopping, or eating disorders. Each of these exits begins with a desire to feel better than how you feel at that moment. The exit seems so promising at first, but what you don't realize is just how far from happiness these behaviors eventually leave you.

Under the Influence

Jared came from a loving, middle-class family, and was given every opportunity to succeed in life. But with a garage full of wholesale-club quantities of beer and a house devoid of much parental oversight, alcohol was easy to get, so he started drinking. As long as he didn't take too much too quickly, no one seemed to notice. There was usually a group of four or five guys who'd find a place to hang out, pool their "resources," and party hearty pretty much as soon as school let out on Friday. If there was a half day or no school on Friday, they'd start early. At first, it was all about the camaraderie of the group, the joint declaration of adulthood, and the fun of sitting around getting drunk with nothing else to do. It was fun back then, and somehow it never seemed to get completely out of hand. When Jared moved out on his own after graduation, his drinking became more of an issue. Now he had an apartment where he could drink whenever he wanted. He had acquaintances old enough to buy beer and more than happy to help him out. Most of his drinking buddies from high school had moved on, gone off to college somewhere, or just drifted away. He'd moved into the apartment with Mike, the only one from the group he still hung around with. With different work schedules, though, about the only time they spent together was when they were drinking and watching sports. Each day after work, Jared came in to the apartment, set down his keys, went to the refrigerator, popped a beer, grabbed the remote, and clicked on the television. No matter what else happened, there was always a beer handy to help it along. Back in high school, drinking seemed like freedom. Now it was a daily requirement.

Alcohol is one of the most promoted products in our culture. Not only are the individual brands of alcohol advertised heavily in all forms of media, but also there is an aura about drinking itself that is secondarily promoted. Regardless of the brand, drinking alcohol is packaged with a specific type of adulthood—young adulthood. Drinking is in this way identified with the unfolding freedoms of the young and newly adult. Ads for alcohol portray young, attractive men and women, often promoting alcohol as a pathway to sexual activity. In these approaches, alcohol does not so much point to *happiness* as it does to *pleasure*. Drinking is a disguise for happiness because it promises to make you feel good. At first, drinking appears to deliver because it disguises (or better yet, it drowns out) your unhappiness. However, the more you drink, the more you need. The more you need, the worse you feel. While it is possible for many people to consume alcohol responsibly, the potential for it to become a dead end is very real, especially for those who have demonstrated a lack of control where drinking is concerned or those with a genetic predisposition to alcoholism.

The term *alcoholic* is still commonly used, but the actual diagnostic wording regarding alcohol has changed into two different subgroups—*alcohol abuse* and *alcohol dependence*. You no longer need to be falling down drunk in order to have an issue with alcohol. Alcohol abuse occurs when your use of alcohol has a negative effect on your life but you haven't yet developed a physical dependence. At The Center, we often work with people who are at the stage of alcohol abuse. They've usually been involved with some sort of alcohol-related driving incident, such as driving under the influence of alcohol (DUI) or an alcohol-related accident. Alcohol abuse occurs when, because of your drinking, you have problems performing at work or school; your drinking drives a wedge between you and your family, loved ones, or friends; you drink even when you know you shouldn't, such as driving after drinking or drinking even though you're taking medications that tell you not to. Alcohol abuse is when you continue to drink, all the while stubbornly ignoring the warning signs. You drink because you want to even when it's causing you problems.

The second diagnostic definition is *alcohol dependence*. Dependence is an appropriate word because at this stage, your body has become dependent upon the alcohol in order to function. You no longer drink just because you want to; you drink because you have to. Forget drinking to make you feel good; you drink now so you don't go into withdrawals and feel like you're dying. This is physical dependence on alcohol.

Alcohol dependence is identified by *cravings, loss of control, physical dependence*, and *tolerance*. According to information from the National Institute on Alcohol Abuse and Alcoholism (NIAAA), craving is defined as a strong need, urge, or desire to drink.[1] Loss of control is defined as not being able to stop drinking once you've started.[2] The physical dependence identified plays out in withdrawal symptoms such as nausea, sweating, anxiety, and the shakes after you stop drinking.[3] Finally, tolerance means you need to drink more and more alcohol to get drunk.[4]

In Washington, a woman was arrested recently after hitting two parked cars. She came up with the highest blood-alcohol level ever recorded in the state—.47. A former Seattle police officer, this woman was surely aware of Washington's blood-alcohol limit of .08. Her percentage was almost six times as high. For people without a tolerance for alcohol, this level is lethal.

According to a newspaper article at the time of her arrest, of the 350,000 blood-alcohol tests done in Washington since 1998, only 35 had ever come up with a reading over .40. No one before had ever gotten a .45.[5] Because of her tolerance to alcohol after years of drinking, this woman was able to breathe, move, and be combative while most other people would be comatose or dead. Pleading guilty to two counts of DUI, she asked the court for forgiveness and is expected to receive one year in jail for each charge.[6] If she is able to achieve sobriety during her incarceration, she should look upon this as a blessing; she was headed down a road to death, either hers or someone else's.

This woman was certainly an extreme case, and, fortunately, a large national study has shown a decrease in the number of people in this country who are alcohol dependent. That's good news. Unfortunately, this same study also shows that the number of people who abuse alcohol is rising.[7] That's not so good. In my line of work, I have come to believe that one of the reasons people turn to alcohol is to self-medicate from a variety of other issues, such as depression, anxiety, and eating disorders. Sometimes people turn to alcohol to numb out the stresses and pressures of life. If happiness no longer seems a viable option, a short-term fix like having a drink—or two, or three—becomes more and more attractive.

The High Life

Janice was a drug addict. She hid her drug use very well. She ran a successful small business, was a member of her children's PTA group, and went to church on Sundays. Yet she was so depressed that she needed her drugs to function, to get going in the morning, to turn off at night, and to concentrate. Terrified of being without them, she made sure she kept a stash in her purse at all times. When her husband questioned her sometimes-erratic behavior, she put it down to stress and "female issues." Janice did not consider her drug abuse to be a problem; she considered not having her drugs to be a problem. After all, these drugs were legitimate; she'd gotten them from her doctor. They came in a thin brown bottle with a white childproof cap, not some sort of baggie. She paid for them with her credit card, not a roll of cash. When she wanted more, she went to a pleasant, sage-painted office, not a dark alley. Janice was an addict, but she didn't consider herself one.

At The Center, we still see our fair share of "traditional" drug addicts, those people who are addicted to marijuana, cocaine, or heroin. These illicit drugs still have a potent and devastating effect on the lives of family, friends, and neighbors. They're still out there, active. Marijuana continues to be the most commonly used illegal drug in the United States.[8] According to the National Institute on Drug Abuse, 25 million Americans age twelve and above used marijuana at least once within the past year.[9] This same study, in 2006, found that 6 million people age twelve and above used cocaine at least once within the past year, with 1.5 million abusing crack, a form of cocaine that can be smoked.[10] The numbers for heroin are smaller, with 560,000 people age twelve and older using heroin within the past year.[11] No, these drugs haven't gone away. They've just been joined by another group—prescription drug abuse.

Prescription drug abuse occurs when a legally prescribed medication is used for something other than its intended purpose or in nonprescribed doses. In 2006, just over 16 (16.2) million people age twelve and older misused a prescription medication such as a painkiller, tranquilizer, stimulant, or sedative.[12] That puts this type of drug abuse right behind marijuana as the most commonly abused category. It's certainly what we've seen over the past several years treating drug abuse at The Center.

People are abusing a cornucopia of pharmaceuticals, all with tongue-tying names. According to the NIDA research, the most prevalent are the opioids, including oxycodone (Oxycontin), propoxyphene (Darvon), hydrocodone (Vicodin), hydromorphone (Dilaudid), meperidine (Demarol), and diphenoxylate (Lomotil). If those weren't enough, there are the depressants, including barbiturates such as pentobarbital sodium (Nembutal) and benzodiazephines such as diazepam (Valium) and alprazolam (Xanax). The stimulant category includes dextroamphetamine (Dexedrine) and methylphenidate (Ritalin).[13] Misuse of these medications, as well as even extended use for some, can bring about dependence and addiction.

This can be a deceptive road to travel, because a physician's prescription of these medications gives them the impression of being legitimate. This impression can remain, even when you are misusing and abusing your prescription. These are not harmless substances. Anything strong enough to help you in the correct dosage is strong enough to harm you in the incorrect dosage and needs to be monitored very carefully. Some of these drugs are only to be used sporadically or for a short period of time because they carry the high potential for physical dependency. They are, at best, a short-term solution. Once a physical dependence has been established with these drugs, it is necessary to taper off the dosage with medical supervision. Doing otherwise is dangerous.

These drugs are potent and able to effect immediate physical changes, such as inducing sleep, reducing anxiety, alleviating pain, and making you alert. There are no harmless shortcuts with these drugs. In some ways, they may be the most attractive of signposts, pointing the way to instant effect. The problem is, when you're whizzing down the road at eighty miles an hour, it's hard to read all of the fine print. And it's the fine print that comes back to haunt you.

Given the potent physical effect alcohol, illegal drugs, and prescription drugs can have, it's not a stretch to recognize the deleterious consequences of misuse and addiction to these substances. These have a strong "steer clear" warning to them that many in the Christian community heed. After all, Scripture is pretty specific when it says, "Do not get drunk" (Ephesians 5:18). You can figure out that if God doesn't want you drunk, He doesn't want you stoned or high either. These are addictions that compete with God's Spirit for control in your life. Even with all the red flags associated with drug and alcohol addiction, Christians still get caught up. Even knowing these substances can be harmful, people fall into the pit of addiction with them all the time.

These are by no means the only addictive dead ends that lead people off track. There are others that advertise as being fairly harmless, but just like drugs or alcohol, they have the potential to ensnare a person in the trap of addiction.

Jackpot

Like many, Randy thought having lots of money to solve all his financial problems would make him happy. His motivation to have money and get it fast led him to gambling. Randy could feel the sweat beginning to soak through his shirt, even though it was relatively cool inside the casino. He'd just won a large pot playing Texas Hold 'Em. Scooping up the chips, he breathed a sigh of relief. He really could use a win tonight. Things were a little tight. Sales hadn't been so great the last couple of months, and his daughter's orthodontist expected a payment on the tenth. As he told his wife over and over again, he didn't gamble for money, but a couple hundred extra this month would be nice. He heard a voice inside his head say, "Randy, just get up from the table now, cash in your chips, and go home." He thought about that for a minute and then replied to himself, "I'm winning, so I should stay here a little longer, just to see what happens." Somehow, he kept forgetting that usually when he told himself that, what happened was he lost.

I wrote an entire book devoted to the subject of gambling titled *Turning the Tables on Gambling: Hope and Help for an Addictive Behavior* (see the resource list for more information). In the years since that book was written, things haven't gotten any better. In fact, they're worse.

In 1992, the last survey on gambling showed that thousands of our citizens had problems with gambling, with hundreds of thousands expected to be adversely affected in the future. How many are there now? I don't know. There hasn't been a study done in over fifteen years. This is during a period of time when the money generated by gambling has exploded, especially with the construction of tribal casinos.

Though Washington State receives literally millions of dollars in revenue from its own state-sponsored gambling, and gambling constitutes over a billion-dollar industry, it contributes a pittance to help those addicted to gambling. A couple of years ago, the state legislature allocated around half a million dollars toward a program to help problem gamblers. They expected about 200 people to sign up. According to the news article at the time, 226 people signed up with a waiting list of 150. The program got started, people got helped, and then the state pulled out of the funding in the middle of the program.[14] Now, the most the state does is fund money to provide public awareness ads, signs in casinos, and a hotline that goes to a nonprofit council on gambling. The message from Washington State, it appears, is that if you have a problem with gambling, you're on your own.

(In the Rest Stop section at the end of this chapter, you'll have an opportunity to answer a series of questions to help you determine if gambling has become a problem for you.)

Job Security

Paula looked up at the clock. It was after seven, and her son's program at school started in less than fifteen minutes. Luckily, her husband said he'd get the kids fed and Caleb to school early. She was supposed to meet them there, having explained she needed to finish up a project at work. Her husband had been less than pleased, given this was the third night in a row she hadn't made it home in time for dinner. Paula had argued this was an emergency situation that would be handled by week's end. Her husband countered with the fact that her job had contained "emergency situations" for more than six months, ever since she became a manager. Paula wanted to concentrate just on what was happening today and find a way to get everything done she needed to. Her husband, with his exasperated tone, made it clear it wasn't just about tonight and the school program but her increasing pattern of later and later nights. With all the stress she was under at work, Paula was furious he'd use this time to pressure her about working so much. After all, it wasn't like she had a choice. Glancing up at the clock, she realized seven had come and gone. Flying around the office to distribute her workflow, she hastily locked the door and dashed to her car. If she stood in the back of the auditorium, instead of trying to sit with the rest of her family, she could probably give the impression she'd been there the whole time but they just hadn't seen her. She just hoped Caleb's solo wouldn't be within the next twenty minutes, or she'd miss it. He insisted she promise him she'd make it, and she had. Driving as fast as she could through the side streets, Paula realized the only obligations she felt comfortable breaking on a regular basis were those to her family. Stressed, guilty, and late, she told herself angrily they'd just have to understand.

Behaviors become addictive when they are continued, even in the face of negative consequences to important aspects of a person's life. Often, whether or not a behavior is addictive is measured against whether it has a negative impact on someone's ability to work. But what happens when work itself becomes addictive? This is colloquially called *workaholism*, with the "ism" part meaning a behavior that's way out of hand. When the demands of work overtake obligations of self-care and your relationships with others, it's a problem.

It's said that people vote with their feet. I also believe that people vote with their *time*. Time is the new commodity, the new treasure, in this culture because so many people seem to have so little of it left over. So, how a person spends his or her time says a great deal about what they value. If time is the new money, it might be instructive to reword an admonition from Jesus in Luke 12:34, switching *treasure* for *time*: "For where your *time* is, there your heart will be also." What you spend your time on indicates what you really care about.

I firmly believe people should care about their jobs. It's what I expect from myself and from those who work for me. However, there can come a point where you are out of balance, investing too much time in one aspect of your life to the detriment of others. I guess the biggest place I've seen this played out where work is concerned is in the emptiness and longing I've heard from adult children whose fathers, generally, but also mothers sometimes, simply were unavailable to them because of work. No matter how old the adult is, the heartbreak of a child left wanting is unmistakable in her voice, questioning why she wasn't important enough to make an impact on her parent's time. She wanted so much just to spend time with her father or mother. Instead, all she received were adult reasons and grown-up excuses, all couched in words of great import and consequence. Often, she heard, "I really want to spend time with you, but this job is important." She figured out if her father or mother had to spend time on the important things in life and didn't spend time with her, the obvious conclusion was *I'm not important*. This obsessive devotion on the parent's part to work constantly can lead to a plethora of addictive, coping behaviors on the child's part.

In this world of downsizing, two- and three-day vacations, if at all, and the increasing pressure to produce more in the same amount of time, it's easy to understand the stress people feel surrounding their work. Work, however, takes on an addictive quality when you begin to either equate all your successes or bundle all your fears of failure into what you do as opposed to who you are. If you feel you either must work or you won't be recognized and praised, or if you feel you must work so you won't be found out and punished, your work has become more than a job. It has become the source of your identity and security. This is completely at odds with God's desire for your life. Your identity comes from being a child of God, and your security comes from His provision and protection in your life.

Right before you die, do you honestly think you'll be sad because you didn't work more? Or, will you regret the time you'll never be able to recapture with those you love? *Where your time is, there your heart will be also.*

Cyber Fantasy

The airport speaker overhead kept up a repetitious reminder that parking was for loading and unloading of passengers only. Leaving his car for just a second, Dan helped get the luggage on board the cart and tipped the skycap. Kissing Sharon good-bye, he gave a hug to each of the kids with best wishes for a great time at the grandparents.

"I'll miss you," Sharon said wistfully, as she kept a sharp eye to make sure the kids stayed up on the curb, out of traffic.

"Me, too," he assured her as he maneuvered back to the car, closed the trunk, and climbed into the driver's side with a wave. He would miss Sharon and the kids. It was going to be two weeks home alone, but Dan already had plans. A Saturday golf game was already in the works with Steve, along with poker at the house the following Friday night. There were also plans for in between. Instead of hiding and lying and making sure he wasn't observed, Dan looked forward to relaxing and enjoying his other favorite pastime, Internet pornography. By convincing himself that he wasn't going overboard with it, he still looked forward to being able to do what he wanted without worrying about the possibility of discovery. Besides, what else was he supposed to do with Sharon away for two solid weeks? He'd miss her and the kids but planned to make good use of the time. What Dan was looking for was intimacy as a door that could lead to more happiness. What he found, instead, was false intimacy and despair.

Internet pornography has just become an accepted fact of life. When I was writing a book on Internet pornography addiction titled *Hidden Dangers of the Internet*, people were astonished and outraged that the largest moneymaker on the Internet was pornography. There were calls to do something about it, curb it, regulate it. That has proven impossible to do, up to this point, especially given the complexities of Internet pornography—who makes it, where it comes from, who accesses it, the sheer number of people accessing it. The enormity of the task is so great that law enforcement agencies have focused their efforts on child pornography, leaving adult content to, ostensibly, adults. That adult porn is huge business on the Internet is now a ho-hum given. The effects on families, however, are anything but ho hum.

In the last several years, The Center has seen an increase in the number of people calling in with "marital issues" and "sexual issues." Often, the problem is not an affair or infidelity in the marriage. The problem is that one of the spouses—usually the husband, but not always—is addicted to Internet pornography. There is absolutely an alienation of sexual affection but the "other woman" isn't even someone real. Instead, it's a barrage of airbrushed, ultraeroticized, slickly packaged, pornographic images. These images are immensely powerful, with the power to create an addiction.

Here is a quote from the Focus on the Family Web site article about the power of Internet pornography:

> Some of you reading this will become addicted like I was. The porn companies don't mind at all if you become completely addicted to their product. It's great for business. An addicted customer keeps coming back for more. And so they fill their porn with images that will excite you, arouse you and get the hormones flowing. You don't have to shoot up any drug with a needle to get addicted to porn—your body will make its own drugs just looking at the pictures.[15]

Pornography addiction is like any addiction, in that it is progressive in nature. What began as exciting and arousing becomes less so over time, and there is a need to increase the amount, volume, and depravity of the images in order to achieve the same level of stimulation. The first person in this article goes on to admit that he reached a point where viewing was no longer enough, and he was jailed for attempted rape.[16]

It generally starts with one picture, one image, one instance. Porn companies are very clever and find all sorts of ways to push their images onto your computer. They know that a certain percentage of people who inadvertently view a pornographic image will take a second look and then want to see more. To them, it's all a matter of numbers. If they can send out X amount of pornographic images, a percentage of X will come back for more. If the X amount is very large, then it doesn't matter if the percentage number is small. The more images they can put out there, the more people will get sucked in.

There is something enticing about doing something you're not supposed to do. You glance around to see if anyone is watching, and if they're not, you feel a rush of having gotten away with something. No oversight, no account-ability. It's as if you've gotten something for free. You go through red lights at three in the morning when no one else is around. You fudge on your tax return because the chance of anyone ever questioning that amount is infin-itesimal. These are, of course, fairly innocuous examples, but, as people, there is a thrill of being about to get away with something for nothing. It's part of the rebellion of our human nature. When this tendency is coupled with the powerful images of pornography, the compulsion to continue is overwhelming. Even when you know you shouldn't do it, you know it has gotten out of hand, you know you're adversely affecting the relationships in your life, you do it anyway, and you do more of it, and you look for deeper and deeper ways to gain the same stimulation. This is the working defini-tion of *addiction*. Just because it's just you alone in your den doesn't make it any less so. What started out as stimulating becomes scary and humiliating and compulsive. You're no longer getting away with anything; it's getting away with you.

Just My Size

Chelsea felt anxious, disconnected. Nothing seemed to be going right with her life. Work was crazy, her boyfriend hadn't called in three days, and last night she'd had a stupid fight with her mother. She felt antsy, like her skin was crawling, like something bad was about to happen. There was no way she wanted to go home to her boring, quiet apartment, not when she felt this way. She wanted to do something; she needed to do something to take an edge off the, well, edge. What she needed, as she often joked to the other girls at work, was a little "retail therapy." Chelsea always felt better after she went shopping, especially if she could find something unique and fun, something that made her feel special. She wasn't exactly feeling special in any other area of her life, so she'd have to do it for herself. Who cared if her credit card balances were getting high? That's what credit was for. As soon as work calmed down, her boyfriend called and apologized, and her mother got over being so neurotic, things would be fine, and she wouldn't need to let off steam like this. As soon as things calmed down, she'd get caught up—just as soon as things calmed down.

I'm not sure where the term *retail therapy* first originated, but it has come to be commonly used, along with the other "ism," shopaholism. Both of these terms refer to the behavior of shopping as a way to alter your mood. Depending upon the person, this trait can also be linked with impulsivity. So, you go shopping for that blouse you've been wanting but end up with shoes and a jacket to match, all because you had a bad day.

Compulsive shopping is not a trip to the mall every six weeks to get either a new pair of shoes or to replace a worn-out pair of pants. It is a pattern of behavior where you go shopping not to purchase a needed item but specifically to feel better. It's where you end up with drawers and a closet full of items that still have the tags on them. It's where you purchase items that, upon getting home, you realize you're never going to use. It's where you are spending more on shopping than you can afford. It's where, in the absence of some other pressing business or activity, you find your-self shopping, just for the act of shopping. Shopping is an activity; it's not a strategy for dealing with life.

You Can't Eat Just One...or Two

Rita couldn't wait for the kids to leave for school so she could get back into her car. Waiting for her, tucked up against the backseat, safely wrapped in plastic, was the chocolate cake she'd bought that morning along with the milk. It was on the day-old rack, a birthday cake to "Susie" that wasn't picked up for some reason the night before. Rita often shopped early in the morning so she'd be first to find treasures like these on the day-old rack. Usually, she could get doughnuts, pies, cookies, muffins—all sorts of baked goods at a substantial savings along with whatever else she had to buy. The more she saved, the more she could buy without her grocery budget being too far out of whack. Granted, Susie's cake was a little more than she usually spent, but Rita couldn't resist the expanse of creamy whipped frosting and the bouquet of pastel flowers. Even now she could imagine the silky burst of sweetness each one would bring.

The longer it took for the house to empty out, the more she thought about and anticipated the cake. It was her day off, so no one else in the family would be around soon, and she could have it all to herself. By the time the kids got home from school, the cake would be gone, the plastic container washed, cut up into smaller pieces (those large plastic tops were impossible to hide if you kept them intact), and placed in an unsuspecting neighbor's garbage can. By the time her husband got home from work, she'd be dressed with dinner ready, the master bathroom wiped clean of any residual vomit, and the window closed again after being open all day to air out. There wasn't going to be any evidence left. The cake was Rita's secret, one she was not willing to share with anyone, especially her family. She figured this would hold her for at least a couple of days before she'd have to go out in the morning and cruise the day-old rack again.

At The Center, I oversee a team of professionals who treat a number of addictions, including eating disorders. These are some of the most insid ious types of addictions because of the lies they tell you. Anorexia tells you that happiness can be found through restricting food and fluids, through attaining an "ideal" weight. If you can only find a way to become that weight, you'll be happy, you'll be safe. What anorexia doesn't tell you is that once you attain that weight, it's an ever downward target. If a little weight loss is good, more is better. Anorexia doesn't tell you about the constipation, bloating, digestive problems, being cold all the time, pallid skin, fatigue, night sweats, shaking, dizziness, or hair loss. Anorexia doesn't tell you that, as bad as these things are, they pale in comparison to the fear of becoming fat that complicates every effort to return to health. It doesn't tell you how your body begins to consume its own muscle tissue when all other reserves are gone, threatening your heart and your very life.

Bulimia is also a liar. It promises to make you happy by allowing you to eat and eat and eat without consequence. It tells you all you need to do after binging on whatever you want is to purge it away, either through vomiting or laxatives or exercise. It says you'll be able to get away with something—eating all that food and not becoming fat. You can have your cake and eat it too and not gain a pound. What bulimia doesn't tell you is about the nutrient loss due to purging, the rot to your teeth through vomiting, and the esophageal ruptures from gagging. It doesn't tell you about the potassium loss through constant diarrhea, cramping, and bloating. It doesn't tell you about how your body becomes so conditioned to vomiting that it will do so involuntarily, so it becomes a struggle to keep anything down even when you want to. Bulimia doesn't tell you about the hoarding of food, stealing of food, or hiding of food. It doesn't tell you how food becomes the most compelling relationship in your life, crowding out family and friends. Neither anorexia nor bulimia disclose that they mean to control your life completely. Both advertise themselves as a way to gain complete control.

The Center works with both anorexics and bulimics, along with those who compulsively overeat. These are the people who are addicted to food itself. When you eat not because you're hungry but to fill some sort of void in your life, you are addicted to food. Food is your drug of choice if you use it to self-medicate loneliness, sadness, anxiety, fear, distress, discomfort, boredom, or worry. You are no less addicted if you turn to ice cream instead of vodka, sweets instead of marijuana, and starches instead of wine. You may not be hitting the bar after work to down a couple of beers, but what about the fast-food restaurant for a large burger, large fries, and a large milk shake?

Many years ago I wrote what some call a classic book on the treatment of eating disorders, called *Hope, Help and Healing for Eating Disorders*. It has been revised and is still going strong as a force for healing and recovery for people with eating disorders. If anything, since that book was written, I am seeing more and more people come into this category of being addicted to food, without the classic behaviors of anorexia and bulimia. These are people who think about food all day. From the moment they wake, they're consumed with what they're going to eat, how hard it will be to eat what they know they should, how they're tormented to eat what they know they shouldn't, how deprived they'll feel if they don't eat what they want. They go to bed at night, guilty over what they did or didn't eat, how much, and why. They weigh themselves on a constant basis or have surrendered the weight battle and just get fatter and fatter. How much they weigh or how they look determines how they feel about themselves. They are chained to food all day long. On the outside, they may appear to have a weight within a normal range. Inside, they hold a dialogue about food in their minds almost every waking moment. They are, in fact, tormented by food. It is both friend and foe, lover and loather. Never is it an enjoyable, appropriate source of nutrition for the body. Whether an eating disorder or disorder eating, these sufferers are so far from happiness in their lives that they've forgotten what it looks like.

Addictions are compulsive behaviors that take over your life. They can come through outside substances like drugs, alcohol, even food. Or they can come through behaviors that charge up the body's own feel-good responses. They are meant, initially, to bring relief, comfort, excitement, or pleasure. They promise fulfillment and a respite from suffering. They are not a shortcut to happiness; they are a dead end of despair and compulsion. They do not provide control; they take control.

Addictions are also powerful liars. Even with overwhelming evidence to the contrary, an addicted person will swear there isn't a problem or, if there is, it's a problem he or she can control if they really want to. The catch, of course, is that the addiction will not allow them to want to stop. They'll need to find the strength to stop because they have to, not because they want to.

It's time to have a heart-to-heart with yourself. It's time to be honest and take a look at what behaviors may be controlling your life. God is a jealous God who does not countenance any idols in His place. He wiped out entire cultures of people in the Old Testament just to make sure the sin of idolatry did not continue to fester. He's that serious about it. Now, in your own world, you probably don't have a wood or stone image you give offerings to and pray to and ask what your own hands have created to save you. That kind of behavior would seem absurd nowadays. But be honest; if you are addicted to alcohol, don't you look to the drink your own hand has poured to save you from the pain in your life? If you are addicted to gambling, don't you look to the gods of chance and luck to provide you with what you need? If you're addicted to food, don't you look to that food you've made or purchased to comfort you in times of distress? If you're addicted to pornography, haven't you taken your God-designed system of arousal and attraction and prostituted it toward a technology-provided graven image?

These are harsh concepts, I realize. But how are you going to get out of your prison if you persist in seeing it as a paradise? How are you going to get out of your prison if you continue to provide excuse after excuse for why freedom is not possible, when God is standing before you with an open door and open arms? Addictions are liars; they do not want you to see the truth. As you go through the rest of this section, I want you to go through each of the inventories and sets of questions. At the end, there will be a place for you to write down the behaviors you personally are struggling with right now, which may or may not be represented here. My hope is, through this discussion, even if they aren't listed, you'll still come to recognize them for what they are.

Is Alcohol an Issue for You?

Answer the following four questions about your use of alcohol. They come from the National Institute on Alcohol Abuse:[17]

1. Have you ever felt you should cut down on your drinking?

2. Have people annoyed you by criticizing your drinking?

3. Have you ever felt bad or guilty about your drinking?

4. Have you ever had a drink first thing in the morning to steady your nerves or to get rid of a hangover?

According to the NIAAA, a yes answer to even one of these indicates you could have a problem with alcohol. The more you answer in the affirmative, the higher the probability.

Remember also the four signposts to a physical dependence on alcohol: cravings, loss of control, physical dependence, and tolerance. With these in mind, ask yourself the following questions:

1. Do you often feel a strong urge or need to drink?

---

2. Do you find that you are unable to stop drinking once you've started?

---

3. If you stop drinking, do you experience any of the following: nausea, sweatiness, shaking, or anxiety?

---

4. Do you find you need to drink more and more alcohol to feel drunk?

If you have answered yes to any of these questions, you have met one of the criteria for alcohol dependence. Answering yes to any of the questions in this section is a red flag you should pay serious attention to and seek immediate help from a health-care or chemical-dependency professional.

Are Drugs an Issue for You?

If you are using any illegal drug, such as marijuana, cocaine, crack, or heroin, the answer to this question is yes. These drugs are illegal because of their proven harm. If you're using marijuana, don't listen to the arguments that it's no worse than alcohol and should be legalized. It is a mood-altering substance that has the potential for great harm. It is an addictive substance, and your use needs to be addressed by professionals. The same is true for any illegal drug. These will consume and control your life. If you are using them at all, there is nothing more to be said—you need to stop. You will not be able to do so on your own; that is also a lie. If you had cancer, you'd see a doctor. You are chemically addicted, and you need to see a professional who is trained to help you overcome your addiction.

If you are abusing other substances, such as highlighter pens, glue, or inhalants, then see above. These are harmful, addictive behaviors that require the intervention of professionals to assist you to stop. The creativity with which you get high does not negate the detrimental effects of what you're doing. On the contrary, the more creative you get to achieve a high, the greater the damage you could be inflicting. If you go to such lengths to get high and avoid life, there is a definite issue that needs to be addressed immediately.

If you are misusing your prescribed medications, you need to come clean immediately to your doctor. There are medical detox programs available to safely wean you off of these prescription medications. You may need to look for naturopathic or holistic alternatives to achieve similar results in order to avoid the temptation or physical trigger of these types of medications. Only a discussion with your health-care provider can provide you with the specific answers for your specific situation. (As a word of caution: if you feel you have a problem with a prescription medication but the doctor who prescribed it to you doesn't respond to your concern, it's time to get another opinion. It's your body and health; don't feel embarrassed or bad that you're seeking confirmation through another health-care professional or a chemical-dependency professional.)

Is Gambling an Issue for You?

Following is the gambling personality questionnaire I developed for my gambling book. Answering these questions honestly will be valuable to you:

1. Consider the things in your life of value to you. They can include family and friends or activities you enjoy or find meaningful. How much time do you devote to each of these valuable things?

2. How much time do you devote to gambling during a week? Contrast that amount of time with the time you put down for the valuable things in your life.

3. Think about how you feel when you gamble. Are those feelings negative or positive? If they are negative, consider why you engage in an activity that promotes negative feelings. If they are positive, how long do those positive feelings last? Do they outlast the gambling activity itself, or do they dissipate as soon as you have stopped gambling?

4. With busy lives, often decisions must be made about how to spend our time. Think back over the past six months. How many times has a decision about whether or not to gamble come up against a need to do another activity? This could be time spent with family or friends, time spent working, even time spent relaxing or sleeping. How often has gambling won out over these other things, and at what cost?

_____

_____

_____

5. When you think back over your gambling, does it seem like you enjoyed it more at the beginning or now? If it has changed over time, can you remember when the transition occurred?

_____

_____

_____

6. Do you feel isolated from your family or friends when you gamble? Do you feel like they are unable to understand the way you feel about it? Do you feel, by being out of touch with gambling, they are out of touch with you?

_____

_____

_____

7. When other people have questioned you about your gambling, how have you felt? Do you feel they are invading

your privacy, your "private space," by questioning you? Do you feel defensive about your gambling?

_____

_____

_____

8. How honest have you been with others about how much time you spend gambling and/or how much money you spend gambling? Do you find yourself trying to hide or cover up the truth about your gambling?

_____

_____

_____

9. When you are in the midst of gambling, do you ever feel like you are "getting away" with something? How does that make you feel? Bad? Excited?

_____

_____

_____

10. Consider your gambling over the past six months. Now consider your spirituality over the past six months. Has your gambling increased and your spirituality decreased? Have you missed your connection with God? Would you be willing to alter your gambling behavior if it meant being closer to the Lord?

_____

_____

_____

11. Think about all of the things gambling promises. Honestly evaluate how much of a motivation those things are in your life. Do you desire them too much? Is gambling really the way to achieve them?

12. When you are gambling, do you engage in activities you feel guilty about? Do you drink or smoke excessively while gambling? Do you flirt or engage in sexual conversations with other gamblers? Does gambling strengthen your resolve to live a godly life or does it weaken you?

13. If you had to give up gambling or your loved ones tomorrow, which would you choose? Having chosen to give up the first thing—gambling—did you still wish you could somehow continue to have them both? Were you relieved it was only a question and not a reality?

14. If you had to give up gambling or God tomorrow, which one would you choose? Are you sure you haven't chosen already?

I wish I could say that gambling addiction gets the kind of attention and resources as alcohol and drug abuse, but it does not. I encourage you to download a copy of *Turning the Tables on Gambling* for information on resources and recovery. You can also contact Gamblers Anonymous (http://www.gamblersanonymous.org), which has organizations in all fifty states and the District of Columbia.

Is Workaholism an Issue for You?

Most people need to work, and your work may vary from time to time, so determining whether or not workaholism is an issue for you can be difficult. In order to ferret out the depth of the issue, I think it would be helpful to take some questions from the section on alcoholism.

1. Have you ever felt you should cut down on the amount of time you're working?

2. Have people annoyed you by criticizing how much time you spend working?

3. Have you ever felt bad or guilty about how much time your work takes away from other commitments, such as family?

4. Have family members asked you not to work so much?

5. Do you ever feel resentful of the amount of time you feel you need to work?

---

6. Do you ever feel like you're trapped in your work, to the point that you want to work less but don't feel you are able to?

---

7. Do you receive the majority of your affirmation and praise from others due to your work?

---

8. Do you feel others identify you for what you do instead of who you are?

---

9. When you take the time to stop and factor how much time you spend working, are you surprised at the amount?

The concern of family and friends can provide a voice of reason when trying to decipher if workaholism is an issue in your life. Happiness is found in living a life in balance with your responsibilities and obligations.

Is the Internet an Issue for You?

If you are viewing Internet pornography, you need to take steps to stop it—now. Pornography always takes you further than you ever want to go. It is one of the strongest addictions to battle. This is not an issue of gratification. God does not allow this activity. Viewing images of other people for sexual gratification is prohibited. Jesus put it this way: "But I tell you that anyone who looks at a woman lustfully has already committed adultery with her in his heart" (Matthew 5:28). God condemns adultery, and He condemns pornography of any kind, Internet or not.

If you are viewing Internet pornography and have tried to resist the urge but have failed, I urge you to seek out the help of a trained counselor or therapist. Pornography addiction is progressive and needs professional intervention. Be brave, put aside the shame, and contact a professional counseling agency that can help you work through the issue. There are more resources available for getting help than ever before. For more information about the intensive recovery program for pornography addiction at The Center, please go online to www.aplaceofhope.com, or call our referral line at (888) 771-5166.

Is Compulsive Shopping an Issue for You?

This is a materialistic, consumer-driven culture, so it can be difficult at times to determine if you've crossed a line from a harmless purchase to a compulsion to acquire. Perhaps asking yourself the following questions can help you interrogate your own reasons for what you do.

1. Do you find yourself shopping even when you don't have a specific need?

2. Why do you shop compulsively?

3. What is the payoff for you?

4. Do you have clothes in your closet or drawer that you have never worn? Why?

5. Do you find yourself buying more of a particular item (such as shoes) than you realize you'll ever really need?

6. How do you feel after you've gone on a shopping spree?

_____

7. Do you find yourself shopping for other people, even if they have not expressed a need for you to do so?

_____

8. When was the last time you left a store even though you didn't find what you were looking for?

_____

9. Has anyone ever talked to you about how much you spend on shopping, either in time or in money?

_____

_____

_____

10. How many credit cards do you have in your wallet? How much credit card debt do you currently owe?

_____

_____

_____

There are studies that show people actually feel better about themselves when they're wearing or using something new. That's pretty normal. It becomes a problem, however, when you are unable to feel good about yourself unless you're wearing or using something new. Feeling good about acquiring things should not be a substitute for feeling good about yourself. You cannot buy your way into happiness or comfort or security or selfworth. You'll only spend more money than you can afford and still come up empty. The hole you're trying to fill isn't in your closet; it's in your heart.

I have found there are very specific reasons why a person turns to "retail therapy" to feel better. I can tell you the real thing—professional therapy— is much more effective and less expensive in the long run.

Is Food an Issue for You?

Food has a proper place in our lives, yet it has the potential for getting out of hand, so it needs to be monitored. Paul, in 1 Corinthians 6:12 said that even though certain things were permissible, he would not be mastered by them. I have seen far too many people during the course of my professional life who allowed themselves to be mastered by food. In each case, their relationship with food went off track when they gave food power to provide them with something other than nutrition, either a sense of power and control through anorexia, as a salve for emotional wounds through bulimia, or as the ultimate comforter through compulsive overeating.

Food is designed to provide nutrition and fuel to power our daily activities. God designed it to be pleasurable and a blessing to us. Eating disorders and disorder eating moves food out of its proper realm into a role it was never meant to assume. Food today is used to relieve boredom, reward behavior, alleviate loneliness, reduce stress, provide companionship, and supply pleasure, as well as to punish, withhold, and control. Food becomes the medium people use to fill their voids, vent their frustration, and funnel their rage. For many Christians, it becomes an acceptable drug of choice, without the stigma of other addictive behaviors. To help you understand if food has moved out of its God-given realm and into an inappropriate place in your life, answer the following questions, and be sure to explain *why* you answer the way you do.

1. How often do find yourself eating something even when you're not hungry?

2. Are you concerned about your weight? Why or why not?

3. Do you tend to think about food during the day, what you'll eat and how much?

4. Did you grow up in a home where you felt you needed to be perfect to be accepted?

5. Did your mother or father express a high degree of concern about his or her own physical appearance?

6. As a child, do you remember receiving comfort through food?

7. When engaging in social activities, do you enjoy those where food and especially desserts are provided?

8. Have you ever deliberately overeaten, even though you felt uncomfortably full?

9. If you have a pattern of overeating, do you "make up" for it by either restricting, using laxatives, or excessively exercising?

10. Do you regularly take diet pills or diuretics?

11. Do you smoke or drink in order to avoid eating?

12. What types of foods do you find yourself eating over and over?

13. Do you hold a belief that you're fat even though others do not hold the same opinion?

14. Do you prefer to eat alone instead of with other people?

15. Do you eat differently with other people than you do when you're alone?

16. Have you ever felt defensive about your eating?

_____

_____

_____

17. Have you ever felt tired of thinking about food and weight all the time?

_____

_____

_____

18. Do you find yourself repeatedly eating foods you know aren't good for you because they feel good to eat?

_____

_____

_____

Food can become an obsession, either the desire to consume far more than your body needs or the need to restrict what you eat in order to reach an ideal weight. You need not be rail-thin or morbidly obese to be obsessed with food, what you'll eat, how it will taste, how you'll feel, and fear that you'll eat what you shouldn't. When food is disconnected from all the other reasons you eat and is returned to the realm of nutrition, you take back the power you've given it over your life.

Making a Three-way Turn

If you're like most people, you've developed a pretty good denial system and blind spot where addictive issues can hide out. Only by opening up that denial system and exposing those blind spots to the truth can healing begin to occur. Addictive behaviors cannot get you to a place of happiness in your life. They can only retard and stop your progress altogether. It's time for you to make a three-way turn and get off the dead-end road. No matter what you struggle with, it is possible to find your way back onto the right road again.

Through an honest look at what you're doing, how often you're doing it, how you feel when you're doing it, and how you feel when you don't, my hope is you'll be able to determine the depth of the issue in your life. If you still have doubts, ask a trusted friend or loved one what he or she feels about this activity and whether or not it is a positive or a negative in your life.

Don't give up hope! Praise God for His wisdom that can help you overcome these detours and dead ends, and find your way back to true fulfillment and happiness in your life. Now that you're aware of the problem areas in your life, it's time to begin an intentional plan of action, leading to the happiness you seek. Over the next four chapters, we'll examine specific areas in your life that can affect your outlook—your emotional state, your relationship with others, your physical well being, and your spiritual state.

Chapter 6

CHOOSE YOUR STATION
WISELY (EMOTIONAL)

OST DRIVERS ENJOY LISTENING TO A CERTAIN RADIO station when they're driving, and if you are fortunate enough to have a programmable radio in your vehicle, then you can program in your favorite talk and music stations. This way, when you're driving down the road, you can select a favorite genre of music or a favorite radio personality to hear. But what (or who) you listen to is important because you are allowing the music (or person's commentaries) to influence what you think. As the adage goes, "Garbage in, garbage out." If you listen to enough negative music or vulgarity, eventually that type of negativity will begin to infiltrate other areas in your life. It's the same with life; if you continue to listen to the little voice inside your head that tells you that you can't do it or that you're not smart, eventually you begin to buy in to that lie.

It's like a radio station in your car that never loses reception. Whether you want to listen or not, it's constantly on, continuingly commenting, interpreting what's going on around you, so choose your station wisely.

For many of you, the station you're glued to is truly a blast from the past, your own version of *Cruisin' With the Oldies*, except these "oldies" are the negative messages and perceptions from your childhood. You know every word, every note, every beat of their litany of negativism, all played with an overarching theme of anger, guilt, and shame. No matter how sunny the day is, how open the road, how marvelous the view on the horizon, if you're listening to this station, your outlook is clouded and there's so much noisy, scratchy, irritating static, it's impossible to tune in to happiness.

Turn It Up to Turn It Off

If there's one thing about this background drumbeat of negativism I've observed over the years, it's how pervasive it can be in a person's life without them really realizing it's there. Because it's on all the time, it becomes part of the backdrop of their emotional lives. They fail to realize its presence and power over how they interpret their circumstances. Because they hear it all the time, they stop paying attention to what it's really saying. Because they hear it all the time, they stop hearing it.

I read a newspaper article about the tragic death of a teenager who failed to hear the train that killed her. This young seventeen-year-old wasn't deaf; in fact, she was talking on her cell phone when she died, run over by the train. She was walking to have her nails done, crossing over the train tracks near her home. According to the story in the *Seattle Times*, police said it appeared she "was engrossed in her phone conversation and failed to hear the approaching train or its whistle. She lived near the tracks, and police suspect she may have become used to the noise."[1] The noise of the oncoming train, the shrill warning of the whistle, even the honking of a nearby motorist didn't break through to this young woman. Familiarity with her surroundings obscured the danger. The article went on to say that people who live around train tracks can simply become so used to the noise that they fail to notice it. Said a police spokesperson, "After a while, that noise just doesn't exist."[2]

This teenager didn't recognize the danger bearing down on her because of its utter familiarity. It's the same with the background noise of negativity that so many people have running inside their minds. After a while, it becomes so familiar that they stop "hearing" it and fail to recognize the danger it presents to their lives and happiness.

So, how do you hear something you're so used to that you've tuned it out? The answer, I've found, is to turn up the volume. Now, that may seem counterintuitive. It seems like you should just turn it down so you *really* can't hear it or turn it off completely. The problem with this station, however, is no matter how low you think you have it, it's still loud enough to cause problems, and unless you deal with the messages, you can't turn it off. The answer isn't to minimize it or ignore it. You have to turn up the volume so you can recognize what's really being communicated.

Name That Tune

This soundtrack you've been living with wasn't recorded overnight. Instead, it's a compilation of messages you've heard, impressions and impacts you've assimilated, and conclusions you've reached over the course of your life. It's like a top-forty countdown, except these aren't the best songs you've ever heard; they're often the worst. Do you remember the list of situations that can lead to insecurity from chapter 4? (See pages 75–78.) These "life lessons" become your "top forty" and form the basis of the messages that make up your background noise.

These messages have the ability to overpower the positive things you feel and that happen in your life by the sheer momentum of their negativity. These messages have created a well-worn groove in your mind, allowing them easy access to your subconscious and conscious thoughts, where they color how you feel about yourself and think about what happens to you.

Amy grew up in a household where the "noticed" child became the target of verbal and emotional abuse by an angry father. The way to survive growing up was to be unnoticed. Blanket pronouncements of incompetence and worthlessness were common. Amy grew up hearing she wasn't good enough, wouldn't amount to anything, couldn't do anything well enough, and wasn't pretty enough to be of much use to anyone. If she did well at school, her father said it was because the teachers were stupid. Amy's father was always right in his pronouncements. Any arguments to the contrary were quickly and vehemently countered, with sarcasm, insults, and threats. Amy learned to keep her mouth shut, to hide what she was doing, hide who she was, and lay low. She distrusted attention and accolades, convinced she'd gotten away with something whenever anything good happened. She tried extremely hard to do everything right so that nothing could be held against her, all the while fearing she wasn't up to the task. When positive things happened at work, they were a source of anxiety and fear instead of satisfaction and celebration. If Amy could have picked out her "top forty," to *Name That Tune*, she would have put down:

- I learned no matter what, I'm just not good enough.

- I learned to become resigned to failure.

- I learned I am the problem.

- I learned what I do is never good enough.

- I learned the thoughts of others are more important than my own.

- I learned the lesson of my own inadequacy.

- I learned to wrap my pain in shame and hide it away.

Of course, Amy had never stopped long enough to really *listen* to what she was telling herself. This self-dialogue was so ingrained that Amy stopped recognizing it years ago. These "lessons" formed the framework for how she interpreted the world and provided reasons why bad things happened to her. They warned her not to expect good things, and Amy considered them protective, so she wouldn't get hurt when things didn't turn out like she wanted. As far as Amy was concerned, it was better to be resigned than rejected.

I've known many people like Amy over the years. These are well-meaning, good people who developed some pretty elaborate coping skills in order to survive and make sense of difficult circumstances. Because the negative messages they carry around inside them are so deep seated, it isn't always an easy or comfortable process to uncover their true meanings and influence. It requires courage, commitment, and a safe environment where truth is honored and supported.

Patience, Perseverance, and Practice

Rooting out the negative messages and bringing them up to the surface where they can be examined requires patience. It simply takes patience to work through these issues. These negative messages are crafted out of the ignorance, arrogance, hostility, and, far too often, sin of others. They are powerful and deceptive and burrow deep into your heart, mind, and spirit. It takes patience to unravel them back to their point of origin in order to hold them up to the light of truth.

This also requires perseverance. The white noise of these messages acts to cover painful truths. You must persist in unraveling the truth, even when it is painful, unpleasant, or uncomfortable. It can be extremely difficult for adults to place themselves back in the state of mind of childhood, where many of these events and messages originated. You spent your childhood running from the unpleasant and hurtful truths, protecting yourself from them. Adulthood was supposed to mean being able to crawl out from under and finally move beyond them. You may have grown up, moved out, and moved on but find that the messages remain, stuck in your head, affecting everything you do and feel today. As difficult as it is, you must have the perseverance to continue to work through the messages, one by one, and really listen to what they are saying. When you really listen to them, you expose them. Once exposed, they are ready to be examined, understood, and placed into their proper context.

Finally, this process requires practice. It is not enough to say, "Just stop believing the lies." Listening to and leaning on these negative messages have become routine, habit, and a pattern. They spring into your mind without conscious thought. Once you've learned to understand them for what they really are and where they really come from, you still have to deal with the powerful pattern they've established in your life. Each day, you must prac-tice intentionally acknowledging and rejecting the messages, choosing to believe something else instead. With this practice, you are erasing the old negative messages and recording over new positive, uplifting ones.

A New Song

God never intended for you to have your mind filled with negative, destruc-tive messages created through the damage of others. For every lie these messages spew, He holds fast with His truth. His truth is positive, uplifting, empowering, and refreshing. God knows every negative thing you say to yourself; He hears the words of despair you utter and offers words of encouragement instead.

You say, "I learned how much one person can hurt another."

God says, "My command is this: Love each other as I have loved you. Greater love has no one than this, that he lay down his life for his friends. You are my friends if you do what I command" (John 15:12–14). God, knowing how much people can hurt each other, commands each of us to love one another instead.

You say, "I learned that no matter what, I'm just not good enough."

God says, "My grace is sufficient for you" (2 Corinthians 12:9). God, understanding your weakness, makes His abundant grace available to you.

You say, "I learned it is possible for someone I love to stop loving me."

God says, "God is love" (1 John 4:8); "Never will I leave you; never will I forsake you" (Hebrews 13:5). God, who is love, has promised never to leave or forsake you.

You say, "I learned to become resigned to failure."

God says, "I can do everything through him who gives me strength" (Philippians 4:13). God's ability to succeed is stronger than your ability to fail.

You say, "I learned what it feels like to be on the outside."

God says, "But you are a chosen people, a royal priesthood, a holy nation, a people belonging to God" (1 Peter 2:9). God has always meant for you to be part of His family, His plan—the ultimate insider for eternity.

You say, "I learned I am the problem."

God says, "Who will bring any charge against those God has chosen? It is God who justifies" (Romans 8:33). God, who knows the truth in all things, is the defender of those wrongly accused, including you.

You say, "I learned up is down and down is up."

God says, "Jesus Christ is the same yesterday and today and forever" (Hebrews 13:8). Because of sin, this world will often seem upside down, with nothing sure and secure. God, through Christ, promises and affirms the opposite, giving your life foundation and security.

You say, "I learned a home is not a refuge."

God says, "Take my yoke upon you and learn from me, for I am gentle and humble in heart, and you will find rest for your souls" (Matthew 11:29). Over and over again in the Old Testament, God is called a rock and a refuge. God, through Christ, promises to be both refuge and rest for you.

You say, "I learned the world is a scary place, not to be trusted."

God says, "Do not let your hearts be troubled. Trust in God; trust also in me" (John 14:1). God knows the world is an untrustworthy place, so He offers Himself and His Son as the appropriate repositories of your trust; and God, unlike the world, is faithful with your trust.

You say, "I learned how quickly things can change."

God says, "He who is the Glory of Israel does not lie or change his mind; for he is not a man, that he should change his mind" (1 Samuel 15:29). God is your rock, and He does not change. Note that God does not promise things won't change; He only promises that He will not. This life comes with storms; God offers Himself as your anchor.

You say, "I learned that what I do is never good enough."

God says, "And God is able to make all grace abound to you, so that in all things at all times, having all that you need, you will abound in every good work" (2 Corinthians 9:8). God is able to work through you to accomplish amazing and extraordinary things. Look at the number of times the words *all* and *every* appear in that one passage. Say it over to yourself this way: "And God is able to make all grace abound in me, so that in all things at all times, having all that I need, I will abound in every good work." It's perfectly appropriate for you to personalize Scripture; it was written with you in mind.

You say, "I learned that the thoughts of others are more important than my own."

God say, "Do nothing out of selfish ambition or vain conceit, but in humility consider others better than yourselves" (Philippians 2:3). God knows the only way to have a true heart of humility is based upon an understanding of your own value and worth first so you can extend it on to others. After all, one of the great commandments of God is to love your neighbor as yourself (Leviticus 19:18), which presupposes that you love yourself. You were told others were more important than you. God says, out of love, consider others as better than yourself. It is an attitude of love and service that God commands, after first demonstrating how it is done in the person of Jesus.

You say, "I learned the lesson of my own inadequacy."

God says, "For it is God who works in you to will and to act according to his good purpose" (Philippians 2:13). When God is working through you, there is nothing you cannot accomplish; you are more than adequate.

You say, "I learned to wrap my pain in shame and hide it away."

God says, "As a mother comforts her child, so I will comfort you" (Isaiah 66:13). God knows the depth of your secret pain and promises comfort and restoration through His unfailing love. God doesn't want you to hide your pain; He wants you to bring it to Him, as a hurting child runs to his or her mother, so He can comfort you.

You say, "I learned to fear it could happen again."

God says, "I have told you these things, so that in me you may have peace. In this world you will have trouble. But take heart! I have overcome the world" (John 16:33). There are no empty assurances with God. He too knows it could happen again, and He promises to be with you through it all.

I'd like you to go back to what you wrote in the Rest Stop for chapter 4. In that chapter you began the process of identifying the *how*, *why*, and *who* of the anxiety and worry in your life. These make up the negative messages that cycle throughout your mind, shadowing how you feel about yourself and how you interpret what happens to you in life. Each negative message needs to be confronted and a new script created, one based on love and truth. Each lie, each distortion must be countered with the truth. This is a very biblical thing to do.

Do you remember when Jesus was tempted by Satan during His time of fasting in the wilderness before He began His public ministry? Satan would distort the truth in order to try to trap Jesus, but Jesus would counter the lie with the truth.

> Then Jesus was led by the Spirit into the desert to be tempted by the devil. After fasting forty days and forty nights, he was hungry. The tempter came to him and said, "If you are the Son of God, tell these

stones to become bread." Jesus answered, "It is written: 'Man does not live on bread alone, but on every word that comes from the mouth of God.'"

—MATTHEW 4:1–4

Next, Satan tries to use Scripture to get Jesus to act outside of God's will and plan.

Then the devil took him to the holy city and had him stand on the highest point of the temple. "If you are the Son of God," he said, "throw yourself down. For it is written: 'He will command his angels concerning you, and they will lift you up in their hands, so that you will not strike your foot against a stone.'" Jesus answered him, "It is also written: 'Do not put the Lord your God to the test.'"

— MATTHEW 4:5–7

Finally, Satan tries to use bribery to tempt Jesus.

Again, the devil took him to a very high mountain and showed him all the kingdoms of the world and their splendor. "All this I will give you," he said, "if you will bow down and worship me." Jesus said to him, "Away from me, Satan! For it is written: 'Worship the Lord your God, and serve him only.'" Then the devil left him, and angels came and attended him.

—MATTHEW 4:8–11

Distortion, half truth, and outright lies must be countered every time with the truth. Satan uses the same tactic today to weaken your resolve and hamper your ability to be about your work in this world for God. Satan didn't want Jesus to succeed; he doesn't want you to either. Scripture calls Satan "the father of lies" (John 8:44), and the negative messages you hear in your head have his fingerprints all over them. You must reject them and turn instead to God's truth to counter their destructive influences.

Through all of the chatter and static this life puts up, one truth should always ring loud and clear: God created you; He loves and values you. Don't let anyone else take that truth away from you! Using the negative messages from chapter 4, I'd like you to begin to write a specific counterpoint phrase to each. For each, I've provided an example. I want you to write at least one more for yourself. Use what you know from Scripture to help you if it's difficult for you to provide a counter.

- I learned how much one person can hurt another.

- Counter: I choose to act differently; I choose to show love toward others.

_____

_____

- I learned that no matter what, I'm just not good enough.

- Counter: I do not need to be perfect for others to love me.

_____

_____

- I learned it is possible for someone I love to stop loving me.

- Counter: I choose to be in loving relationships with others, accepting this as a risk because God will always love me.

_____

_____

- I learned that favorite things can be taken away by those who love me.

- Counter: Knowing how easy it is to be hurt, I will treat others with gentleness and compassion.

_____

_____

- I learned to become resigned to failure.

- Counter: I am not perfect, but I am not a failure. I choose to learn and grow from my mistakes.

- I learned what it feels like on the outside.
- Counter: Because I know what it is like on the outside, I will treat others with compassion, knowing I am accepted by God.

- I learned I am the problem.
- Counter: I am not a problem; I am a person and deserve to be treated with love and respect by others and myself.

- I learned up is down and down is up.
- Counter: I choose God as my rock, even in topsy-turvy times.

- I learned a home is not a refuge.
- Counter: God is my refuge and the head of my home.

- I learned the world is a scary place, not to be trusted.
- Counter: God is my security, not the things of this world.

- I learned how quickly things can change.
- Counter: God is my anchor in the storms of life.

- I learned that what I do is never good enough.
- Counter: I do not have to be perfect to be good enough for God.

- I learned that the thoughts of others are more important than my own.
- Counter: I choose to respect myself so I can extend that respect to others.

- I learned the lesson of my own inadequacy.
- Counter: I accept I am not perfect and love myself anyway.

- I learned to wrap my pain in shame and hide it away.
- Counter: My pain is not a cause for shame; it is an avenue for healing.

- I learned to fear it could happen again.
- Counter: God is in control, and I choose to trust Him.

I'd like you to take some time here and write down any negative messages specific to you and your circumstances that have not been covered above. Take time to turn up the volume of your own negative messages and write down any that haven't been countered yet.

- I learned

- Counter:

- I learned

- Counter:

_____

_____

- I learned

_____

_____

- Counter:

_____

_____

Again, recording over those negative messages will take patience, perseverance, and practice. If you find it too difficult a task, I encourage you to seek out a trusted friend or loved one. If you have a background of abuse and trauma, I urge you to seek out a professional therapist or counselor to assist with this process. Assisting you in this great work is why I do what I do, and it's the same for those I work with and my colleagues across the country. Look for those who are associated with the American Association of Christian Counselors (www.aacc.net), or check for counselors in your area who have developed a trust relationship with your local church.

You will be amazed at how you feel and the world looks when you are not weighed down by the drumbeat of negativity that you've been carrying around inside you. And once you've ridden your internal life of these negative messages, you also want to make sure those around you are singing the same positive song!

Chapter 7

DON'T GIVE UP THE WHEEL (RELATIONAL)

MOST PEOPLE ARE PRETTY PARTICULAR ABOUT WHOM THEY allow to drive their cars. So, it's always been amazing to me how cavalier people can be with whom they allow to drive their lives. Someone who would never dream of picking up a hitchhiker on the side of the road will invite virtual strangers to have tremendous control over their life and happiness. Other people will cede control over to people who have no real business behind their wheel in the first place. On this pursuit of happiness, whom you allow in the car with you, especially behind the wheel, can make all the difference in whether or not you ever will arrive at your destination.

Have you ever allowed a rude driver or an inconsiderate comment or an outburst by a co-worker to ruin your day? I'm talking about the kind of incident where it came out of nowhere and interrupted an otherwise normal day? It caught you completely off guard when it happened, and then you couldn't stop thinking about it for hours afterward. Like a small pebble in your shoe, you kept feeling it irritating you the rest of the day. The person who cut you off or made the remark or pitched the fit moved on, but you didn't. Here is someone who doesn't know you or barely knows you, and yet you've given them power to negatively affect your entire day. Why in the world would you do that?

I've found the answer in many cases is because the action or the comment or the outburst taps into and echoes that negative background track spoken about in the last chapter. You give these instances power over you because whatever happened fits into the overall themes of your negative messages. They fit right in with the picture of your world drawn by that negativity. Otherwise, you'd wonder what was wrong with that guy who flipped you off while driving instead of feeling guilty for doing something wrong yourself. Otherwise, you'd figure you just misunderstood the comment and put it out of your mind instead of dwelling on it. Otherwise, you'd stand up for yourself against the outburst and shut the other person down instead of shutting down yourself. As hard as it is to put events like these into proper context with people you barely or don't know, imagine how hard it is to do with those you are in real relationship with.

Along for the Ride

In this life, you have a variety of relationships: family, extended family, work, acquaintances, and friends. Some you can choose, and some you can't. In all of your relationships, it is important for you to be in control and set the tone of the relationship.

Family

Natalie pulled up to the curb and sat a moment before turning off the engine. She couldn't wait too long or her mother would be out the door, asking her why she wasn't coming in the house. Natalie knew she'd been spotted as soon as she pulled up because she saw the living room curtains swing back into place; her mother was waiting for her. Grabbing the sack of tomatoes beside her, she took a deep breath, reminded herself to be calm and in control, and stepped out of the car.

True to form, her mother was out the door on the porch before she was halfway up the steps. "Hi, Mom," Natalie said, giving her a hug. "I brought these tomatoes from my garden for you."

"Come inside," her mother directed her. "Your father's waiting for you." Natalie knew she arrived just at the time she'd said, but, somehow, even when she was on time, her mother could still make her feel late.

As they entered the house, her mother asked her, "When are you going to do something with your hair? It always looks like such a mess."

"Oh, Mom," Natalie replied, kissing her father on her way to the kitchen. "I like it this way. I'll cut it when I'm ready."

"Well, you should be ready now," her mother softly commented, loud enough for Natalie to hear. "How is your work going?"

Natalie never told her mother how things really were at work because her mother could take even the best situation and find a way to pronounce dire warnings. Natalie's mother saw herself as a disaster detective with an innate ability to recognize potential problems and a duty to inform Natalie not only of their existence but also the precise way she needed to solve them. To Natalie, work was work, not a battle to be fought each day. She saw her co-workers as allies, not adversaries. It was just a different way to look at the world. So Natalie glossed over how things were going and spoke in pleasant generalities, realizing she wasn't giving her mother much to go on.

"What's wrong with your tomatoes?" her mother asked, looking into the bag and for more fertile fields. "They were much bigger last year."

"I went with a different variety this year. Hopefully they'll do better on the deck because they're smaller, and I think they ripen quicker. Here, Dad," she said, throwing a firm round tomato to her father who'd just come in the doorway from the living room. "Bite into that and tell me what you think."

"Delicious!" he proclaimed, smiling as the seeds gushed out and down his chin.

"You're going to get it all over your shirt!" her mother protested unhappily. She never liked it when Natalie's father got in the mix with his sunny disposition and eternal optimism, both of which she found burdensome.

After several hours of catching up, laughing with her dad, and fencing with her mother, Natalie was ready to depart.

"I love you," she said to them both as she stepped out the front door onto the lighted porch.

"This time, call me during the week," her mother instructed her.

"I will, Mom. Probably won't be until Thursday, but I'll touch base with you then."

"Drive safely home!" her mother warned.

"I always do, Mom," she assured her, turning at the sidewalk to wave good-bye. There they were: her mother frowning and her dad smiling. Some things never changed. It was a good visit.

Family ties are the most binding, the most complicated, and can ultimately be the most hurtful or the most satisfying. Helping people navigate family relationships is a large portion of my work. When family works well, it provides support, stability, encouragement, and love. When family doesn't work well, it complicates, hinders, constricts, and entangles. When family doesn't work at all, it leaves a person adrift and severely compromised in life.

It is not possible to have the perfect family. The reason for this is simple: families are made up of people; people aren't perfect, so no family will be perfect. The fact that a perfect family does not—cannot—exist in no way ameliorates the deep desire for one. This is the longing of the inner child to be loved and cared for in every way and in every way perfectly. This longing is strong and can survive against tremendous odds. I have worked with individuals who grew up in the most dire of circumstances, in abusive and damaging families, who are still tied to a family member through their tenacious wish that the person will somehow, someday, change and treat them as they should.

They continue to maintain contact with this abusive person, all in the hopes that the person will come around and love them. The strength of desire for that wished-for future powers through all of the stark evidence of an unchanged here and now.

Far be it from me to suggest that people cannot change. I've seen it gloriously played out innumerable times in my professional career. There is always room to hope because God is a powerful change agent in people's lives. Change, however, tends to happen slowly, over time, in relationships. It requires a conscious effort, intentional will, and constant accountability. And the change I'm talking about is not a change in the other person; it's a change in you. Hopefully, in damaged relationships, the other person will see a need to change, but you cannot change the other person, no matter how much you want to. You can only change yourself.

A relationship is an equation in which there are two components: you and the other person. If you change the "you" in the equation, you change the equation. If you change the "you" in the equation, you establish control and set the tone for the relationship. This applies to all sorts of family relationships: husband-wife, parent-child, sibling-sibling, and so on. When you change yourself, you change the dynamic of the relationship and provide an opportunity for the other person to make positive changes also. That's the hope anyway. With you changing for the good and the other person changing for the good, you move toward a healthier relationship.

Note that I didn't say "perfect relationship." A healthy relationship is not a perfect one. If a healthy relationship was so narrowly defined, by definition, none would exist. It is possible to have a healthy family relationship. This is a relationship in which perfection is not expected or demanded.

Go back to the scenario with Natalie that began this section. Natalie has a healthy relationship with her mother and father, not a perfect one. Even though Natalie's mother is argumentative and negative, Natalie's relationship with her is healthy because Natalie is in control. She does not allow her mother to overwhelm her with her negativity. She stays positive and upbeat, choosing to maintain the relationship out of love, understanding her mother's personality. Natalie deflects her mother's negativity away from herself without rancor, while maintaining her own opinions, actions, and reactions. Natalie consistently affords her mother the opportunity to reevaluate her negativity. In this way, Natalie acts as a change agent herself in the relationship.

Natalie's relationship with her mother is a healthy one even though Natalie's mother's does not have a healthy relationship with herself or others. How can there be a healthy relationship if one of the parties is unhealthy? Natalie's relationship is healthy because Natalie herself is healthy and sets the tone for her side of the relationship. Based upon this, Natalie determines the boundaries and parameters for her interaction with her mother. The health of the relationship is controlled by Natalie and not her mother.

This concept is especially important when dealing with relationships between family members. As the saying goes, you can choose your friends but not your family. Yet, family remains extremely important and, whenever possible, there is value in holding on to and strengthening family ties. On the other side, family can be the arena where people "relax," act "themselves," and, as a result, treat each other poorly. I have seen family members who treated me with the utmost respect and politeness turn around and speak to family members disrespectfully and rudely, all within the same breath. You would think that family, because they are family, would be afforded greater love, honor, and respect than casual acquaintances or strangers but, sadly, sometimes this is not the case.

For those of you with families that work well, you should thank God for such a blessing. The strength of your family relationships should act as motivation to, as Hebrews 10:24 says, "spur one another on toward love and good deeds" within your family. Each person, being imperfect, can strive to act in a more loving, patient, gentle, caring manner. This bond of love and affection can then flex with the addition of new family members and weather the inevitable storms of life.

For those of you with families that don't work so well, you have some challenges ahead of you. The first is, you need to work toward rewriting those negative tapes talked about in the last chapter. Many times those tapes were written and broadcast in childhood, by the very same family members you are in relationship with today. You need to allow yourself time, apart from the relationship, to write over those negative messages with positive, affirming truths. These become the basis of your side of the relationship, overwriting and supplanting any lingering negativity in the relationship. Whenever the other person's negativity threatens to become too overwhelming for you, you'll need to withdraw for a time to recoup and recover. This may mean that for you to have a healthy relationship with a difficult family member, you may need to maintain limited contact. For you, a healthy relationship may be one that is kept strictly within very defined boundaries until you have healed and are healthy enough to engage in anything more significant. Your new, positive inner dialogue must be stronger than the old, negative patterns of your past. When this happens, as with Natalie, you'll be able to control your side of the relationship and allow the relationship to continue under your predetermined parameters.

Just as you gave God thanks for a family that works well, you can also ask God to be with you, as a change agent in families that don't work so well. You can ask Him for patience, protection, perseverance, and guidance. You can pray specific prayers for specific people, asking God to change attitudes, actions, and hearts. You can ask for wisdom to know how much contact is advisable for you to engage in.

For those of you with families that didn't work at all, you may not have the option, as an adult, to continue within those relationships. If you grew up in an abusive home, with abusive family members, continuing in relationship with the abusers may not be an option. You have no obligation to allow yourself to continue to be abused just because it's family. In this case, the healthiest relationship you can have with an abuser is no relationship at all. This isn't to say that you attempt to erase them from your mind. On the contrary, you acknowledge who they are, what happened in the past, and, whenever possible, extend as much forgiveness as you are currently able, but you are not obligated to present yourself to the other person for further abuse. This is appropriate and healthy. The hope of change and the power to effect so great a change lies firmly in the hands of God. This is not your burden to carry. You were not responsible for the abuse in the past, and you are not responsible to "fix" it in the present or future by downplaying it or dismissing it or pretending it didn't exist. If and when the abuser shows remorse and repentance, a true change of heart, then the context of the relationship can be reevaluated.

Whenever possible, deal with family members with as much grace and forgiveness as you can, recognizing the universal failure of all to meet expectations. There should be few actions that cause you to break relationships, but you should stick to those few unwaveringly. In this way, you are helping your family to understand that you are in the driver's seat of how you are treated. You need to be able to limit or withdraw relationship if a family member violates your boundaries. Otherwise, err on the side of grace and love. After all, they're family.

Extended family

I make a distinction between intimate family, such as spouses, parents, children, and siblings, from more extended family, which can include cousins, aunts, uncles, grandparents, and even in-laws. Put another way, the difference is who shows up for dinner on a weeknight and who shows up for dinner at Christmas. Sometimes, extended family includes people you barely know, due to the diaspora common in many interstate families.

These people may appear to have a right to barge on over and grab the wheel of your life out of your hands because you share the same last name or progenitors, but they really don't. The further removed they are from you or the smaller amount of time they have spent with you, the less power over your life and happiness should be given. If your Aunt Paula, who hasn't seen you in eight years, makes a disparaging comment about your spouse or your weight or your career at a holiday get-together, you are completely within your rights to disregard it. However, if your grandmother, who has seen you regularly since birth cautions you against taking that job, at least listen attentively and consider what she says. But if an extended family member attempts to use that family connection to take advantage of you or to impose upon you or to belittle or disrespect you, you may need to close off that relationship on your end. Extended family members deserve a special place in your life, as long as their conduct toward you warrants continued contact.

Work

I think the second largest area of relationship problems people come to me about, after family, is work. This isn't difficult to understand once you factor in that many people spend more time during the week with co-workers than they do with family and the financial incentives inherent in employment. Add into that the differences in position involved in most work settings, and work relationships begin to get very interesting.

"Jack! Get over here!" The call came from across the loading dock. From the tone of voice, Jack knew it couldn't be anything good. "What is it this time?" he thought to himself. Hopping down off the forklift, he dodged the general chaos of the loading and unloading going on and walked over to his supervisor, Larry.

"What were you thinking?" Larry asked, gesturing his arms as if Jack was supposed to know what in the world he was talking about. As he was still several feet away, he just put his hands out and shrugged with a look of puzzlement on his face.

"You double-booked bay three, and now we're gonna have a backup on our hands! A driver idle and too much to be unloaded before the shift ends, which means overtime if we want to get it cleared out. What were you thinking?" There was the question a second time, but Jack knew it was rhetorical. Larry didn't really care about the circumstances or what Jack was thinking. He always assumed that when something went wrong, it was

Jack's fault, or anything Jack set up was bound to go wrong. Rarely did he look into the particulars before he blew up.

Tamping down the familiar knot of anger and frustration in the pit of his stomach, Jack took a deep breath and began to explain. He knew, from experience, he'd only have a short amount of time to plead his case. "The noon shipment didn't show up until almost a quarter to two, and the four o'clock was already on its way, so there was no way to stop the process. That's why I pulled three people from Andy's team over to expedite getting the late delivery handled. They'll be done by four, and if we all work together, we can get everything put away and wrapped up before shift change."

Even though his explanation was reasonable and showed initiative and creativity on his part, Jack knew none of that was going to be acknowledged by Larry in the slightest. Instead, he stood for the next couple of minutes listening to a general tirade about the problems with changes to the schedule, slackers at work, and the insensitivities of management, none of which did anything to solve the problem. Jack felt just like he did growing up, listening to his father berate him for things equally ridiculous and out of his control. Back then, he'd kept his mouth shut and his face stoic because he needed a roof over his head. Now, he needed the paycheck.

With a wave of disgust and dismissal from Larry, Jack walked back to the forklift even more energized to get the work done. Anger kept burning inside him the rest of shift. Even successfully handling the two shipments by the end of the day didn't really help because he knew Larry would never acknowledge it. If Jack was right, nothing else was ever said. If Jack was wrong, he heard about it for days. He dreaded the ride home, where he'd review each of his actions over and over again, looking for anything that might prove he'd slipped up and Larry was somehow right... that, after all these years, his dad was somehow right.

Work isn't family, but it's still relationship. Work involves different people of different backgrounds, skills, and temperaments all coming together to accomplish a common goal. They do this multiple hours per day, often in stressful circumstances. There are differences in roles and responsibilities, positions and power, personalities and perspectives. How well each person individually and collectively does his job has significant financial impacts. Society places a great deal of value on not only what you do but also how well you do it. That's a whole lot of pressure rolled up into a job. The more the pressure, the higher the stress; the higher the stress, the more a person's work life can begin to affect and overtake their personal life. Once work overtakes your personal life, it's pretty easy to look up and realize a co-worker or boss has wrestled control of your happiness away from you.

It is not difficult to imagine how a work situation, in which there is a disparity in position, can imitate a family relationship. Bosses can some-times treat subordinates like their own children. They can also treat them like they themselves were treated growing up. Subordinates can some-times react to bosses or supervisors in the same way they did to a parent or sibling. With a boss as a parent and co-workers as siblings, workplaces can become surrogate sites for family dynamics and sibling rivalries to be played out. Work relationships simply can have a way of triggering old familial relationships, especially dysfunctional ones. When this occurs, the secondary work relationship gains an unfair advantage through the tie-in to the primary family relationship. The only way to sort it out is to learn how to separate the two.

Work is a contract between an employer and employee. The employee agrees to give energy, expertise, effort, and time to the employer in exchange for an agreed-upon wage. This is a limited contract and has numerous built-in legal safeguards regarding conduct, reimbursement, expectations, etc. While the law certainly can and does provide protection for workers in many areas, it is up to the worker to protect himself or herself personally from being unduly influenced by what goes on at work. It is up to you to put guardrails up around your work, to help keep it from spilling over and overtaking your personal life. Employers will not do that for you.

This can be especially difficult for those individuals who grew up to believe that their value and self-worth derive from what they do as opposed to who they are. For these individuals, there is no such thing as a good day at work because there's always more to be done. For these individuals, the thoughts and opinions of those they work with take on out-of-proportion importance. A negative comment about one area of work by a co-worker can turn into a total condemnation of all areas of work. The desire to please the boss, often as a surrogate parent, compels them to demand an ever greater performance in order to achieve an elusive state of perfection and parental affirmation.

When this happens, the person becomes more concerned with how others feel he or she is doing, as opposed to what they are actually doing. This can interfere with work productivity, morale, and job satisfaction. When these suffer, the person as a whole suffers, and what is going on at work becomes the driving force in the person's life. The enjoyment of family, friends, recreation, and other pursuits are all tainted by this negative shroud of work dissatisfaction and the constant pressure to do more.

I speak from personal experience when I say that it is of utmost importance to have a balance between work life and personal life. Earlier in my career, I learned about this the hard way. My book *Becoming Strong Again* was written after coming back myself when the emotional exhaustion and fatigue from my work life totally overtook my personal life.

Work, because of the large role it plays in life, has a tendency to want to flood over its banks. Because of fear of failure, you end up doing more than you should. Because of past hurts, you are acutely sensitive to the unintentional actions of others. Because of insecurity, you pay more attention to the negative things said about you than the positive things. Because of fear of rejection, you stay silent more often than you speak up and build up a brimming supply of festering frustration. Because of fear of the unknown, you stay and suffer at times when you should trust and move on.

Work should not be in the driver's seat of your life. It should be firmly relegated to the backseat. It is part of your life; it certainly is along for the ride in your life, but it is not who you are, nor should it determine how valuable you are. Your satisfaction from work should come from who you are expressed within what you do, whatever it is you do. When you derive your sense of satisfaction from who you are, expressed through work, activities, and relationships, you provide yourself an anchor even when things don't go as planned.

Acquaintances

Acquaintances are people you know but, for whatever reason, have not developed into friends. Often it's because of circumstances or timing or just time. It takes time to develop friendships, and in a busy world, finding the time can be difficult. Because these people have not developed into friends does not mean their impact on your life is insignificant. For those of you who have trouble seeing yourself as competent, valuable people, the thoughts, opinions, and prejudices of acquaintances can take on undue force in your life.

Remember, these are people who are casually acquainted with you. They don't really know you. They haven't heard your story or know your background or, through time and affection, come to understand who you are. They know bits and pieces about you and are often content with this fragmented knowledge. It is not their desire to come to know you better, for reasons that may have absolutely nothing to do with you and everything to do with their life circumstances. These people interact with you on a limited, sporadic basis. Be pleasant, be polite, but don't grant them more control over your life and how you feel about yourself than what is appropriate. Interacting with you on a limited basis twice a week does not make them an authority to you, your life, and your value. Therefore, listen to what they have to say cautiously, like you eat fish. Enjoy any meat that's there, but pick out and discard the bones.

Friends

There are instances, of course, when casual acquaintance becomes something else, something more, and turns to real friendship. Friends are those you choose to attach yourself to, to love and trust. There is a decision involved. If you have grown up in a difficult family without real love and respect among the family members, it is through friendship that you can gather to yourself the deep, uplifting, and satisfying relationships that bring meaning and strength to your life.

Because friends are those individuals you have chosen to be in deep relationship with, it behooves you to choose wisely. Your friends should be a source of strength, encouragement, laughter, and support. When you're wrong, they should tell you, love you anyway, and encourage you to do better. When you're right, they should expect it, acknowledge it, and celebrate it.

Beware the friend who competes with you, belittles you, makes a habit of criticizing you before others, or seems to base his or her friendship on what you contribute to it. If your friend consistently appears to use you to elevate himself or herself, then you are useful, but you are not a friend.

Again, go back to those negative messages. If your friend echoes those criticisms, insecurities, and negativity, this person is not your friend. A true friend is one who supports, encourages, and uplifts. Then, based upon that foundation of love and support, a true friend can tell you when you're going the wrong way in your life. A true friend cares enough about you to warn you of any danger your actions or attitudes might represent. Proverbs 27:6 says, "Wounds from a friend can be trusted, but an enemy multiplies kisses."

You need friends who will love you enough to gently tell you the truth. Sometimes family members are simply too close to you to be able to detect a potential problem. Friends, though close, have the benefit of increased distance and can be invaluable in pointing out possible dangers ahead.

There is something else extremely valuable in a friendship. It is not merely what you can get from the friendship but also what you are able to give. Friends give to each other a certain level of access, of permission to speak honestly and exchange deep thoughts, feelings, and emotions. The gift of who you are, in your innermost thoughts, may not always be desired or appreciated by family members, but it is the foundation of the deepest friendship. This foundation is reciprocal. It is the two-way nature of this sharing that cements the bonds of friendship. In the Old Testament story of the friendship between Jonathan, the son of King Saul, and David, who was destined to become king in Saul's place, the New American Standard Version says, "The soul of Jonathan was knit to the soul of David, and Jonathan loved him as himself" (1 Samuel 18:1). This bonding together of two people in friendship must be done through mutual love and respect.

This is the type of friendship to strive for. If it can be with family members, so much the better. However, if this level of friendship is not possible through family or extended family, it is still possible to grow and develop through others. It's been said that the best way to gain a good friend is to be a good friend. Watch for reciprocity in your growing friendships. Those who answer your commitment to the friendship with commitment of their own are the ones to continue forward. If your commitment is answered with repeated selfishness, negativity, or a sense of entitlement, then move on.

Relationships can be a source of deep satisfaction, joy, and happiness. I truly believe that's one of the reasons God created them. God places you into a family and wants you to have friends. He calls you His child and wants to be your friend Himself. Relationships are meant to support you, not drag you down. Think of that old summer favorite, a gunnysack race. This is where two people are literally tied together. The right leg of the one is placed in a sack with the left leg of the other and then tied. The two people now have "three" legs. In order to run the race successfully, they need to be in sync with each other. When the two people cooperate and help each other, they successfully run the course. When the two people don't cooperate or help each other, they generally end up in a heap on the ground.

In order to be successful in relationships, it's important to evaluate who you're tied together with and whether or not you're both cooperating. In this Rest Stop section, I want you to take time to evaluate your current relationships—your family relationships, work relationships, friendships, and acquaintances. I want you to honestly appraise them to see if they are helping you get where you want to go on the road to happiness or if they're hindering you and holding you back. You're going to do this by listing the positive and negative aspects of each relationship. (Remember, there are no perfect relationships, so it's appropriate for there to be pros and cons in even the best of relationships. That's part of life.) Because each person will have a different number of relationships to evaluate, I've provided an example below of the type of table I'd like you to use. You'll need to draw this on a separate piece of paper to have enough space to do it properly.

Relationship	Positives	Negatives	
Family			
Work			

Friends			
Acquaintances			

Start with your family relationships and name each of them. Of course, you'll want to include all your intimate family relationships such as spouse, siblings, children, and parents. Also, include any significant extended family relationships. It's up to you to determine if an extended family relationship is significant enough to include. If the person has an impact on your life, go ahead and include him or her.

In the second column, I want you to write down how that relationship is a positive in your life. You get to determine what you consider a positive. In the third column, write down how that relationship is a negative in your life. Again, you get to determine what and why it is negative.

Give yourself plenty of room to write, and don't try to do this exercise as quickly as possible. This isn't a timed test. You may have to take a break and come back to it. That's fine.

Go through your intimate and significant extended family members. Then, go on to significant work relationships. You should include any direct bosses or supervisors and those co-workers you have contact with each day. You can also include work itself as a relationship, because some times positive and negative aspects of work come from the work or job itself and are not specifically attached to any one individual. Next, move to your friends and be honest marking in the positive and negative columns. Finally, move to acquaintances, and put down only those acquaintances who are significant to you in either a positive or a negative way.

Go ahead and work through this relationship grid, and then come back to the text and continue.

You'll have noticed, of course, that the last column does not have a heading. What I'd like you to do is use this column to determine what changes may need to be made. Look first for any of those relationships whose negatives far outweigh the positives.

For example, if you have a family relationship that is presently skewed in the negative direction, you may want to consider limiting contact with that person. Or, if there is a particular family member who provides you with a great deal of positives in your life, you may also want to evaluate if you are doing all you can to strengthen and support that connection.

If your work situation is extremely negative, even though there are positive people and aspects of the job, you may want to consider a change in employment. Or, if you realize you really do like your work environment but there are some negative people, you may want to attempt to either relocate away from those individuals or, if that is not possible, develop an intentional strategy for being in control of your interactions with those people.

If you realize you have a friendship that is overloaded in the negative column, you may want to propose changes in order to maintain the friendship. Or, if you see a very positive friendship, take a moment to determine what you can do today to make it even better.

Finally, take a look at your acquaintances. There may be some there with real promise to turn into a deeper friendship. These are ones to look at and explore. If there are those who are overly negative, it may be time to jettison them in favor of others more positive.

I recognize that thinking about, evaluating, and writing down this information is not a small task. However, few people, I've found, ever devote the energy and take the time to really evaluate their relationships and the positive or negative effects they have on their lives. Relationships have a tremendous effect on our ability to experience and enjoy happiness in life. It's worth the time and effort to think about and evaluate such a potent force.

I also recognize that knowing what changes to make and how to make them may be more than you feel comfortable or competent to do. If so, don't be ashamed or discouraged. This is where counselors and therapists come in. These professionals are trained to help you navigate situations and decisions just like these. They won't do it for you; instead, they'll help you discover the best way to do it for yourself. You'll still be in control but with professional support and guidance.

You may feel comfortable and competent to make many of the changes indicated through this inventory. However, there may be one or two that require assistance. Depending upon the type of changes indicated and the specific relationship involved, you may be able to enlist the help of a trusted family member or friend to assist. Where this is not possible, please don't hesitate to seek out professional counsel and help. This isn't something you need to do on your own. Find someone you trust, and work together to successfully make the changes you've determined will do you good. Toxic people and toxic relationships pollute the air of our lives and smother our ability to experience happiness. Go over your list and see where it may be time for you to clear the air.

Chapter 8

MAKE SURE TO SEE YOUR MECHANIC (PHYSICAL)

Y OUR BODY IS THE VEHICLE YOU USE TO GET AROUND IN LIFE. Like any vehicle, if something isn't working right or well, you take it to a mechanic—or do you? Are you one of those people who drive around for miles with the "check engine" light on? Is the oil change sticker on your windshield faded and weathered with age, with the mileage of the next visit long since passed? Do you have to reintroduce yourself to the mechanic every time you take your car in because it's been so long since the last time? Do you drive around with knobs falling off, bulbs out, belts squealing, and brakes shimmying? Do you avoid taking your car in for service because you're sure things are so bad it's going to cost you more than you can afford to fix it?

It's amazing to me how many people think of their bodies in the same way as a car. You grow complacent with aches and pains and just assume that's the way you're supposed to feel. You know you're due for that yearly physical, but it's been eighteen months and you still haven't called for an appointment. If you do go in to see your doctor—only when really sick— the doctor spends more time looking over your chart than looking you in the eye, in order to remember when in the world you were seen last. You walk around with sore feet, strained back, lousy sleep, and excess fat. A doctor is the last person you want to see, because you're afraid of all the bad news you'll get and, worse, all of the changes you'll be pressured to make.

What happens to your car if you put off routine maintenance and avoid getting it repaired when needed? It falls apart and stops running. That's pretty much what happens with your body too, especially as you age. Some people, through the lottery of genetics, can put this off longer than others, but eventually neglect and time catch up to everyone. You are not an exception. The physical laws of the universe are not going to be suspended just for you, not where either of your "vehicles" is concerned. Neglect your car and it stops running. Neglect your body and it stops performing. Neither situation is bound to make you feel very happy.

Is Your "Check Engine" Light On?

Yes, happiness is in the mind, but your body has a tremendous impact on your ability to be happy. If you feel lousy all the time, that's a significant barrier to overcome. You become irritable, depressed, lethargic, and frustrated. It's hard to be happy when that's how you feel.

Julie sat in her car a minute, collecting her thoughts. She was exhausted after another long day at work. It was only Tuesday, and she had no idea how she was going to get through the rest of the week. Luckily, her husband had called and picked up food on his way home so she didn't have to cook dinner. The kids were off doing who knows what. With a sigh, she gathered up her things from the car and went inside. Walking up the steps to the front door got her winded, and she pushed the realization out of her mind. Forty pounds overweight didn't help, and with no change in sight, neither did dwelling on it. She didn't have the energy or the will to diet. Frankly, food was one of the few things left that she really did seem to enjoy and look forward to during the day.

The pizza was already half gone as she entered the kitchen. Her husband, engrossed in something on television, acknowledged her entry with a quick, "Sorry; couldn't wait for you to get home to eat. You can nuke it." She was just glad he'd stopped for food and wasn't about to complain. Besides, she really liked pizza and looked forward to sitting down with the paper, a large soda from the fridge, and several slices. After dinner, she went to the cabinet, pulled out whatever bag of cookies was still left from the last shopping trip, and transferred herself to the couch to join her husband. Before long, she was drifting off to sleep between the commercials, which were always so much louder than the rest. Intermittently, she and her husband would talk about their day, about work, but it was usually pretty negative. This gave her a chance to vent. They both weren't very happy with their jobs and batted around their dissatisfaction between them.

At nine-thirty, she'd had enough of sitting there and decided to head on up to bed. Her husband always seemed to stay up later, but Julie hadn't slept well the night before—actually, she hadn't slept well for several nights—so she wanted to get in bed early in case tonight followed suit. As she hobbled upstairs on protesting knees, she wondered how in the world she was going to make it through the rest of the week. Sometimes, it just didn't seem worth the effort.

There are physical conditions, beyond a person's control, that negatively impact the ability of the body to function properly. I think everyone can agree with that. But before you automatically put yourself in that category and determine there's nothing you can do about it, the key point in that sentence is "beyond a person's control." You have a great deal more control over your body and how you feel than you may think. I've found far too many people just give up where their bodies are concerned. They seem to acquiesce to a gradual decline, willing to accommodate the deterioration instead of taking a few simple steps to improve their overall health. Notice, I said "simple," not "easy."

The Science of Health Isn't Rocket Science

If you've been alive and even moderately alert over the past several years at a minimum, you've been inundated with health information. Frankly, it's everywhere—on the news, in magazines, in books (I've written a few of them myself), on the radio, on television, and plastered all over the Internet. While there is quite a volume of information, some of which can be confusing, I've found there are a few core principles to health that are applicable to everyone, no matter your circumstances or situation in life.

For some of you, a discussion of health is the farthest thing from happiness you can imagine. The reason is probably because your health isn't where you want it to be and it makes you unhappy. This isn't just a case of dissatisfaction, although that certainly could be present. When your body functions properly, you are designed with the ability to be happy, to weather storms, to overcome trials, to be resilient. When your body isn't functioning well, it compromises your ability to maintain emotional equilibrium. Health and happiness are linked together. There is physicality to happiness.

What this means is, with a few simple commitments to health, you can increase your body's potential to assist you along the road to happiness. There are five basic things you can start doing today that will improve your health. These don't require fancy pills or complicated formulas or special equipment. They do, however, require commitment and making intentional lifestyle changes. They require will and resolve. They do not, however, require perfection. Instead, think of these changes as a series of baby steps. Go gradually, grow consistently, and you'll keep moving forward.

The five basic things you can do aren't rocket science. They won't be difficult for you to understand or believe in. They are: (1) choose healthy food in appropriate portions; (2) adopt a more active, less sedentary lifestyle; (3) support your body with nutritional and hormonal support, where indicated; (4) develop the tools to experience true sleep; and (5) stay hydrated. There, nothing earth-shattering. Yet, I will tell you that adopting these simple changes can have profoundly positive effects, both to your overall health and your mood.

Factor Your Fuel

God always intended food to be fuel for the body. He also meant for it to be a source of pleasure; that's why He made food to taste good. As usual, the good God intended has been corrupted by the practice of people. This happened from the very beginning. In the garden, Eve looked at the fruit she knew she wasn't supposed to eat and saw that it looked good, was good for food, and made one wise (Genesis 3:6). The first two were legitimate food reasons. The third was a nonfood reason. All of these reasons, of course, were trumped by God's declaring this tree and its fruit off-limits.

Food today isn't forbidden by God, but that doesn't stop people from choosing food for nonfood reasons. Now, people don't necessarily eat to become wise, but they eat for comfort, to relieve stress, to temporarily overcome boredom, because it's pleasurable, as a form of rebellion, and in the name of convenience. The more nonfood reasons people have to eat, the more they eat. The more they eat, the larger they become. The larger they become, the more dissatisfied they are and the harder it is to experience and maintain a sense of personal happiness.

In my previous book *The Body God Designed*, I encouraged readers to utilize an easy-to-find tool in order to eat more healthfully. This tool is the U.S. government's food pyramid found at www.MyPyramid.gov. The government's food pyramid is a dietary guideline for all ages and activity levels. Here's a graphic from the Web site:

The food pyramid outlines the daily recommended amounts you should consume in different food categories. The part on the far left of the pyramid represents grains (bread, cereal, crackers, rice, pasta, etc.). The next part over represents vegetables, and the next part represents fruits. The little thin sliver represents fats and oils, while the bigger next wedge represents milk and dairy products. The last wedge represents protein. Using nutritional and medical research, the pyramid outlines how much is recommended daily from each category. Utilizing a tool on the Web site, you have to put in your age, gender, and activity level to customize your own pyramid and to show how to either gain, maintain, or lose weight. This customized pyramid gives amounts, suggested foods to eat, and portion sizes. It gives guidelines on sodium intake and how to handle "discretionary calories," that small category involving desserts and sweets.

The MyPyramid.gov Web site is full of great nutritional information, easily accessible to most people, written in understandable, not scientific, language. You can also print up a daily meal planner sheet that helps you track what and how much you're eating. (For a tour on how all this works, you can link to the meal planner through the main Web site or go to http://www.mypyramidtracker.gov/planner/sitetour/USDASiteTour.html.) You can also register and work with the site's meal tracker, which helps you daily assess both your food intake and your physical activity. All of this is free, available through the Internet, courtesy of your tax dollars at work through the U.S. Department of Agriculture. It's an amazing tool and one I heartily encourage you to visit and use as a way to assist you in making healthy food choices.

The bottom line for healthier eating, which you'll find in my books or through the pyramid, is to eat more grains (with whole grains being the best), more fruits and vegetables (with darker vegetables being best—just think peppers and broccoli as opposed to celery), more lean sources of dairy and protein, and less oils and fats (with more of the good sources of fat like olive oil and flaxseed oil and less of the saturated and partially hydrogenated fats). With all of that healthy eating going on, there isn't much room left for things like highly processed foods, packaged convenience or snack foods, junk food, or "discretionary calories" like cookies, cakes, pies, and the like. Having these items occasionally is realistic. Eating them consistently, daily, is not realistic for healthy living.

God designed your body to use the food you eat as fuel to power your body's functions. If you consistently put lousy gas in the tank of your car, it wouldn't run properly. It may still get you down the road, but you'll experience pings, burps, smoke, hesitations, and lack of power. It will gum up your engine parts and increase the amount of pollution in the air. Do this long enough, and you could find yourself calling a tow truck on the side of the road. It's the same way with your body. An occasional treat is not going to cause you problems, but if you live on a diet of high-calorie, high-caffeine, low-nutrient foods, your ability to physically perform will be compromised.

I've just gone over the tip of the iceberg (or the pyramid) of healthy eating. I encourage you to pick up a copy of one of my books that contain information on healthy eating (*The Body God Designed*, *Thin Over 40*, or *The Total Temple Makeover*). Each of these books takes you on a journey of discovery for healthier living and gives you the tools you need to make better choices. Right now, I want you to acknowledge what you really know to be true, that you need to commit to eating more healthfully. It really does make a difference in how you feel.

Get Up and Go

While it's great to eat a healthy variety of good foods, your body was designed to *do* something with that food. It was designed to *use* it. In order to feel better, you need to get out and get moving. This culture is a sedentary one. People drive instead of walk, take elevators instead of stairs, ride buses instead of bikes. Instead of getting out and being active, the preference is sitting in a chair and watching television or sitting at the computer. Instead of getting up out of the chair and switching the channel, there are controllers to do that job for you. It's considered the height of inconvenience to have to move ten feet. You get up in the morning and go from a bed to a chair, to a car seat, to a chair, to a car seat, to a couch, to a bed. The emphasis has switched from participating to observing, becoming passive and sedentary. All of this is bad news for a body that was designed to get out and get moving.

One of the best ways you can increase your health is by embracing opportunities during your day to increase activity. Park your car at the farthest point possible and walk to where you are going. Whenever possible take the stairs instead of the escalator or elevator. Bring a pair of comfortable shoes to work and get out and walk midday. In the morning, instead of a jolt of sugar and caffeine to get you going, get up a little earlier and take a walk or exercise. Instead of calling a co-worker while at work, get up and go to where he or she is. In the evening, after dinner, instead of lounging on the couch or in a chair, get up and go outside. Take a walk or do a little gardening, weather permitting. Take the kids to a park; walk the dog. Whenever possible when running errands, make that phrase more reflective of the activity. *Run* the errand or at least get out and *walk* the errand.

If you're able, join a gym or engage in regular, routine exercise, combining strengthening and cardiovascular exercises. Strengthening exercises build up lean muscle, which acts as a metabolic booster. Lean muscle uses more energy than fat, even sitting around doing nothing, so the more lean muscle you have, the more calories you burn just by taking up space. Cardiovascular exercises also help boost metabolism and help keep your heart, lungs, and circulatory system in shape.

Somewhere along the line, *exercise* became a dirty word for many people, especially as they got older. It's OK to admit you're one of them. For you, it may have occurred as the demands of career and family began to compete heavily for time priority in your life. It may have occurred when an injury curtailed some physical activity you were engaged in, and you never did pick up the slack with anything else. You may never have been one for much physical exercise, having never developed the habit or pattern growing up. If this is you, it's fine to admit. You have the ability to change and begin to look for and adopt a more physically active lifestyle. This doesn't mean you must commit to running the Boston Marathon next year. What it does mean is that you'll need to look over and evaluate your level of activity and come up with doable, concrete ways every day to increase it (more about that, ironically, in this chapter's Rest Stop).

Boost Your Octane

People today have pretty stressful lives. I know I do, with the demands of running The Center, writing and speaking, commitments to my faith community, to say nothing of being my wife's husband and my kids' dad. It's a lot. I dare say I'm not that different from you. Because life is stressful, with many demands on time and energy, sometimes the nutrition derived from a daily diet is not enough. If you don't eat nutritious food in the first place, then you're really operating from a deficit. If you overstimulate your body with jolts of calories and caffeine, you create internal stress to augment the normal, everyday, external stresses of living. If you take prescription medications, you can compromise your body's ability to break down and assimilate whatever nutrition you do take in. If you abuse laxatives, prescription medications, drugs, or alcohol, you are constantly leeching nutrients from your system.

Even for those of you who already have a pretty good handle on healthy eating, it may still not be enough. Since 2002, the American Medical Association (AMA) has recommended adults take a multivitamin supplement daily. At The Center, our whole-person approach to recovery is firmly grounded in the need for and efficacy of nutritional support and supplementation. An individualized plan is created based upon medical testing to determine nutritional deficiencies and the best ways to correct those deficiencies. We use a variety of specialized nutritional products to help bring people back up to optimum nutritional levels. The results in health are very gratifying and are a significant part of our intensive recovery programs for a variety of mental-health and chemical-dependency issues.

While these are individualized plans, there are a couple of common-sense nutritional supplements that make sense for the vast majority of people. The AMA may recommend a single multivitamin, but I believe a better multivitamin and mineral formula is one that is taken over the course of the day, involving more than a single pill. Because most nutrients in supplement form are water-soluble, a percentage of them simply are flushed down the drain during the course of a day. In order to assist in greater absorption and assimilation, your multivitamin serving size should consist of several tablets or capsules, taken at intervals during the day. You also want to look for a formula that maximizes bioavailability. It's not just what nutrients are in the supplements but how easy it is for your body to absorb and make use of those nutrients. Otherwise, most of your nutrients will end up down the drain and of no benefit to you.

In addition to a good multivitamin and mineral formula, many people have found health benefits from taking an EPA/DHA supplement, sometimes called a fish oil supplement. EPA (eicosepautoic acid) and DHA (docosahexanoic acid) are omega-3 fatty acids. Dietary sources of these omega-3s are cold-water fish (like salmon), whole grains, fresh fruits, vegetables, olive oil, and garlic. Omega-3s are really good for you, with a whole host of benefits. Research is being done on the use of EPA and DHA to help with depression, Alzheimer's, ADHD, overall brain function, and lubrication for the digestive system and for joint function. If you go to the Web site for the National Institutes of Health and search for EPA/DHA, there are over two hundred articles listed from research around the world. It's pretty impressive.

Omega-3s, as essential fatty acids, are well established as beneficial. You can take them in capsules over the course of the day or as a liquid (this is the most efficient delivery system, but be cautioned, the taste requires a little getting used to. The liquid form needs refrigeration, which is good because the taste seems to be less "fragrant" when cold.) As more and more people come to understand the health benefits of taking a supplement containing EPA and DHA, technology keeps getting better. The potency of the supplements, I believe, will only increase.

Get Your Rest

You need your sleep. If you don't get it, your body operates under stress. Sleep deprivation has been linked to increases in depression, cardiovascular disease, diabetes, as well as memory and cognitive problems. This isn't a pretty picture. Recently, the *Seattle Times* (one of my hometown papers. The other is the *Seattle Post-Intelligencer*. I live in one of the few cities in the country with two daily newspapers. As an aside, they've been in legal battles with each other for years, with the outcome and the victor as yet to be determined) ran an article heralding the completion of an extensive study on sleep by the Centers for Disease Control.[1] According to this study by the CDC, which looked at a variety of issues relating to sleep including obesity, the healthiest (i.e., thinnest) people slept more than six hours a night but not more than nine hours a night. Apparently, the study found that if you sleep too little, it's a health issue, and it's also a health issue if you spend too much time in bed. Kind of a Goldilocks sleep solution—not too big, not too small, but just right. I guess that doesn't surprise me. What does surprise me is how many people begrudge getting seven or eight hours of sleep a night. They believe sleeping less makes them more productive. Oh, you may be awake more hours during the day, but your ability to function well during all that extra time awake is compromised. When it comes to sleep, less is definitely not more.

Operating under a sleep deficit isn't a cause to brag about how little sleep you need. It's a cause of concern. Lack of sleep causes your brain to be, well, tired and sluggish. You have a harder time making cognitive connections while you have an easier time making mistakes. This rather intuitive conclusion comes from an article I read in a publication by the American Academy of Neurology chronicling research done with residents in medical training programs who are known for getting notoriously little sleep.[2] Reading this article made me decide that whenever I'm in the hospital next, I'm going to make sure the physician has the proper medical credentials and a good night's sleep!

The older (and, hopefully, wiser) I get, the more I realize sleep needs to be prepared for. When I was younger, I used to be able to go Mach 10 until the wee hours of the morning and literally fall asleep in a matter of minutes. Now, however, I need time to transition myself into sleep, to set the stage for a good night's rest. I used to be able to sleep in just about any position I found myself in. Not so much anymore. Now, I actually need several conditions met to be able to sleep—like having it dark and actually being comfortable (oh, for the joys of youth!).

In my book *Thin Over 40*, I mentioned several suggestions from Dr. Michael Vitiello, who is a psychiatry and behavioral sciences professor at the University of Washington in Seattle, regarding how to maximize your ability to sleep. They matched what I've come to believe myself and observe from working with clients at The Center. They are:

- *Keep to a regular sleep schedule.* I try not to vary, by much, the time I go to bed and wake up each day of the week, including weekends. This establishes a pattern for my body to adjust to.

- Prepare your sleep environment:

    1. Keep it dark.

    2. Keep it quiet.

    3. Keep it a comfortable temperature.

    4. Sleep on a good-quality, supportive mattress.

    5. Have good airflow in the room.

I find I simply am not able to have good sleep if there are lights on everywhere, with noise blaring, in a room that's either frigid cold or stifling hot, on a thin, lumpy mattress, all the while feeling like I'm suffocating. Imagine that. Every single one of these conditions makes perfect sense and is well worth the effort to put into effect.

- *Do not use tobacco or alcohol from the late afternoon on.* The nicotine in tobacco is a stimulant, and alcohol negatively affects your quality of sleep. At The Center, we teach and model nicotine cessation. Frankly, I see no positive reason for using tobacco of any kind. As for consuming alcohol, for those who are able to do so in strict moderation, that's fine. However, we see a great many people who turn to alcohol to self-medicate other issues and work with those individuals to develop the tools and pattern of sobriety.

- *Keep your bedroom your bedroom.* Don't turn it into an auxiliary television room, computer room, or workstation. Your bedroom should be a place where you give your mind permission to rest, turn off, and go into "sleep" mode.

- *Try warm milk if you have trouble sleeping.* This may be an old remedy, but it really does have properties that can help you sleep. You can also use a small glass of noncaffeinated hot tea. Keep any liquid consumption limited to around 4–6 ounces or you'll end up waking up during the night to use the bathroom!

- *Turn the clock around so you can't see it.* Fixating on the changing time isn't exactly going to enhance your ability to relax and fall asleep.

- *Take a hot bath or shower just prior to going to bed.* Some people find this very relaxing, as a precursor to sleep. Allowing your body to physically relax will assist your mind in triggering it's internal shut-off switch.

I've also found that reading, for many people, helps them relax, tune out from the events of the day, and give themselves permission to relax. It's important to choose your reading material wisely, of course. Personally, I find reading Scripture is helpful (this is why my Bible study is not done at night!) to relax and fall asleep. Knowing I have a loving Father who never sleeps, to whom I can turn over the events of the day, my worries, and concerns, allows me to relax at the end of even stressful days. In the same vein, prayer can also be a wonderful way to both say "good night" to God, to relax, and to go to sleep.

You may be one of those people who really want to experience good sleep but don't. Sometimes, for everyone, sleep can be elusive, but if this is a pattern for you, I encourage you to consult with your physician. At The Center, our naturopathic doctors work with people to identify the reasons—both physical and environmental—that hinder sleep and create strategies to help. There are nutritional supplements that can be taken that enhance sleep by assisting the body in producing serotonin, the neurotransmitter responsible for the sleep cycle. Sleeping poorly isn't something you should learn to put up with. Instead, it's a critical area for your health and needs to be aggressively addressed with health-care professionals. If the suggestions listed above do not provide the results you're looking for, look further and get the help you need. It's not just a good night's sleep; it's the foundation for everything that happens in the day that follows.

Drink Up

Lately, there's been some nay-saying to the conventional wisdom about drinking a lot of water. I'll let the debate rage around me and just go with what I've observed, which is that people feel better when they're hydrated. If you get dehydrated, you can feel lethargic and lightheaded. The debate has even extended over what you can drink to satisfy your fluid intake. Again, I'll let the debate continue elsewhere and just go with what I believe. When you're thirsty, I prefer for people to just drink water. It doesn't come with all of the chemical baggage of other liquids (caffeine, calories, poly-syllabic ingredients). The more activity you engage in, the more water intake you should have. It's been generally accepted that people should have around four to eight glasses of water a day.[3] However, if you're thirsty, drink more water. If it's hot, drink more water. If you're ill, drink more water. It's pretty simple. Water is good for you, and other liquids should be consumed in moderation.

Get a Checkup

What I've talked about here are a few common-sense, easy-to-understand suggestions for improving your health. I am not, however, a physician. Before you make any significant changes to your health habits—and certainly if it's been over a year since you've seen your physician or if you're contemplating starting a structured exercise routine—I encourage you to touch base with your doctor. Find out how you're doing physically, from either a medical doctor or a naturopathic physician. There are medical tests that can be run and read by your physician that will provide insight and information into how your body is *really* doing. Together with your physician, you can partner to make the changes necessary to increase your health. The better you feel, the easier it is to anticipate, experience, prolong, and appreciate happiness. When you feel better, it's easier to be happy. Depression, fatigue, lethargy, aches, and pains all interfere with your ability to be happy and can be addressed and treated by your physician. Don't let a fear of the mechanic keep you from getting your car into the shop. The cost, in the long run, of not going in may be more than you really want to pay.

OK, it's time for another personal inventory. It's time for you to really evaluate how you're doing on the things talked about in this chapter. Hopefully, you've read over them and agreed to their general benefits. There may be some of you, however, who are reluctant to evaluate them when it comes to your own life. Being able to nod generally in agreement can be quite different from analyzing your own life and habits and determining specific changes that need to be made to achieve more healthful results. It's OK to be reluctant, but I want you to do it anyway. After you've done so, choose one positive change you can make and integrate into your life. As soon as that one change is no longer a change but simply the way you live, go on to the next. Again, these are baby steps you're taking. Each change you successfully integrate will give you encouragement, motivation, and strength to take on another. In this way, you're building up a scaffold of change and a firmer foundation of health for happiness.

Let's take a look at how you're doing on the food front. I'd like you to start by remembering what you had to eat and drink over the past twenty-four hours. Using a grid like the one below, write down each type of food you ate and beverage you consumed (yes, all of the food and drink—don't leave anything out). Next indicate if you ate that food for fuel (for it's nutritional characteristics) or if you ate it for some other reason, and be sure to think about and identify the reason if you can (comfort, boredom, stress, convenience, rebellion, etc.). Do this also for whatever you had to drink. I have found people sometimes forget a great deal of caloric intake can occur from what they drink. By just switching mostly to consuming water, people have been able to make significant adjustments in their overall daily calories.

Type of Food/Drink	Fuel	Other

What are you able to determine, based upon your eating and drinking? Is the majority of food/drink intake due to nutritional needs, or are you eating/drinking because of other reasons?

Pick out one area where you are eating/drinking for a reason other than nutrition. Think about how you could meet the need that doesn't require food. Could you take a walk, call a friend, read a book, listen to music? What could you do instead? The next time you're tempted to eat in order to fill that need, switch to plan B.

I also encourage you once again to go to www.MyPyramid.gov and take a look at the information and tools available for free on this Web site. Even if you just print up a meal plan and attach it to your refrigerator, it can help you keep in the forefront of your mind how and what you should be consuming each day for a healthy diet. The sooner you start to eat better, the sooner you'll start to feel better. When you feel better, it's easier to be happy.

Next, think about your activity level during the day. Trace over your steps from the time you get up to the time you go to bed. Do you regularly find ways to avoid additional physical exercise? How can you increase your amount of physical activity within your daily routine? I'm not talking about anything major or a structured exercise routine here, just ways you can take more steps, move more, during the day. Many people I've worked with have become quite creative and really have fun finding ways to be more active. It's a source of encouragement and accomplishment. They also tell me it's a lot easier than they thought. Write down three immediate ways you can increase your amount of physical movement through the normal course of your day. Here are a few suggestions to get you thinking: park farther away and walk; walk instead of taking a bus or car; take the stairs instead of an elevator or escalator; take a walk before, during, or after work/school/home activities; walk between work/school areas; or do yard work or housework more quickly.

I can increase my physical movement today by:

1. _____

2. _____

3. _____

If you're on a roll and can think of more than three, write them down! Put them on a sticky note or several sticky notes where you'll see them and begin to integrate them immediately. This will help you to cultivate an active mind-set instead of a sedentary one. It's just a way for you to look at your world a little differently—at *you* a little differently. When you see yourself as an active, physical person, you'll look for ways during the day to reinforce that.

If you decide, after trying this for a while, that you really are enjoying increased daily activity and decide you want to adopt a more structured exercise routine, please consult first with your doctor. This is especially vital if you have been inactive for several years or have a health condition that needs to be factored in to your exercise routine. Believe me, your doctor will be thrilled to assist you with this task (or should be) and can provide medical insight and guidelines for how best to integrate a more structured exercise routine into your life. Regular, prolonged exercise releases physical compounds called *endorphins*, which are known as the body's natural opiates. Endorphins are basically "feel-good" chemicals. Simply put, exercising helps you feel better, not just physically but emotionally as well. Remember, when you are moving your body, you are using it as it was designed to function. It's happy; you're happy.

Are you regularly taking a multivitamin formula and an EPA/DHA supplement? If not, I encourage you to go to our Web site at www .aplaceofhope.com and look at the Hope Store for information on the products we carry. You can also look for supplements at a local health-food or supplement store. Buy the best product you can for the money you have to spend. Ask about the amount of bioavailability built into the product. Look at the ingredient list, and ask questions about things you don't understand. Nutritional supplements vary greatly in quality and efficacy—they can be a tremendous physical benefit or a significant waste of money. Don't just pick up the first bottle you see at the grocery store. Do a little research (or just call The Center).

Next, think about how you're sleeping. If the truth is, not that well, it's time to intentionally start putting into practice the suggestions listed in this chapter. It may mean you'll need to get a light-canceling shade for your room, or remove a television, computer, or workspace from your bedroom, or change when you consume alcohol, or give up smoking. It may mean you'll need to intentionally gear down for bed instead of running around like a rodent on a wheel right up until the moment you turn out the light. It may mean you'll need to get a new mattress or a fan for your room. It may mean you need to cut down on your activities and responsibilities during the day so you can devote the proper amount of time to sleep. Purpose to make the changes you need to prepare yourself and your room for better sleep. The benefits are huge compared to the costs.

Here are the suggestions again, in a form you can use to evaluate your personal space:

Sleep Condition	Positive Changes
Sleep schedule	Go to bed and wake on a similar schedule daily, including weekends.
Darkness	Keep room dark for sleeping, regardless of time of day.
Quiet	Reduce as much noise as possible for sleeping. Use white noise or fan if environment is noisy beyond your control.
Temperature	If it's too hot, open a window or use a fan. If it's too cold, increase heat or blankets.
Mattress	Buy the highest quality you can afford with the most support you're comfortable with. Test it out first, whenever possible.
Airflow	Get as much natural air in the room as possible. If opening a window is not possible, use a fan to circulate air.
Distractions	Remove television and computers from the room. Whenever possible, do not use your bedroom as a work area. If necessary, put away all papers and work products in drawers at the end of the day.
Alarm clock	Move this away from you. You won't be able to fixate on it while getting to sleep, and it will be far enough away that you'll actually need to get up to turn off the alarm!
No tobacco or alcohol late in day	Avoid use of both of these past late afternoon or early evening.
Warm milk or tea	If you're having trouble relaxing and falling asleep, try a small glass of warm milk or hot noncaffeinated tea.
Hot shower or bath	Take a hot bath or shower to help your body relax and prepare for sleep.
Read or pray	Read a book or the Bible or pray to relax prior to falling asleep. Avoid personally disturbing reading material, as the goal here is to read something relaxing, not scary or intense!

If after implementing these changes you still are not experiencing restful sleep, it is time to call in reinforcements. This is definitely a discussion you should have with your physician. There are even specialists in sleep available to assist your physician in diagnosing and providing solutions to your individual situation. Sleep deprivation is a stress and a toll on your body, mind, and spirit. It needs to be recognized, addressed, and treated as part of an overall strategy of improved health.

All of these things are important to your health. Your health is important to your ability to experience happiness and fulfillment in life. Go back through and identify those changes you are excited about and know you can implement immediately. Put those on your "to do" list right now, and tackle them one at a time. For the others, keep implementation as your goal, and intentionally work toward making these a part of your life. Don't shortchange yourself in this area. Any effort you put in will bring you exponential dividends.

Chapter 9

GOD AS YOUR NAVIGATOR (SPIRITUAL)

AVE YOU EVER GOTTEN LOST, THROWN UP YOUR HANDS, AND wondered aloud, "Where in the world am I?" Many people have discovered the wonders of a Global Positioning System, or GPS. Using a system of twenty-four satellites, the GPS triangulates a handheld device to this satellite system and shows you exactly where in the world you are. It's pretty handy. There are handheld devices and GPS units built into cars. The GPS was initially set up for military use, but after the tragic downing of a commercial jetliner in 1983, President Ronald Reagan opened it up for public, commercial use. Now you can buy a small device with a screen that will give you precise directions to anywhere in the world. You can even choose a male or female voice with a foreign language, and the unit will "speak" to you. You can even link the device to your computer with Google Earth and have actual pictures as you drive of where you're going. I think this would make me carsick, but I'm sure some of you would find this a must-have feature.

In my line of work, it's amazing how many people don't know exactly where they are, metaphorically speaking. It's impossible for them to get where they're going, because they have no real inkling of where they are in the first place. They need, for their personal, emotional, and spiritual lives, a way to navigate. Now, a GPS is a relatively new marvel; God has been providing this service to people for millennia. God, in some ways, is like a spiritual GPS. He knows how to help you get from where you are to where you should be. If you need help navigating your way to happiness, don't leave home without your spiritual GPS. Oh, but be careful how you use it.

I've known of several people over the course of my professional career who wanted to treat God just like a GPS unit. If I'm honest, I have to admit that I've done so myself. I want God, like a GPS unit, to tell me how to get to my desired destination. I've gotten myself lost, in a mess, and realized I needed help to find my way out. So I called out to God—as my spiritual GPS—and asked Him to help me get to where I really wanted to go. Of course, I didn't ask Him if my intended destination was any better than my current one. I didn't really want His opinion; I just wanted His help and divine power to get me out of my jam. I just wanted to be able to input my own data and with His help arrive at my chosen destination. It's somewhat akin to the God-as-Santa-Claus syndrome. All I wanted to do was tell Him what I wanted and for Him to miraculously provide it. I wanted His *provision*, not His *perspective*. This is God as *device* not *deity*, as *servant* not *sovereign*. This puts me firmly in control, and then I wonder why things don't turn out and I'm not very happy.

In the depths of my despair and need, I call out to God, delineating in detail the best way to solve my problem, and then I wonder why God and His (my) solutions don't appear as a genie from a bottle. This isn't spirituality; it's fantasy. It's not biblical; it's delusional, to say nothing of disrespectful, disobedient, and rebellious. God is not really just a spiritual GPS device. It's not His job to get me out of my messes. He can and will because He loves me, but He was not created for me. I was created for Him. In the powerful words of Rick Warren in *The Purpose-Driven Life*, it's not about me. In the same way, it's not about you. When God is truly your spiritual navigator, you may drive the car, but He is in charge of the direction you go. It's your job to follow His leading, even if it's a direction you're not thrilled to be taking. With God as your spiritual navigator, it's not about you. Instead, you need to give up control, listen to God, do what He tells you, and trust Him to make it all come out OK in the end.

Paper-Bag Directions

There's a woman I work with who will openly admit that she can't find her way out of a brown paper bag. She calls herself *directionally challenged*. Now that her children are grown, she has no one to help her find her car in the mall and grocery-store parking lots, which adds quite a bit of adventure to her shopping experience. She lives by MapQuest for any trip over a half a mile. Even when she gets to her destination, she will often exit the complete opposite of the way she came in. Driving at night is a problem because she can get even more turned around. She has learned not to trust her own instincts since they are invariably wrong, or, put another way, she has learned to trust that her instincts will always be wrong. While I'm glad I'm not afflicted by such directional confusion, I have to admit that I can learn a lot from her.

In a spiritual sense, I'm *directionally challenged* because of my humanity. Proverbs puts it this way in both chapter 14, verse 12, and chapter 16, verse 25 (I'm stubborn, so I need the repetition): "There is a way that seems right to a man, but in the end it leads to death." Simply put, I'm not the best judge of the direction I should take, and neither are you. In fact, even thinking you can always know which way to go is ludicrous at best and arrogant at worst. A little later in Proverbs, even wise King Solomon wrote: "A man's steps are directed by the LORD. How then can anyone understand his own way?" (Proverbs 20:24). How, indeed? In truth, I want to direct my own steps and just have God take over when I get into really significant trouble. This is what I fight against on a daily basis, asserting control and sovereignty over my own life, even when I know well Jeremiah 10:23: "I know, O LORD, that a man's life is not his own; it is not for man to direct his steps." I know that, but I still want to direct my steps anyway.

This dilemma means I must continually, intentionally give over control of the direction of my life to God. I think this is what Jesus might have meant when He said, "If anyone would come after me, he must deny himself and take up his cross and follow me" (Matthew 16:24; Mark 8:34; Luke 9:23—there's that repetition again). The Luke passage adds that you need to pick up your cross *daily*. (A single day at a time is about all I'm good for, and even then I have trouble sometimes.)

If you believe you are competent enough to direct your own steps, you are operating under a delusion. It might work for a little while and will probably make you happy. You'll be cruising down the road of life with the top down, radio blasting, singing your freedom song at the top of your lungs, and before you know it, you'll be sailing off the edge of a cliff marked divorce, disease, abandonment, financial problems, relationship issues, health struggles, or you fill in the blank. Or you'll be jetting along at Mach 10 with the wind in your hair and the landscape a blur, only to find yourself out of gas and lost in a spiritual wasteland. It's time for you and me to face the truth of Jeremiah 10:23 and submit to God's authority and direction over our lives.

Are You Listening?

Once again, I'm reading through the Bible in a year. OK, to be honest, I'm a little bit behind in my daily reading, but I have every intention of catching up. (No matter when you're reading this book, I'm probably just a little behind so any prayer you offer up for me at this point would be most appreciated.) I've been reading through the Book of 1 Samuel. If it's been awhile since you read this story, here's the short version: Samuel, as a boy, is brought to Eli, God's priest at Shiloh, by his mother, Hannah, to serve the Lord. This is because Hannah couldn't have children initially but prayed to God, who allowed her to give birth to Samuel, so she dedicated him to the Lord, literally. As a small child, she dropped Samuel off at the tabernacle where he became Eli's helper. One night as Samuel slept, he kept hearing someone call his name. Waking up and thinking Eli was calling him, Samuel ran to Eli to find out why he called. This happened twice in succession, and each time, Eli told Samuel to go back to bed because he didn't call him. Finally, on the third time, Eli figured out that it was God who was calling Samuel. (Every time I read this story, I'm really impressed that Eli figures out it's God and not just a dream of Samuel's, especially because at the beginning of chapter 3, it says this sort of thing was not exactly commonplace in Israel at the time.) Eli told Samuel that the next time God calls him, he should answer this way: "Speak, LORD, for your servant is listening" (1 Samuel 3:9).

This should be your attitude when asking God for directions: "Speak,

LORD, for Your servant is listening." Notice I said *should*. Instead, I have said things like, "Speak, LORD, for Your servant is listening *for what I want to hear*," or "Speak, LORD, Your servant is listening, *but I may or may not do what You say*," or "Could You speak up, LORD, *I can't hear You over the noise of my own desires*." These may be honest answers, but they're not satisfactory ones to give to God when asking for help and direction. They won't get you where you want to go. Then, you won't be happy, and God won't be pleased.

God explains this attitude and its consequences in Jeremiah 7:23–24:

> But I gave them this command: Obey me, and I will be your God and you will be my people. Walk in all the ways I command you, that it may go well with you. But they did not listen or pay attention; instead, they followed the stubborn inclinations of their evil hearts. They went backward and not forward.

Backward and not forward doesn't get you to your destination.

You need to listen to God and pay attention. As a father, I completely understand why *listen* and *pay attention* are combined. My sons are still fairly young, so their attention span is about as long as the life of the average fruit fly, which is to say extremely short. They will clamber and jump for my attention, just so they can ask me a question, a question they must have the answer to at that very second or something really, really bad is going to happen. I can never figure out what, but they are sure it will. So, after they ask their question, I start to answer it. It is, then, amazing to me how quickly they can stop paying attention to my answer. A second ago they were dying to have me answer the question, and a second later they're drifting off in distraction. I get so frustrated sometimes that I just want to quote Scripture: "Listen, my sons, to a father's instruction; pay attention and gain understanding" (Proverbs 4:1). I haven't actually used this one yet, but I've memorized the verse, just in case. Maybe you should memorize it too. When God speaks, listen, pay attention, and gain understanding.

Following Instructions

I'm pretty good at following instructions, at least some of them. I have a tendency, though, to predetermine how long any set of instructions should be. I'll hang with them that long, but if they go on much longer, I start looking for shortcuts, thinking surely I could have designed better instructions than the ones I have. This leads, of course, to things that are put together *mostly* right and any number of small, leftover parts and pieces whose functions are vaguely guessed at. I keep them all, just in case. However, once they go into the container with all the others, it's pretty much impossible to pick the right ones out again. If a problem crops up, I usually just call Kevin, my handyman, and he sorts it all out in the end.

It would be better, of course, if I just followed the directions—all of the directions—through to the end. This concept is a biblical term called *obedience*. In our culture, obedience brings up images of small children and training classes for dogs. It does not, however, often conjure up adult obligations and certainly not any obligations to God. Whatever society says, obedience means doing what God wants, not necessarily what you want. It means God is in control and you are not. This isn't easy to do, and it doesn't come naturally. Again, it's why you need to commit to pick up your cross *daily*.

Why would you voluntarily pick up a cross daily, with all that metaphor conjures up? I understand the concept of the self-sacrifice of Jesus, and that's probably the "Sunday school" answer to that question—I pick up the cross to be like Jesus. Jesus, in addition, understands a concept that's more in line with the human condition—the concept of motivated self-interest. Hebrews 12:2 says, "Let us fix our eyes on Jesus, the author and perfecter of our faith, who for the joy set before him endured the cross, scorning its shame, and sat down at the right hand of the throne of God." One reason you should obey God is because it produces a beneficial outcome in your life. There is a positive reward at the end of the obedience. God is still the God of Jeremiah's time; if you obey God, things go well with you and you end up going forward, not backward; that's positive. People, of course, are still like people of Jeremiah's time and do the opposite, to deleterious effects.

Up to this point, you've heard a lot of talk about journeys and cars and road trips and rest stops. You've heard freeway analogies and fuel metaphors. For all of that, this is your life you're reading about. You want to find happiness in this one life you've been given. It's important; I venture to say there is nothing more important to you than your life and to be happy. There's nothing more important than your life; there's nothing *but* your life to give up in order to find happiness. That's what obedience is all about— giving up your control of your life and giving it over to God so that it can go well with you and you can go forward, not backward.

I don't think there is anything harder in this world to do. If you're having trouble with the concept of obedience, I understand. I feel the dilemma, the struggle, myself. The way I want to go is to hang on to the control of my life, to keep my life in order to save it. Do you remember the first verse of this chapter? It was: "There is a way that seems right to a man, but in the end it leads to death" (Proverbs 14:12; 16:25). What you think should work out won't; it ends in defeat. What appears to be a defeat—giving up control to God—ends up working out. Jesus puts it this way: "Whoever tries to keep his life will lose it, and whoever loses his life will preserve it" (Luke 17:33), and again, "The man who loves his life will lose it, while the man who hates his life in this world will keep it for eternal life" (John 12:25).

If you love your independence and think holding on to it will lead you to life and happiness, you are wrong. You must give up your independence, give up your control, listen and pay attention to God, and then be obedient to do what He says. This is the way you preserve your life and find happiness. Because this is so hard to do, it requires another tall order; it requires trust.

Trust the Navigator

Webster's dictionary defines *trust* in the following ways: "1 a: assured reliance on the character, ability, strength, or truth of someone or something; b: one in which confidence is placed."[1] In order to obey what God tells you to do, you need to be able to place your confidence in Him. That confidence is based upon His character, ability, strength, and truth.

God's character is clearly shown through the names He gives Himself. These are descriptors of His character. Regent University has a wonderful Web site at www.bible.org that outlines the names of God.[2] They are:

- *Elohim*—This is the plural version of the term *El*, which means "strong one," and refers to majesty. It is plural, signifying the triune nature of God.

- *El Shaddai*—"God Almighty." God is almighty, or as Luke 1:37 says, "Nothing is impossible with God."

- *El Elyon*—"The Most High God," stressing God's strength, sovereignty, and supremacy.

- *El Olam*—"The everlasting God." God does not change, nor does He wear out.

- *Yahweh Jireh*—"The Lord will provide." Note it doesn't say *might* or *could* or *may provide*; it says *will*.

- *Yahweh Nissi*—"The Lord is my banner." This signifies God as leading the charge in battle and providing victory.

- *Yahweh Shalom*—"The Lord is peace." This peace is global and personal (Isaiah 26:12).

- *Yahweh Sabbaoth*—"The Lord of hosts." God is the commander of the heavenly armies; He has spiritual resources at His command.

- *Yahweh Maccadeshcem*—"The Lord your sanctifier." God has sanctified you; He has set you apart for His purposes.

- *Yahweh Ro'i*—"The Lord my shepherd." (See Psalm 23, one of the most beautiful poems ever written.)

- *Yahweh Tsidkenu*—"The Lord our righteousness." God provides what you and I are unable to provide on our own.

- *Yahweh Shammah*—"The Lord is there," signifying God's personal presence. He is not a way-out-there, disconnected deity; He is there with you.

- *Yahweh Elohim Israel*—"The Lord, the God of Israel." You are included as a spiritual descendent of Israel.

- *Adonai*—"Master, authority, provider." This is also in the plural form, signifying God's triune relationship.

- *Theos*—"God." This is a Greek word, identifying God as the one true God, as unique, as transcendent, as Savior.

- *Kurios*—"Lord." Another Greek word, signifying authority and supremacy.

- *Despotes*—"Master," with the connotation of ownership. First Corinthians 6:20 and 7:23 remind you that you were bought with a price and are not your own.

- *Father*—I thought it was interesting that this form of the word is found only 15 times in the Old Testament but 245 times in the New Testament. Whatever else and whoever else God is, He is your heavenly Father.

Put all of these together, then, and this is who you are being called to place your confidence, your trust, in. What better place can you think of in which to place your trust? (You'll have an opportunity to actually answer that question in the Rest Stop coming up.)

According to the dictionary definition of *trust* given earlier, God has the character, ability, strength, and truth to be worthy of your trust. There is, however, a secondary definition I'd like to explore. It is "dependence on something future or contingent."[3] Do you remember Hebrews 12:2 mentioned earlier? It says, "Let us fix our eyes on Jesus, the author and perfecter of our faith, who *for the joy set before him* endured the cross, scorning its shame, and sat down at the right hand of the throne of God" (emphasis added). "For the joy set before him" points to this shading of definition for the word *trust*. Jesus endured because He was absolutely sure of and dependent upon something in the future, that *joy*. Jesus trusted God for what had not yet occurred. This future joy tomorrow helped Jesus endure today.

In the same way, you can trust God not only for what He can do for you today but also for what He will do for you tomorrow and into eternity. If all of this sounds too good to be true, too much like an evangelical infomercial, let me just say a couple of things. First, I agree, it does sound too good to be true. However, God is truth, so while it is entirely too good for the likes of me (and you, if I may be so bold), it is true. You can count on it; you can trust in God. Secondly, it becomes easier to understand and accept if you'll concentrate on the last word of the names of God, one of the two I added. Concentrate on God as *love*. God is trustworthy with your life and future and happiness because He *loves* you. He has demonstrated that love to you in the most graphic way possible, in the most compelling, convincing, convicting way possible—by sacrificing His one and only Son in your place so you can be made righteous and able to enter into intimate fellowship with this amazing, all-powerful, almighty, loving Father.

Remember, it's not about you; it's about God. You can trust Him because He has put in motion this eon-spanning, intricate, creative plan to outwit evil and death, slavery and bondage, sin and torment. All you have to do in response is, again, give up control, listen and pay attention, obey and trust.

Receiving the Instructions

I've often thought how nice it would be to literally have God as my navigator; for Him to lay or sit or stand or walk right beside me, saying things like, "Oh, don't go over there!" or "This is the one you should pick—definitely!" or "Just walk away. Don't look back; just walk away!" How great would it be to have God right next to me all the time? Of course, then God would see when I mess up, or argue with me when I deliberately make the wrong choice, or be there even when I'd rather He left me alone for a little bit.

This is just my way of compartmentalizing because God *is* always with me, around me, aware of me. I just don't always hear Him say, "Oh, don't go over there!" or "This is the one you should pick—definitely!" or "Just walk away. Don't look back; just walk away!" His direction to me is not always that easy or clear or definitive. Sometimes I have to look really hard to see what direction to go and listen very intently to hear His voice, and sometimes I still am not sure of the instructions. Sometimes it takes work and effort on my part to put myself in a position where I can hear God. Some people call this effort "spiritual disciplines." It's not my purpose here to try to answer doctrinal questions or step on denominational toes, but there are several things that I have found to be very helpful in my own life and in the spiritual lives of those I've counseled. I pass them along to you, like a piece of well-cooked fish (very biblical)—enjoy what you're able, and pick out what you're not.

Pray. This is your conversation with God. How do you know where He wants you to go or what direction to take to get there? Ask. Many people I know pray and talk to God pretty much on an ongoing basis during the day. They make themselves *aware* of Him and constantly touch base in prayer. Others find it helpful to designate a special time and place for prayer, one that is private and quiet and allows for introspection.

Meditate. This requires you to remain still and focused on a central theme or thought. It allows your mind to open up and for God to speak to you directly regarding the subject of your meditation. Of course, once you open your mind to God, He can decide what He wants to convey, so just be prepared; He may not follow your checklist.

Read. You're already aware that I'm reading through the Bible this year (OK, I'm a little behind so far, but I'll get there). Have you read the Bible all the way through? If you have, I'd encourage you to do it again, with the goal of asking God to reveal Himself to you through what you read. If you haven't, you're in for an adventure. The Bible says that Scripture is "God-breathed" (2 Timothy 3:16), so get ready to be blown away!

Journal. Keep a small notebook with your Bible. This is so you can write down your thoughts, prayers, questions, and God's answers. For many of our clients at The Center, we provide a journal for them to use during their recovery process. For those who embrace it, the journal becomes a conduit for their thoughts, feelings, and emotions. It becomes a real-time record of their journey to recovery. In the same way, a spiritual journey can become a real-time record of your faith journey. You would think that with something so important, so foundational, to a person's life, you'd remember every step along the way, but trust me; you won't. You will forget. Keeping a journal will help you remember how far you've come and, more importantly, remind you of God's faithfulness to you in your journey.

Study. Sometimes I don't understand what I read. It doesn't just jump out off the page into my comprehension. I have to really study the verse or the passage or the book in order to understand what God is saying. Could God just zap comprehension into my brain? Sure, and He has, but I also believe there is a value to spending time in studying and examining the Scriptures.

Seek counsel. This isn't something you have to undertake by yourself. God has placed books (like this one, if I can modestly say), Web sites, and materials in your path, to help you gain spiritual understanding. He also uses godly people to provide counsel for those seeking it. Proverbs calls these people *the wise.* Seek out wise, godly counsel if you have a problem or question you can't seem to find an answer to. The solution isn't somehow discounted because you didn't come up with it yourself. There are no points taken off for looking on someone else's paper or talking to your neighbor during a test in your life! So go ahead and ask for help.

Listen. As you've read already, you need to listen and pay attention. Listening requires you to do two things: stop talking yourself and focus on what the other person is saying. There is a time to cry out to God, and there is a time to be quiet. Ecclesiastes 3:7 says there is a time to be silent and a time to speak. Notice that the silent part comes first. There is a time to be quiet and wait for God to speak.

Your religious background may speak to you in other ways about how to find and receive instruction from God. These are from my own and are offered respectfully to you. Whatever your background, you may still need a little help to put all of this into perspective. If your emotional or relational life is compromised, you see a therapist or counselor. If your physical life is compromised, you see a physician. If all this spiritual information is simply too overwhelming for you, seek out a professional. That is, seek out spiritual counsel through specific people or a religious organization you trust. If you have trouble finding one you trust, keep looking and watching until you find one you do.

Before I get to the Rest Stop section for this chapter, I want you to think about one more word—*faith.* Hebrews 11:1 says, "Faith is being sure of what we hope for and certain of what we do not see." When dealing with God and scriptural things, you aren't always going to have everything tied up in a neat little theological package. You aren't always going to hear God as clearly or as loudly or as often as you want. During those times, you need this word *faith.* Hebrews 11:6 goes on to say:

And without faith it is impossible to please God, because anyone who comes to him must believe that he exists and that he rewards those who earnestly seek him.

When you don't understand what God wants for your life, have faith that you will. When you don't know which direction to go, have faith and be patient. When you don't hear God as clearly as you want, have faith that the truth will be revealed. When you don't hear God at all, have faith that He's still there and cares for you.

Turning over your life to God as the navigator is not an easy task, as I've said. It requires you to give up the control over your life, to listen to God and pay attention to His answer. It requires you to commit to being obedient and trust even when you don't like it or understand it. Before you jump right in on these things, I think it's a good idea to look at each one of them and determine what barriers might exist to successful implementation. You may want very much to do these things but find it hard to follow through. There may be assumptions, attitudes, or behaviors that hinder you in any or all of these areas. Before you can go forward, you need to figure out what might be holding you back.

Giving Up Control

There are people I come into contact with professionally who are controllers. They share many of the following characteristics:

- These are people who require a great deal of personal control over their lives.

- They are most comfortable when they know exactly what is going to happen and when.

- They are not spontaneous, easygoing people. Surprises are met with suspicion and hostility instead of with joy and delight.

- If an event does not happen just the way they planned or envisioned, they become upset and disappointed.

- If they are not in charge of an event, they are extremely uncomfortable. They either will attempt to assert control over some aspect of the event or withdraw and become sullen.

- They attempt to control the behavior of others by their own negative behavior, using hostility, sarcasm, anger, guilt, and shame to try to get their way.

- They tend to believe their perspective is the only correct one and are reluctant to accept different perspectives from others.

- They have been hurt in the past by the actions or attitudes of others and believe they can avoid pain in the future only by having firm control.

- They are extremely uncomfortable being wrong and rarely admit it, even when it is obvious.

- They spend a great deal of their time concentrating on the problems, issues, and lives of other people, generally with a condescending and superior attitude.

- They do not confess their faults to others but expend effort to either cover them up or pretend they don't exist.

- If confronted with a wrong, they will respond with excuses, reasons, and rationales, seeking to make the person who confronted them the one in the wrong for bringing it up in the first place.

- They are self-righteous in personal and religious matters.

How much do you see yourself in these descriptions? Be honest with yourself and admit even when you can see yourself partially reflected. The more of a controller you are, the harder it will be for you to give up control over your own life to God. Be aware that I've known very many religious people who are also controllers. They have all the outward appearances of piety, but instead of allowing God to control their lives, they retain control by personally interpreting what God wants—for themselves and others.

Write down the top three to five characteristics you see in yourself. These are characteristics I want you to be especially aware of. Ask God to reveal the depths of these characteristics in your life and expose the damage to you. Often, He will put you in contact with someone else who has the very same characteristic. This will allow you to begin to understand how your behavior and attitude affects other people. So, don't be surprised if some difficult people come into your life! Thank God for them, and learn how deeply the need for personal control is affecting your life. As you gain understanding, intentionally unclench your fists and let the control go. Start with small, everyday things, working up to bigger challenges. In all of these things, seek out professional counsel when appropriate to help you fine-tune your personality. There's no shame in wanting to become a better person, a more accepting child of God.

Listen and Pay Attention

Look over the list of ways you can look for God to speak to you. Again, they are:

- Pray
- Meditate
- Read
- Journal
- Study
- Seek counsel
- Listen

If you're already doing some of these, congratulations! Rededicate yourself to the task. If one or more of them have become stale or rote, switch it up.

- Choose a different place or time to pray or meditate.

- Try using a journal to record your prayers or meditations.

- Read a different translation of the Bible. Try one that you've never considered before.

- Switch it up. Be more structured with your study if you haven't been studying the Bible much, or, if you've been very diligent, change your study topics for the next six months; be more spontaneous. Start opening up the Bible at random, and study from there.

- Find a wise, godly person who you can be open and transparent with, seeking accountability and a sounding board for spiritual matters.

- Spend some time each day just calming your mind, opening it up, and listening to what God might want to say that day. Whenever possible, go outside and walk in order to get out of your environment and into His.

- Pay attention to what God is saying to you. Write it down as soon as you hear it. Use your journal or keep a small spiral notebook or pocketbook with you or available so you can make sure not to lose what you hear. Make sure to put it by your bedside, as God often has used the time of either going to sleep or upon waking to capture my undivided attention. (My wife, LaFon, sometimes hears a word from the Lord at odd hours of the night, so if you're like her, this will be very handy.)

Look over the list again, and star those you are currently doing. Put a circle by one or two you haven't been doing but are convicted that you need to start. Put an X by any you know you should do but somehow you've never been able to commit to. Consider working with an accountability partner on those with an X by them. This would be someone you like and trust, who can gently help you work through the barriers to any of these you know you should be doing but repeatedly don't.

Lastly, write down any additional ways you understand God can speak to you that aren't listed, and then go over them with the same star, circle, and X evaluation. Again, my list is by no means the definitive one, so if you wish, include any that are a part of your faith tradition.

Obey

Once you've begun to set aside your need for control, to listen to God and pay attention to what He's saying to you, you will start having a way to evaluate whether or not you are being obedient. It seems that one of the ways to determine your commitment to obedience can come—not through the things you should do—but through the things you shouldn't do. Over the course of this book, you've probably read about behaviors, attitudes, and actions you know you need to stop or modify. They could be regarding how you speak to yourself, your emotional equilibrium, or the emotions you choose to employ on a regular basis. They may be with how you treat other people or allow other people to treat you. They may be with what you should or should not be eating, or your level of physical activity.

God, hopefully, has been speaking to you all through this book. So, now you're at the obedience part. How are you doing? What is God asking you to do or to stop doing? Pick out three changes you believe He is asking you to make, and write them down next to the numbers below.

Next, write down the challenges these changes may present. Then, consider what reinforcements you might bring online to assist with the challenges. What can you do to meet and overcome those challenges? These could be things you need to do yourself or help you need to request of others. The goal here is to not accept defeat! (I'd recommend the first reinforcement under every challenge needs to be *prayer*.) Your goal with this part of the Rest Stop is to see what positive changes you can make in the next thirty days. Keep track, keep focused, keep working, and keep praying!

1. _____

Challenges:_____

Reinforcements:_____

2. _____

Challenges:_____

Reinforcements: _____

3. _____

Challenges:_____

Reinforcements: _____

Trust

For many of you, your reason for retaining control, for not wanting to listen or obey God, may have to do with a basic lack of trust. For whatever reason, you don't trust God to be careful with your life. You're afraid of what will happen to you if you give over control. You've placed more reliance and trust in other things than in God, and you're not ready or willing to give those things up. OK, it's time to be honest about the trust factor.

I'd like you to write down five reasons you have to trust God.

1. _____

2. _____

3. _____

4. _____

5. _____

Now, write down up to five reasons you have not to trust God.

1. _____

2. _____

3. _____

4. _____

5. _____

Which list took you longer to complete? The first or the second?

OK, more lists. I want you to write down five things, besides God, you put your trust in.

1. _____

2. _____

3. _____

4. _____

5. _____

I've added a number six below. This is so you have a second chance to write down that one thing you didn't want to put in the list above. This could be something you really do *not* want to acknowledge, articulate, or own. It's your own personal eight-hundred-pound gorilla in the corner. You know it's there, a part of your life, but you've gotten very used to just pretending it really isn't there. You don't want to acknowledge it, and you certainly don't want to write it down anywhere! Just do it anyway. Now is the time you're thinking about it and have the opportunity to be honest.

6. _____

You've just listed five, hopefully six, things you have chosen to place your trust in, apart from God. Now, I'd like you to write *why* you trust those things. What about them has proven to be worthy of trust? Realize some of these can be considered "good" things in and of themselves. They only take on a negative connotation when you trust in them more than you trust in God, when you rely on them in your life more than on God. Food, for example, is a good thing; it was given to you by God. But, if you are trusting in food to give you comfort and pleasure in this life, your relationship with food needs to be addressed.

You could be trusting in family more than God to take care of you. Family is a good thing, but if you are neglecting your relationship with God and substituting relationship with family members, you are shortchanging God, and this needs to change.

Going to church is a good thing. Scripture tells you not to neglect getting together with others to worship God (Hebrews 10:25). However, going to church can become a substitute for a relationship with God, which is certainly not what God intends.

After reading over these examples, are there any others you'd like to add to your list? If so, go back and make changes. This is your list, for your introspection and insight. As such, don't be surprised if you hear God speaking to you right now. If He is, listen, pay attention, and gain understanding.

Faith

Finally, I'd like you to consider your faith, as it is at the present time. This is not so you can critique it, to either bop yourself on the head or pat yourself on the back. Rather, it's just for you to provide yourself with a snapshot of where you think you are right now. Answer the following questions:

1. How much faith do you think you have in God? Go ahead and come up with a descriptor.

2. If God could do one thing for you to have more faith, what would it be and why?

3. If you could erase one thing from your past to help you have more faith, what would it be and why?

4. Are you the sort of person who needs to see something to believe in it?

5. How much are you like the man spoken of in Mark 9:24 who exclaimed to Jesus, "I do believe; help me overcome my unbelief!"

I firmly belief that the ability to increase faith is a gift from God. It is, therefore, certainly a subject for prayer and petition. Like the man above, it is perfectly reasonable to be able to say to God, "I have faith; help me overcome my lack of faith!"

Keep looking over this evaluation you've done, and keep working toward and praying for improvement. Again, think baby steps instead of huge, ground-swallowing leaps. You may get some of those—I certainly pray you do—but don't become discouraged if the pace is slower. You will be growing, learning, and drawing closer to God. Growing, learning, and drawing closer to God are the rewards. Relax, and enjoy the ride.

Chapter 10

THE ROLE OF OPTIMISM IN BEING HAPPY

I T'S ONE THING TO ARRIVE AT HAPPINESS; IT'S ANOTHER THING to stay there. If you're like me, I'm sure you've experienced that high of happiness due to circumstances, only to find out how quickly that high can dissipate. It is possible, however, to arrive at a state of happiness and stay there, instead of just stopping by for a quick visit.

A state of happiness is really a state of mind. It is a way of looking at the world and circumstances. One of the key components to this state of mind is learning to exercise optimism. In a pessimistic, negative world, this can be quite a challenge.

Undoubtedly, you have heard the adage about the difference between an optimist and a pessimist. The optimist sees the glass as half full, while the pessimist sees the glass as half empty. The pessimist chooses to focus on what is not in the glass; the optimist chooses to focus on what is. The operative word here is *chooses*. An attitude of optimism or an attitude of pessimism is a choice. Read this small vignette.

> Good morning, Pamela. How are you today?
> Lousy, Tracey. I got up late.
> But you're here on time.
> Yeah, but I didn't have time to do my hair right or iron the pants I
>   wanted to wear.
> You look fine to me.

Well, it's probably going to rain anyway, so doing my hair would
    have been a total waste of time.

It might rain, but it's sunny now.

It won't stay that way for long. I won't be able to get outside anyway.
    I have to work through lunch to get ready for that presentation.

I'm sure you'll do great. You always do.

The copier's down, so even if I get finished in time, I'll have to go
    over to Kinko's to run the presentation folders.

Conner called the copier guys already, and they said they'd be here
    this afternoon. It'll probably be fixed by the time you need it. If
    it's not, I'll be happy to run over to Kinko's for you.

Well, I'm waiting on Bill's part to finish, so even if the copier comes
    back online, it's still going to be down to the wire. I don't know
    why I always have to put these things together. It's so stressful!

Being asked to present is a wonderful opportunity! If they didn't
    like what you did, they wouldn't ask.

I don't know why they ask. It seems like only a third of what I
    suggest ever gets implemented.

It must be gratifying, though, to be able to affect company policy
    even that much.

Gratifying? No, not really. It's stressful, nerve-racking, and mostly
    futile. I'm hoping they'll stop asking me.

Well, cheer up! With your attitude, they probably will!

Have you ever had this kind of conversation with someone? If you have,
I'm sure it was a little irritating, whether you were the pessimist, Pamela, or
the optimist, Tracey. If you're the optimist, it can be irritating to have the
other person be so negative. If you're the pessimist, it's definitely irritating to
have the other person be so positive. The difference is Tracey will get over the
irritation a lot quicker than Pamela!

If you ask a Pamela why she's so negative or a Tracey why she's so positive, each will probably tell you that's just the way she is. People often believe
they are either born optimists or born pessimists. I firmly believe optimism
and pessimism are learned responses to life. Granted, the learning may
have started very early, so it can seem like you've been that way all your life.

The good news is, if you've learned to be pessimistic, you can change. And the first step toward change is admitting the way you are now.

If you are a pessimistic person, I want you to be able to proclaim it, to own up to it, and to accept it. What I have found over my years in practice is that pessimistic people often don't see themselves that way. In fact, while they view everything else as being universally negative, they tend to view their pessimism as positive. Instead of interpreting themselves as pessimistic, they instead see themselves as pragmatic, realistic, more informed and enlightened, savvy, and smarter. For them, a pessimistic response to the world is seen as protective and even superior to the optimist. Because they approach life believing the worst in circumstances and in people, they feel they are better prepared for whatever life throws at them. They live a guarded, cautious, defensive life. Problems, difficulties, inconveniences, and downright disasters are expected. They live their lives in perpetual fight-or-flight mode. Life, for the pessimist, is a battle to be confronted, factored, and endured. Every good thing that happens is an unexpected, short-lived surprise. Every bad thing that happens is confirmation of the correctness of their pessimism. Since people tend to want confirmation of their own opinions, they choose to focus on the bad things that happen.

Pessimists have what I refer to as a critical spirit. It refers to a person whose inner default mode is to be critical or negative. In *The Message*, Eugene Peterson uses the phrase "critical spirit" in translating Matthew 7:1–5:

> Don't pick on people, jump on their failures, criticize their faults—unless, of course, you want the same treatment. That critical spirit has a way of boomeranging. It's easy to see a smudge on your neighbor's face and be oblivious to the ugly sneer on your own. Do you have the nerve to say, "Let me wash your face for you," when your own face is distorted by contempt? It's the whole traveling road-show mentality all over again, playing a holier-than-thou part instead of just living your part. Wipe that ugly sneer off your own face, and you might be fit to offer a washcloth to your neighbor.

Picking on people, jumping on their failures, and criticizing their faults appears to be a positive, proactive position for pessimists. However, as this passage shows, doing so says more about your own faults than the faults of others.

Please don't misunderstand me. I have been in the counseling business too long to think that pessimists don't have very specific reasons for being this way. I have heard, literally, hours of reasons why a pessimist's attitude is really a good thing in his or her life. However, in my experience, I've found the reasons to spring from a deep well of pain, injury, abandonment, neglect, humiliation, abuse, and disappointment. Is it any wonder, then, with this kind of well, that what bubbles up in the life of a pessimist is bitterness and negativity?

Pessimism can seem like a more rational approach to life. There are problems, heartaches, catastrophes, and disasters in this world. There is disease and death. There are struggles, challenges, and defeats. When looking at the world, it can easily appear to be half empty, and what is there can appear very bitter. With such a worldview, pessimism can appear to be the most pragmatic approach possible. This is the worldview of the *wounded heart*. Pessimism, then, is a response to woundedness. No matter how superior you attempt to color your pessimism, it springs from pain, from a time in your life when you felt anything but superior. As long as you surrender to pessimism, happiness will only be short-lived in your life.

A pattern of pessimism can be very difficult to give up because it seems safe. If you've been wounded, it appears smart to venture out cautiously, carefully, defensively. Pessimism appears to be just the armor you need to engage a hostile world. Do you remember the scripture from the last chapter that talked about a way that seemed right but really led to death? Pessimism is one of those ways. It can seem very right to the wounded person, but it leads to death, a death of optimism. Pessimism becomes not an armor keeping the world out but a prison keeping you in. Pessimism is a world that says the worse thing that can happen to you is to be hurt by someone or something else. This is a world where hate triumphs, where evil flourishes, where wrongs outweigh rights, where oppression is standard and disappointment is the order of the day.

There's only one problem with this worldview; it's a *world*view. It's a view completely obscured by this world. It presupposes that all there is or is ever going to be is this world, with all its faults and problems. This is the type of world described in Ephesians 2:11–12. It is a view "without hope and God in the world."

But you do have hope, and God is in the world, so this worldview is a lie. Since the underlying assumptions of your pessimism are a lie, it's perfectly logical, rational, pragmatic, enlightened, and savvy to reject it and instead base your response to life on the truth. And what is truth? From the last chapter, you know that God is truth. Instead of a *world*view, have a *God* view. With a God view, your response to life can change from pessimism to optimism.

Exercise Your Optimism

Exercising your optimism may not seem natural at first. It may seem forced and manufactured. It may even seem foolish. You may even be called a *Pollyanna*. This term, meaning "a person characterized by irrepressible optimism and a tendency to find good in everything,"[1] comes from a novel of the same name by Eleanor Porter, written in 1913. The little girl in the story, Pollyanna, learns a game from her father called "the glad game." The goal of the glad game is to find the positive in every situation and concentrate on it and be thankful for it. A variety of negative and pessimistic characters in the novel are initially skeptical and derisive toward Pollyanna and her optimistic outlook. At the end, of course, Pollyanna wins over the hearts of the town of Beldingsville, improving their lives by spreading the benefits of optimism.

This change from pessimism to optimism is going to take practice. Your optimistic muscles have atrophied, while your pessimistic muscles are as pumped up as Mr. Universe. At first, it's going to feel pretty rocky, putting all your emotional weight on those shaky optimistic muscles. Again, baby steps. Start slow, start small, and play "the glad game" yourself. Begin to exercise your optimism one step at a time.

This is probably going to require that you have a Pamela-Tracey conversation with yourself. For every Pamela moment you have, you're going to need to come up with a Tracey response. For every pessimistic, negative thought, worry, or fear that pops into your mind, you're going to need to intentionally stop and search for a positive, optimistic response. You're going to need to go around saying, "Yes, but…" to yourself on a continual basis.

Yes, I did miss the bus, but another one will be along in fifteen minutes.

Yes, I did just get cut off on the freeway, but I don't have to let someone else's bad driving bother me.

Yes, the store is out of my size in the shoes I want, but they can order me the right size from another location.

Yes, the dog chewed my couch cushion, but I wanted to add some new color to the room anyway.

Yes, I was asked to do something at work I really don't like to do, but I'm glad I have the job and enjoy the people I work with.

Yes, I didn't get everything done I wanted to today, but there's always tomorrow.

Yes, I ate more cookies than I wanted to today, but this can help motivate me to make better choices tomorrow.

Yes, I'm tired and cranky, but I can choose to respond better than I feel.

Yes, I snapped in anger at my children, but I can apologize and ask for forgiveness.

Yes, I was laid off from work, but I am a valuable, employable person and am able to find and secure myself a new job.

Start out acknowledging the truth of how you feel. Feelings are your interpretation of events. However, feelings are not the last word on the subject. You may not be able to change the circumstances, but you can change how you feel about them. This is where the practice comes in. Acknowledge your initial feelings, and then intentionally choose how you are going to respond. You cannot dictate circumstances, for the most part. You can, however, dictate your response. Pessimism is a reaction; optimism can be a response. Even if your first reaction is pessimistic, you can choose to follow that up with a more optimistic response. This transformation to an optimist from a pessimist will take time. Give yourself that time through consistent baby steps. Begin with the smaller, more inconsequential events in your life, like missing the bus or your dog eating a couch cushion, and work your way up to more significant events like how you treat your family or respond to a job layoff.

Besides telling yourself, "Yes, but...," you will also need to tell yourself no in order to change from a pessimist to an optimist.

No, failure is not just one mistake away.

No, everybody is not out to get me.

No, it's not better to always expect the worst.

No, it's not better to be safe than sorry.

No, I am not the reason for everything that happens.

This process goes back to what you read in chapter 6, "Choose Your Station Wisely (Emotional)," dealing with all the negative messages that clutter up your thinking and keep you from expecting and experiencing happiness in your life. Those negative tapes are a large part of why you react to the world negatively. They teach you what to look for (negative things) and reinforce the negative interpretation of what you see and experience. The more you learn to rewrite those negative tapes, the smoother your transition from pessimist to optimist will become. And remember, it's not just erasing the old, negative tapes; you also have to rerecord new, positive ones. In order to do this, it's not enough to tell yourself, "Yes, but...," or "No." You must also tell yourself, "The truth is..." As you open yourself up to God as your spiritual navigator, the truth will begin to flood into your life. Instead of a bitter well of woundedness, you will be drawing from a spring of living water.

Again, you will need to have internal Pamela-Tracey conversations with yourself in order to move you beyond a pessimistic worldview and into an optimist God view. Here's how this might work: If you were hit with something pretty significant, like the loss of employment, your initial feelings are pessimistic as you consider this event nothing short of disastrous. However, you can intentionally decide to focus on the positive, even while acknowledging the circumstance:

Yes, I was laid off from work, but I am a valuable, employable person and am able to find and secure myself a new job.

Pessimism, however, will probably not give up with just one positive affirmation from you. The Pamela in you will probably counter with doubts, insecurities, and dire predictions of no one else wanting to hire you. In order to shield yourself from this level of disappointment, you may be tempted to just sink into depression, fearing the worst. Don't give in! Counter with one of your "no" statements:

No, it's not better to always expect the worst.

In order to bolster your "no" statement, which will probably continue to be battered by pessimism in quiet moments of doubt, counter with strong truth from God's Word. Hebrews 4:12 reminds you that the Word of God is living and active, sharper than any double-edged sword. God's Word becomes your defender of optimism against the assault of pessimism! When despair, defeat, and doubt threaten to overwhelm your best intentions, defend yourself with Scripture:

> I can do everything through him who gives me strength.
> —PHILIPPIANS 4:13

When you defend yourself with Scripture, you tap in to the truth and power of God. He becomes your shield and fortress, your refuge in times of trouble— all of those beautiful metaphors in the psalms. Read them, learn them, memorize them, use them, integrate them into the very core of your being and you will erase over your pessimism with God's optimism.

In John 4:1–42, there's a beautiful story of the meeting between Jesus and a Samaritan woman. If anyone had reason to be a Pamela, it was this woman. First of all, she's a Samaritan, an ethnic distinction which made her despised by the Jews. In addition, she's a woman with more men in her life than husbands, not an endearing characteristic at this time in history. She's a woman, which presented its own gender issues in her culture. Lastly, she's at a well at noon, during the hottest part of the day. I've heard it speculated that she wasn't exactly well liked in the community and went out to get water at this inconvenient and uncomfortable time to avoid other people.

All in all, this Samaritan woman had plenty of reasons to be negative. When Jesus first went to her, she was. He asked her for a drink of water, and she rudely asked Him what for. Up came the bitterness—He was a Jew; she was a Samaritan. He was a man; she was a woman. Why did He even despoil Himself to speak to her? (That's the sarcasm that can easily accompany pessimism as a shield.) They proceeded to have a very interesting conversation over water. She thought He was talking about the water in the well, and Jesus was talking about Himself as the living water. It's one of my favorite conversations recorded in Scripture because of the honest give-and-take between the two. For all her negativism, this woman doesn't hold back how she feels! And Jesus doesn't allow her negativity and rudeness to deter Him from continuing this vital conversation.

At the conclusion of the story, Jesus confronted this woman to change from the bitterness of negativity into the optimism of hope. Jesus spoke truth to her and named Himself as Christ, the Messiah. He treated her as someone worthy to be spoken to in the first place (contrary to the prejudice and tradition of the day) and as someone worthy to hear the truth. She was transformed from someone who avoided people to someone who proclaimed the truth she heard, and she is actually believed by the people in the town. This woman went from someone without hope and God in her world, to someone with a personal encounter with Jesus.

Truth can become a fountain of living water, washing out the bitterness of a pessimistic life. God can be your fountain of life, so you can say, "Within me is the fountain of life. His light shines through me." If your waters are bitter, if your light is dim, turn to God to provide living water and light into your life.

If you are unsure of what truth is, turn to God and take His word for it. When it's time to say, "The truth is...," turn to what God has to say. Again, I encourage you to find your own truths revealed in Scripture and make them your own. Let them become truths you live and operate by. Many years ago, I claimed a truth from God for The Center. It is from Jeremiah 29:11:

> "For I know the plans I have for you," declares the LORD, "plans to prosper you and not to harm you, plans to give you hope and a future."

Another of my favorite truths is found in the Book of Lamentations:

> I remember my affliction and my wandering, the bitterness and the gall. I well remember them, and my soul is downcast within me.
> —LAMENTATIONS 3:19–20

"Hold on," you may be saying right now. "This is pretty negative!" Yes, it is, but wait; there's more.

Yet this I call to mind and therefore I have hope: Because of the LORD's great love we are not consumed, for his compassions never fail. They are new every morning; great is your faithfulness.

—LAMENTATIONS 3:21–23

Jeremiah, in the midst of the total and complete destruction of everything he'd ever known—his country, his city, his life—remained an optimist because he understood the truth of God's love, compassion, and faithfulness.

Whatever you have experienced in your life, whatever has led you to respond with pessimism, you can change. God is able to give you the truth, the ammunition you need to face life with optimism. There's more to this life than this world. To be an optimist, commit yourself to Colossians 3:2: "Set your minds on things above, not on earthly things." To become an optimist, live by Philippians 4:8: "Whatever is true, whatever is noble, whatever is right, whatever is pure, whatever is lovely, whatever is admirable—if anything is excellent or praiseworthy—think about such things." Step by step, situation by situation, thought by thought, allow God to turn your well of pessimism into a fountain of optimism.

As I said, I believe it's very important for you to acknowledge your pessimism. Even if you consider yourself a fairly optimistic person, there are pockets of pessimism in just about everyone. I'm known as a very positive person, but I will be the first to admit there are areas in my life where I react with negativity and pessimism. My negativity and pessimism act as scabs over areas of pain and hurt. I continue to work through these areas day by day, step by step, turning them over to God and becoming strong enough to hope. You are not immune to such areas in your own life. So, no matter where you are on the spectrum, I encourage you to look inward and acknowledge your areas of pessimism. Take the time to evaluate yourself and write down the areas where you react with negativity.

This could be toward members of your family generally or in specific situations. You could be pessimistic about your job or financial security. You could be pessimistic toward your health or your ability to adopt a healthier lifestyle. You could be pessimistic in your approach to God, believing it's not possible for God to love you or for you to grow closer to Him. You could even be pessimistic about your ability to change in any significant way. Whatever it is, write it down! (Don't just *think* about it, actually write it down. By writing it down, by physically forming the letters and putting them on paper, you acknowledge the truth of it. Write it and own it. Then you can begin to change it.)

You may put down just a few or be able to fill an entire page. The number isn't the issue; being honest and specific is. For some of you, it may be beneficial for you to go back to chapter 6 and look over the Rest Stop for that chapter. Your negativity, your pessimism, springs from many of the things talked about in that chapter. Rereading what you wrote may allow you to include things you might miss or stimulate thought for this exercise. Also, take your time. This isn't a timed test. You may need to take a walk, pray, and meditate in order to complete this section. Pessimism can be such an ingrained, comfortable response to life and circumstances, it can become invisible. One of the best ways to get a read on your areas of pessimism is to ask a trusted friend or loved one. If you are in a relationship, this would be a good person to ask. Since opposites generally attract, you may be in a relationship with someone who is more optimistic than you are or is optimistic where you are pessimistic. Ask this person what he or she thinks your areas of pessimism are. Don't be defensive, and don't necessarily take what the other person says verbatim. Rather, use the answers to cause you to think and examine yourself.

Once you've acknowledged your areas of pessimism, it's time to consider why you've developed this negative response. Specifically pray and ask God to give you a spirit of discernment and courage to accept the truth.

Under each of the areas of pessimism you list, I want you to come up with at least one underlying assumption or belief that you have used to give credence to that pessimistic attitude. Wherever possible and applicable, write down either the event(s) or the person or people you first remember causing you to form that assumption.

Areas of Pessimism

1. _____

    Assumption: _____

    Truth: _____

2. _____

    Assumption: _____

    Truth: _____

3. _____

    Assumption: _____

    Truth: _____

4. _____

    Assumption: _____

    Truth: _____

5. _____

    Assumption: _____

    Truth: _____

This next part of the assignment may take you awhile, but I encourage you to continue with it until it's completed. I want you, in your personal study and prayer time, to begin to identify a truth from God that counters that pessimistic assumption. If you find you are having difficulty discovering these for yourself, I urge you to partner with another person, someone who is godly and trustworthy, to pray and study with.

Lastly, I want you to exercise your optimism. I want you to write down all of the positives you have in your life. James 1:17 serves as a reminder that "every good and perfect gift is from above, coming down from the Father of the heavenly lights, who does not change like shifting shadows." After each positive thing you put down, I want you to write a simple sentence of thanks and praise to God.

Just as writing down your areas of pessimism was important, to make it real and to own it, it is just as important to acknowledge and write down the good and positive things in your life. The glare of the negative can often blind you to the glow of the positive. It's time to turn down the glare so the glow can permeate your life, your heart, your soul, and your mind.

Positives in My Life:

1. _____

   Prayer: _____

2. _____

   Prayer: _____

3. _____

   Prayer: _____

4. _____

   Prayer: _____

5. _____

   Prayer: _____

6. _____

   Prayer: _____

You'll notice that I had you write down at least five areas of pessimism but six positives in your life. This is so you'll recognize that there are more positives in your life than negatives, because God loves you, has compassion for you, and has plans for you, plans to prosper you and not to harm you, plans to give you hope and a future. Count on it.

Chapter 11

The Role of Hope in Being Happy

OPE ISN'T REALLY A HAPPY EMOTION. HOPE IS NOT necessarily a giddy, bubbly, effervescent, here-and-now emotion. It's something much more complex, a response firmly based in the certainty of an unseen future. The dictionary defines *hope* as expecting with confidence.[1] The verb *expecting* clearly indicates the outcome is in the future. Because the outcome lies in the future, it is not visible in the present. Romans 8:24 says, "But hope that is seen is no hope at all. Who hopes for what he already has?" Hope is expecting with confidence something you can't see yet. It's a bit like the explanation of faith in Hebrews 11:1: "Now faith is being sure of what we hope for and certain of what we do not see."

Hope, then, is not a reaction based upon an experienced present but a response based upon an expected future. In this way, hope is like delayed gratification. You may not be experiencing in the present what you want, but you respond to those circumstances based upon what you expect to come to pass in the future. You expect to experience gratification, understanding it's not going to come instantly but rather at some point in the future. You are willing to wait because you expect with confidence that waiting will prove beneficial. In the same way, when things aren't going the way you want, you have to be willing to hope.

Hope, like delayed gratification, is a mature response to life. Listen to the progression, the maturation process:

Not only so, but we also rejoice in our sufferings, because we know
that suffering produces perseverance; perseverance, character; and
character, hope. And hope does not disappoint us, because God has
poured out his love into our hearts by the Holy Spirit, whom he has
given us.

—ROMANS 5:3–5

Hope is a learned response, gained through the school of suffering,
perseverance, and character development. No, it's not giddy, bubbly, or
effervescent, and it's not an adolescent emotion.

In some ways, hope has its most important work as a response to problems and struggles. *Hope* is the watchword of Old Testament people like
Job and Jeremiah, and of David. Each of them experienced hope in the
most profound way during times of great distress and personal turmoil. It
is hope, perhaps most of all, that anchors you deep into the positive and
allows you to weather times of drought and storm.

The Book of Job is one of unremitting suffering. God allows Satan to
remove from Job all of the things in this life you would normally ascribe to
being happy: wealth, possessions, and family. In the span of a single day, all
of that is wiped out. What is Job's response to this utter destruction of his
livelihood and his children? According to Job 1:20–21, he worshiped and
praised God, saying, "Naked I came from my mother's womb, and naked I
will depart. The LORD gave and the LORD has taken away; may the name of
the LORD be praised." This is an amazing, mature response to calamity!

The rest of the book details a series of conversations. Many are between
Job and his three friends, Eliphaz, Bildad, and Zophar, with Job protesting
his innocence of any wrongdoing contributing to all the problems in his
life. There are also conversations between Job and God. Job boldly asks to
present his case in front of God, who agrees and carries on an extended
conversation about His sovereignty over the earth and everything in it. In
the end, Job acknowledges he had no right to challenge God in his circumstances, and he repents. In Job 42, God restores Job and gives him twice as
much as he had before (vv. 10–12). Of course, this restoration is in no way
a certainty to Job throughout his trial. Way before his restoration in chapter
42, in Job 13:15, Job lays out his reason for acting the way he does. He says

of God, "Though he slay me, yet will I hope in him; I will surely defend my ways to his face." So, what was Job hoping for?

The Book of Jeremiah is likewise one of calamity and destruction. It outlines the destruction of Judah by the Babylonians. Jeremiah prophesied about this destruction. He repeatedly tries to alert the people and various kings to the coming catastrophe, but to no avail. It is a book filled with despair and destruction. Yet, it is also a book of hope and future, as Jeremiah 29:11 (my theme verse) says: "'For I know the plans I have for you,' declares the LORD, 'plans to prosper you and not to harm you, plans to give you hope and a future.'" Even in the midst of destruction, God was already promising His future restoration to Jeremiah.

Jeremiah goes on to write the Book of Lamentations, a poetic recitation of the destruction of Jerusalem. Do you remember the verses I mentioned earlier from Lamentations? "I well remember them, and my soul is downcast within me. Yet this I call to mind and therefore I have hope: Because of the LORD's great love we are not consumed, for his compassions never fail" (Lamentations 3:20–22). Jeremiah could look around him, in the face of a vast array of destruction, and have hope. So, what was Jeremiah hoping for?

David was anointed by God to be the king of Israel. When you think of a king, you probably think of palaces and power, feasting and fealty. That's not exactly what David experienced. When God chose David to be king, there was already a king in Israel named Saul. Saul, needless to say, wasn't thrilled about the change in leadership. His response? He set out to hunt David down and kill him. This failed, of course, and David was eventually declared king over Israel. It lasted a little while; long enough for his own sons to grow and rise up against him. David spent a great deal of his time hiding out, running from enemies, and dodging assassination attempts. Being persecuted in this way could have caused David to be a very pessimistic person. Yet, David writes beautifully of his hope in the psalms.

Consistently, in times of trouble and despair, David calls God a source of hope. David says God's Word is a source of hope, His name is a source of hope, and His laws are a source of hope. He says, "May my accusers perish in shame; may those who want to harm me be covered with scorn and disgrace. But as for me, I will always have hope; I will praise you more and more" (Psalm 71:13–14). Through all of his hardship, David chose to place his hope in God. What did David hope for?

David, Jeremiah, and Job all chose to hope for God to provide a positive future. This did not, however, mean they were not fully cognizant of the reality of their present. David was quite clear on the many persecutions and attempts made against his life; he understood the danger he was in. He chose, however, to focus on the hope of God's future for him. Jeremiah was quite clear on the reality of Jerusalem's destruction and Judah's captivity by the Babylonians; he understood God's judgment was absolute. He chose, however, to focus on the hope of God's future redemption for himself and for the people of Judah. Job was quite clear on the serious ramifications of his wretched condition; his eloquence describing his miserable state is considerable and compelling. He chose, however, to focus on the hope of God's future for him, to speak to God face-to-face.

Hope, therefore, is not a rejection of your present circumstance. On the contrary, it is an acceptance of it. For example, this is what is said of Abraham, concerning God's promise that he would have a child in his old age: "Against all hope, Abraham in hope believed and so became the father of many nations, just as it had been said to him, 'So shall your offspring be.' Without weakening in his faith, he faced the fact that his body was as good as dead—since he was about a hundred years old—and that Sarah's womb was also dead" (Romans 4:18–19). I really like that verse. Against all hope, Abraham in hope believed. Without weakening his faith, he faced the reality of his situation and still chose hope. Again, hope is not a rejection of your present circumstances. Paradoxically, as God often works, hope is strengthened in its quality by your present, hopeless circumstances. After all, if the outcome was something you could see or already had, it wouldn't be hope, would it?

What Are You Expecting?

By its very nature, hope is anticipatory; it expects a future outcome. It becomes very important, therefore, to be aware of what sort of future outcome you expect. An optimist expects a positive future; a pessimist expects a negative one. An optimist hopes for the best; a pessimist fears for

211

the worst. Hope and fear battle in your heart for supremacy. In order to be a happy person, the hopeful optimist needs to win.

Now, I have a bit of a problem with the dictionary definition of *hope*, which is to expect something with confidence. I have known many people, myself included, who have expected something with confidence, but that something was anything but positive. I have expected someone to let me down, and they have. I've expected a day to turn out lousy, and it has. I've expected the worst thing to happen only to experience it. Can I actually say I've hoped for these things to happen? My first reaction would be *of course not*! But on second thought, maybe there was a little bit of hope involved.

It could be I was hoping that person would let me down again so my negative opinion of them could be corroborated by their behavior. If I can count on that person's unreliability, it absolves me from ever again taking a risk and entrusting anything again to that individual. I can cross him or her off my list. It makes life (and my scorecard) easier to manage.

There are few things more irritating than being in a terrible mood and having a day full of sunshine and good events. It can make you feel even worse, especially if you've somehow decided you are justified in your dour demeanor. If life is lousy, what right has the rest of the world to strike a positive note? It could be I hope the day will turn out lousy so it will match perfectly my lousy mood. In this way, I am in harmony with the world, even though it's a dirge instead of a dance. After all, when I'm in a lousy mood, it is all about me. Me and my bad mood become the focal point of my world.

There is great tension in waiting, especially for something unpleasant. I have known people who appear almost relieved when catastrophe strikes. Instead of being mortified and troubled, they almost appear calm. They were so certain, so confident, in their expectation of disaster that they react with relief when the worst finally happens. After all, they just knew it was going to happen. Deep down, they hoped for it to happen as a way to put an end to that terrible state of waiting.

In some ways, then, pessimists don't just fear for the worst, but they also hope for the worst. Because they are so sure of bad things happening, when those bad things do happen, it is vindication of their negative expectations, verification of their superior prognostic skills, and justification for their continued state of negativity. When bad things happen, it is a huge *I told you so.*

It really takes no courage to be negative. It takes no great vision to predict gloom and doom. It takes no risk to predict that sooner or later something bad will happen. Pessimists are always right and never happy. In order to be happy, you need to risk being wrong.

Hope can appear to be a huge risk, and the greater the stakes, the larger the risk of disappointment and discouragement. When you look around you and all the signs point to a place without hope, it's a risk to disregard those signs and continue to have hope. Most people need something on which to base their hope, something tangible. So, what do you do when the divorce papers are final, or a loved one's cancer returns, or your attempt at reconciling has been rebuffed for the umpteenth time, or you've failed once again at changing that certain behavior? How do you dare continue to hope?

Here's how: You remember that hope that is seen is no hope at all. You remember that faith is being sure of what you hope for and certain of what you do not see. You remember that even though the worst thing has happened today, there is always tomorrow. You recite and claim the words of Jeremiah in Lamentations:

> Because of the LORD's great love we are not consumed, for his compassions never fail. They are new every morning; great is your faithfulness. I say to myself, "The LORD is my portion; therefore I will wait for him." The LORD is good to those whose hope is in him, to the one who seeks him; it is good to wait quietly for the salvation of the LORD.
> —LAMENTATIONS 3:22–26

Godly hope is no giddy, worldly, wishful thinking. Godly hope is rooted deep in faith and requires courage, patience, and love. You must have the courage to stand up against an impossible reality with the surety of God's sovereignty over the impossible. You must have patience to wait for God to reveal tomorrow the answers you ask for today. You must maintain your love for God in the face of overwhelming pressure to rage, feel bitter, and accuse.

Is hope a difficult thing to do? Absolutely. The more difficult the circumstances, the harder it can be to have hope. But what else is there? If there is no hope, what else is left? Hope is the last fortress to fall. Those who lose hope lose heart. When you lose heart, the pessimist wins.

If this, then, is the victory of the pessimist, I would rather be defeated as an optimist by life's circumstances. An optimist may be knocked down but will always bounce back up. An optimist will choose to continue to hope in the face of overwhelming evidence to the contrary. An optimist will cling to the anchor of hope when the winds of despair buffet and blow. And when the storm is over, the optimist will still be standing in hope. "For his anger lasts only a moment, but his favor lasts a lifetime; weeping may remain for a night, but rejoicing comes in the morning" (Psalm 30:5). A pessimist weeps for a lifetime; an optimist weeps for a night.

You must be in it for the long haul in order to experience happiness. If you focus your sight on the negatives of this world, they are all you will see. Instead, you must lift your eyes to heaven and gaze into the hope and future God has prepared for you. The dictionary says in order to hope, you must expect with confidence. Scripture says in order to have hope, you must expect *God* with confidence. God has been, is, and always will be the reason for you to have hope. It's not about you and your circumstances; it's about God and His sovereignty. You are bound by this life and its circumstances; He is not. God transcends this life and its negativity. Over and over again, He calls you to look to Him in hope of who He is. He asks you to *believe* in Him.

Do you believe? Then have hope. And don't be afraid to say, "I do believe; help me overcome by unbelief" (Mark 9:24). Remember, hope is not a reaction based upon an experienced present but a response based upon an expected future. This is a future planned for you by a loving and all-powerful Father who has said that He wants to prosper you and not to harm you. This is a message He so wants you to know and take deep into your heart. This is the message that will fuel your hope.

What Is the Worst Thing?

What is the worst thing you can think of happening? I can conjure up several in an instant, and just as quickly my mind retreats from the very thought. But I wonder sometimes if the list I could come up with—reluctantly—for the worst things that could happen to me are actually what God would put down. Before this chapter ends, I want you to explore a final idea about hope and about worst things.

Right after Jesus was crucified, if you asked the disciples if the worst thing had happened, they would have said yes. Their world was shaken, their teacher killed, their lives threatened, their hopes for the Messiah dashed, their faith rocked. Their view from Friday evening was bleak and hopeless. All they knew was Friday, for Sunday had not yet arrived.

God, however, is not a Friday-only God; He is also the God of Sunday. He knew Friday wasn't the end of the story. From the disciples' point of view, Christ's dying was the worst thing that could have happened. From the Christian's point of view, Christ's dying is the best thing that has happened. As a limited, finite, weak human being who desperately wants to have hope, I need to rely on God's transcendent point of view. With this point of view, I will be able to see Sunday in the midst of Friday.

God trumps the world. As Jesus was preparing His disciples for His departure, which they really didn't understand until after He was raised again, He told them this: "I have told you these things, so that in me you may have peace. In this world you will have trouble. But take heart! I have overcome the world" (John 16:33). God has overcome the world and all its trouble and negativity. God, in His omnipotence, has the ability to turn the worst thing into the best thing. He is that powerful; He is that loving. Because He is who He is, you and I have hope.

I'd like you to take some time right now and examine your own hopes. What do you hope for? I'd like you to take your time and really think about your life. Write down the top five. Try to cull them down into a single sentence.

What I Hope Will Happen:

1. _____

2. _____

3. _____

4. _____

5. _____

Now I'd like you to look over your list and think about it from a different point of view. You have just written down what you hope *to happen* in your life or in the lives of others. But, on the flip side, you have also named what you fear *won't happen* in your life and in the lives of others. Rewrite these.

What I Fear Won't Happen:

1. _____

2. _____

3. _____

4. _____

5. _____

Look over your hopes and your fears. Which is stronger right now—your hope or your fear? Fear is a very powerful emotion. It has the ability to threaten hope's place in your heart. You must intentionally give your fear over to God. You must believe that even if the worst thing were to happen, God is still reason enough to have hope.

You are not unique in this challenge. It is the challenge of every believer at some point in his or her life. These are times of spiritual crossroads when you must decide if you are going to take the path of fear or choose the road of hope. I cannot tell you the number of times I have watched people in my practice come to grips with this choice. Fear can seem the clearer path; hope can quickly appear to round a bend out of sight. I praise God that so many people have chosen to take the hope and found recovery. It's why, many years ago, our clients began to call us A Place of Hope, and so The Center remains to this day.

When you find an out-of-sight corner coming up on the road to hope, it's good to have something positive to concentrate on. I like to meditate on the promises of God when the road seems unclear. In chapter 8, you looked at the names of God. This was in order to understand and appreciate God's character so you would trust in His guidance and direction in your life. For this Rest Stop, I want you to focus on God's promises. I want you to realize that your hope is not wishful thinking without a rock-solid foundation.

Numbers 23:19 says, "God is not a man, that he should lie, nor a son of man, that he should change his mind. Does he speak and then not act? Does he promise and not fulfill?" These are the questions I want you to answer by going to God's Word.

At The Center, we provide the people who come to us with a variety of small gifts and items, as a way to help them get over their anxiety and fear about recovery. One of the most important items we give is a small book of God's promises. Of all the things we give, it's pretty small and unassuming, but it packs a powerful punch. I encourage you to go to your local bookstore or Christian bookstore and buy a copy of one of these types of books for yourself. There are many varieties; find one that fits your budget. Get it, read it, memorize it, internalize it.

In the meantime, you can also come up with your own personalized list of God's promises to you. One way to help trigger these thoughts is to read through the psalms and personalize what is written there for yourself. Take Psalm 1, for example. It says:

> Blessed is the man who does not walk in the counsel of the wicked or stand in the way of sinners or sit in the seat of mockers. But his delight is in the law of the LORD, and on his law he meditates day and night. He is like a tree planted by streams of water, which yields its fruit in season and whose leaf does not wither. Whatever he does prospers. Not so the wicked! They are like chaff that the wind blows away. Therefore the wicked will not stand in the judgment, nor sinners in the assembly of the righteous. For the LORD watches over the ways of the righteous, but the way of the wicked will perish.

Here is how I personalize this passage and claim its promises for myself:

> When I take the effort to evaluate those I associate with and choose to be swayed by the godly, I am blessed by God.
>
> Reading Scripture is not a passive pastime; it is an active pursuit, filled with delight.
>
> When I am rooted in God, I am refreshed and see the produce of my labor and success.
>
> God is not influenced by this culture but knows who is for Him and who is against Him.
>
> God promises to watch over me and will vindicate me.

Please don't be surprised or disturbed if what you read and interpret as God's promises to you through that passage are different from mine. That's the beauty of Scripture—God is able to speak to you individually. And I will tell you that if I had done this exercise ten years ago, what I wrote down would have been different from today. If I do this ten years from now, it will be different again. God can speak to your heart today, right now, and give you what you need to believe in His promises and place your hope in Him.

Sometimes, in order to set yourself for the future, it's important to go back over your past. I'd like you to think back over a time in your life when something negative happened to you. I want you to go back to that time and remember how you were feeling and what you thought was going to be the outcome:

1. What happened to you?

2. What did you think was going to be the outcome?

3. Did what you think would happen actually happen?

4. Was there anything positive that happened during this time? If so, what was it?

5. How have you changed as a person because of what happened to you?

6. How have you changed in a positive way as a person because of what you experienced?

7. Are you afraid of something similar happening again? If yes, how often do you worry about it?

8. If yes, are you ready to give up your fear to God and ask Him to remove it from you?

9. If you are over the fear, thank God for your deliverance and name another fear you want Him to defeat, as He did this one.

Finally, I'd like you to come up with an affirmation statement, why you choose hope instead of fear. It could be something like:

I choose to hope because God is greater than my fear.

I choose to hope in the midst of my fear because God has promised to be with me.

I choose to hope today and look at the positives instead of choosing fear and dwelling on the negatives because God is a God of the positive.

I choose hope over fear because God has overcome the world.

I choose hope over fear and claim God's victory in my life.

You are welcome to choose one of the examples above or, by all means, pray and create one or more of your own. In order to experience happiness for life, you must grow and mature in your ability to hope in God and His future.

I recognize that some of you reading this may feel the need for assistance in working through some of these exercises. If that is you, please don't consider it a defeat. It just means it's time for you to bring in reinforcements. Depending upon the level of assistance you need, you can turn to a loved one, a trusted friend, or a caring professional to assist you. There are resources available for you to strengthen your ability to hope, to mature, and to grow in your ability to expect God's future in your life with confidence. Don't give in to fear; choose the victory of hope.

Chapter 12

THE ROLE OF JOY
IN BEING HAPPY

I LOVE THE WORD *JOY*. MY FAVORITE CHRISTMAS HYMN IS "JOY TO the World." To me, joy is embodied in how I feel singing that song. The words are so evocative, speaking as they do of hearts preparing room for the Lord and heaven and nature singing at the coming of Christ. In the last chapter, I said that hope isn't exactly a giddy, bubbly, effervescent emotion. Those descriptors are more associated with joy. Joy is an emotional expression of deep satisfaction and happiness.

The dictionary defines *joy* as "the emotion evoked by well-being, success, or good fortune or by the prospect of possessing what one desires," and it is the "expression or exhibition of such emotion." Joy is called "a state of happiness" and the words associated with it are *rejoice, delight, gaiety,* and *bliss.*[1] Wow! No wonder I like this word!

Scriptures also equate joy with strong emotion and extreme happiness. In the Bible, the word *joy* is used almost two hundred fifty times. God, as the source of joy, is tightly woven. Here are just a few of the *joy* verses from the Book of Psalms:

> The LORD is my strength and my shield; my heart trusts in him, and I am helped. My heart leaps for joy and I will give thanks to him in song.
> —PSALM 28:7

> Sing to him a new song; play skillfully, and shout for joy.
> —PSALM 33:3

Clap your hands, all you nations; shout to God with cries of joy.

—PSALM 47:1

Satisfy us in the morning with your unfailing love, that we may sing for joy and be glad all our days.

—PSALM 90:14

Shout for joy to the LORD, all the earth, burst into jubilant song with music.

—PSALM 98:4

There's just a lot of leaping and singing, clapping and playing, shouting and being glad in the word *joy*. It's an in-the-moment, fill-up-your-heart kind of emotion. It's an emotion that demands a physical response. You need joy to be a happy person. Joy is the spark that uses the tinder of optimism to ignite the fuel of hope.

But there's more to joy than just a spark. Think about the last time you made a fire. Maybe you were out camping or having a barbeque in the backyard. The spark ignites the fuel, and fire springs up with enthusiasm. The wood pops and smokes, and the flames spout up into the air. When the fire is flaming, however, is not when you stick in your marshmallows or put on your meat. Instead, you wait for the flame to settle down and the fire to sink deeply into the coals. The true heat reduces down and radiates from within the coals or wood, usually without a great deal of flame. I think joy is a little like this.

Joy is certainly the springing and sprouting into the air of hot emotion, with all the popping and sparks flying into the air. However, joy is also like a banked fire, contained and potent. It is just not possible to continually go through life with over-the-top emotion. Sometimes life is just plain hard. Yet, Philippians 4:4 says, "Rejoice in the Lord always. I will say it again: Rejoice!" That sounds like a command to me. It's taken me awhile to figure out how to reconcile a life that's often hard with a command to always be joyful.

Joyful Hope

What I've come to understand is that for you to rejoice over some of the challenges you face in life, you need to maintain a banked fire of joy. That fire is up to the task of warming your heart at all times and perfectly capable of exploding in fireworks at others. In order to keep the fire going, you need to offer up all of the experiences of your life for joy to consume—the good and the bad, the happy and the sad, the understood and the inexplicable. Just as Pollyanna's father taught her to play the "glad game," God calls us to play the "joy game," which is really no game at all. Rather, it is a way of intentionally responding to circumstances, regardless of the circumstances.

Now, before you go beating yourself up because this seems like a very tall order, indeed, remember that joy is one of the fruits of the Spirit (Galatians 5:22). This is not innate human nature here; rather, it is divine intervention and provision. God Himself is able to empower you with joy as a gift. And in this world, you're going to need it.

Joy, like hope, is most often evident in situations that are far from joyful. When you are joyful over understandable, recognizable, common-place things and situations, it's still joy, but the challenge of the command is having joy when times are hard. The understandable joy is the spark. Inexplicable joy is the coal. Happiness is found in both.

Whenever my hometown baseball team, the Mariners, win, I am filled with joy. It's not the same flavor of joy, though, that I feel when my young son, Gregg, looks up at me and tells me a deep spiritual truth he's learned and just then able to articulate. To see on his face that moment of compre-hension and faith is absolutely precious and fills my heart with inexpress-ible joy. Both can be called joy, but they are different. While I certainly want to experience the Mariner-type of joy in my life, my soul needs to experience the Gregg-type of joy for me to be truly happy.

This type of joy is hard won. It, like hope, is a mature response to life. This kind of joy, also, often comes through experiencing hardship. Romans 5:3 says, "Not only so, but we also rejoice in our sufferings, because we know that suffering produces perseverance." The rest of that passage goes on to say that perseverance produces character; and character, hope. This is also expressed in James 1:2–3: "Consider it pure joy, my brothers, when-ever you face trials of many kinds, because you know that the testing of your faith develops perseverance."

When you learn to rejoice in whatever your circumstances, you strengthen your ability to hope and to persevere. Some days I wish that I could be strengthened just through ease and enjoyment instead of having to go through hardship and suffering. Of course, I realize that my growth as a person most often comes through overcoming adversity. I have no doubt that many of you are nodding your heads in agreement, even as a small sigh escapes your lips. You, like me, learn the hard way.

You also need to realize that God is a realist. Knowing that hardship and suffering are simply part and parcel of your life, He in His wisdom has factored in a way for you to grow, mature, and find joy in the unavoidable things. It's a tall order but is explained, in part, in Romans 12:12: "Be joyful in hope, patient in affliction, faithful in prayer." I'd like to break this verse down, phrase by phrase. It's short but powerful.

In this verse, again, you see hope and joy intertwined. If you need to exist in a state of hope—in a state of expecting but not yet experiencing—you might as well do it with an attitude of joy. If you truly have hope, if you are confident of what you don't yet see, why wait to be joyful? Experience the joy today of tomorrow's hope fulfilled. Because God Himself is the guarantor of your hope, it's a solid bet. You can count on it, so take joy in it!

Next, this verse tells you to be patient in affliction. I admit to having difficulty with this one. I want my affliction to be over *now*. But if I always want my affliction to be over right now, it means for almost the entire length of the affliction—until right up to the very end—I don't get what I want. Doesn't it make sense, then, to learn to be patient within the affliction? This attitude can seem like giving up to some. However, patience and hope are not mutually exclusive; you can be both patient and hopeful at the same time. Patience is submission to circumstances beyond your control, and hope is assurance in one who has control. If you have to take a long journey, impatience is like a pebble in your shoe. You can still walk the road with the pebble, but it makes every step noticeable. When the road is difficult already, why add the pebble of impatience? Being patient allows you to walk the path and focus on the overall goal instead of focusing on each individual step.

It would be impossible for me to handle the first two parts of that verse without the last—be faithful in prayer. Again, this attitude of rejoicing in suffering and being patient in affliction is not part of my general makeup. I need help from God and the Holy Spirit to accomplish and experience this in my life. So do you. This is why you must approach this challenge on your knees, asking God to empower you. Through prayer, you exhibit to God your submission to Him, your belief in His supremacy over your life, and your trust in His love for you. Prayer gives you the power to pull this off, and what a payoff it is! As Paul wraps up this discussion in Romans, listen to what he says in Romans 15:13: "May the God of hope fill you with all joy and peace as you trust in him, so that you may overflow with hope by the power of the Holy Spirit." When you are joyful in hope, patient in suffering, and faithful in prayer, God will fill you with all joy and peace because of the trust you have in Him. This filling up from God allows you to overflow with hope through the power of the Holy Spirit. Having this attitude of joy is not something you can manufacture on your own. It is God at work within you, through the power of His Spirit, to allow you to transcend a natural response to hardship and suffering and respond, instead, with divinely inspired joy. With God at work within you, you will be able to say each day of your life, no matter what comes, "This is the day the LORD has made; let us rejoice and be glad in it" (Psalm 118:24).

This joyful attitude warms your own life and radiates out to warm the lives of others. A truly joyful, optimistic, positive person is wonderful to be around. Because they act in ways that are so contrary to how people usually handle situations, they are immediately noticeable. Others are aware that these people are different. In this way, God is glorified through your ability to exhibit joy in difficult circumstances. Your joy becomes a living testimony to others. You radiate out.

Usually when negative or pessimistic people suffer, they become incredibly inward focused. Their world shrinks and collapses in on itself, coalescing into a self-absorbed core. This core can become so dense with negativism and pain that other people get sucked in and depleted. Interacting with a pessimistic person who tends to always suffer from something can suck the joy right out of you if you're not careful. Being around them makes you feel drained.

I have had the privilege to be around joyful, optimistic people who were undergoing hardship of incredible proportions. I have gone to visit them, fully intending to try, in some small way, to offer comfort and instead found myself receiving much more comfort. Here they are, in dire physical or circumstantial straights, and they end up doing more for me and my attitude than I ever did for them. Their complete reliance on God and the Holy Spirit to get them through the situation is crystal clear. I go to give them comfort, and they wind up giving me hope.

Their attitude is summed up for me in a passage from one of the minor prophets, Habakkuk. It's a small book, only three chapters. Like Jeremiah, it was written at the time of the Babylonian invasion of Jerusalem. Like Job, it contains a series of conversations with God. Habakkuk doesn't understand why God is working the way He is (using the Babylonians to punish Judah and Jerusalem), seeming to allow evil to oppress His people. In the end, Habakkuk comes to understand that God really does have the final say and will make sure justice prevails, even though it will not come about in Habakkuk's lifetime.

At the end of the book, Habakkuk's final words hauntingly echo in my heart as they speak to me of today's hope anchored in tomorrow, of joy expressed defiant of circumstance, of optimism tightly grasped in trust:

> Though the fig tree does not bud and there are no grapes on the vines, though the olive crop fails and the fields produce no food, though there are no sheep in the pen and no cattle in the stalls, yet I will rejoice in the LORD, I will be joyful in God my Savior. The Sovereign LORD is my strength; he makes my feet like the feet of a deer, he enables me to go on the heights.
>
> —HABAKKUK 3:17–19

I don't know what you personally are going through or what might have prompted you to pick up this book. If it was a time of prolonged sadness or tragedy, please know my heart goes out to you. And if it were only my heart I could give you, frankly, it wouldn't be enough. What I can offer you is to embrace the attitude of Habakkuk. Pray and ask God to empower you through His Spirit to experience joy within your situation. For God, nothing is impossible. The reality of this world is set; hardships and suffering are a given. God will not always remove the impossible situation from you, but He is always able to fill your heart with joy.

One way God can fill your heart with joy is through prayer, as you've read. Being in constant communication with God, to receive His Spirit and perspective on life and what you're going through, is integral to a life of joy. Another way to experience joy is through worship. This doesn't necessarily mean only in a religious building or at a religious event. God is worshiped when you offer your life up to Him on a daily basis through the routine events of life. Worship focuses your attention on God and instills reverence and awe. In worship, you acknowledge God for who He is, in all of His attributes. This is the same God who loves you and has promised to care for you. When the world and its problems seem far too large for you to handle, prayer and worship to God can bring it back down to its proper size. When the world and its negativity threaten to suck the joy right out of you, drawing near to God can cause it to flood back into your life. When the road of life gets bumpy, joy acts like spiritual shock absorbers and allows you to still enjoy the ride.

What to Move Aside

As you've seen, joy is something to be experienced in all circumstances. In a way, then, joy transcends circumstances even within the midst of them. You are to have an attitude of joy, no matter what comes your way. So, how do you go about making this a reality in your life, especially if joy doesn't come easily to you? Again, think baby steps. First, I want you to think about situations that most people would consider appropriate for joy. I want you to think about naturally happy occasions, times of celebration or praise. These are the "easy" circumstances where joy should be a given. However, in your case, they may not.

When LaFon and I were teaching both little Gregg and Benjamin to walk, we kept the distance between us small at first and removed any obstacles in their way. In other words, if the floor was strewn with toys, we'd move those out of the way before launching our little one. After all, it was challenging enough for Gregg or Benjamin to get the mechanics of walking down without having to navigate over stuffed animals, books, or plastic toys. In the same way, if joy is an emotion you're unfamiliar with or new to, before you launch out on in baby steps, you may want to remove any obstacles from your path.

One of the biggest obstacles you may need to move aside is perfectionism. Joy is not like your in-laws; you don't have to have everything perfect before joy can come to visit. A woman I know had a daughter who recently got married. The wedding itself should have been an occasion of great joy. Instead, she related it to me in terms of stress, disappointment, and anger. Why? She complained about the color of the groom's mother's dress because it clashed with hers in the pictures. The music was too loud while the vows were too soft. The bride and groom, against her most adamant wishes, chose to smear wedding cake all over each other's faces instead of sedately feeding a small corner of cake to each other. Every objection she raised was inconsequential, in my eyes. She, however, was unable to experience the joy of the event because her focus was on the minutiae and the need for everything to fit into her pattern of perfection. Her obsessive perfectionism cast a pall over this most joyful occasion. She was angry and resentful that others in her family weren't as upset as she was. The wedding was now a source of contention among the family instead of an event of collective joy.

Another obstacle to experiencing joy is fear. What trips people up is refusing to enjoy today because of what could possibly happen tomorrow. This is the domain of the pessimist, who fears what may happen tomorrow regardless of the good that took place today. This is the man whose performance anxiety crowds out any joy at his job promotion. It's the woman who approaches the joy of a vacation to a brand-new destination with the fear of the unknown. This is the man who greets his son's athletic accomplishments with fear as a condemnation of his own age and physical decline. It's the woman who views a move to a new city as an ending instead of as a beginning. Fear has the ability to completely extinguish the spark of joy.

Anger also has a way of putting up obstacles to experiencing joy. Angry people are rarely joyful people. Instead, the intensity of their anger incinerates the beginnings of any other emotion, including joy. Anger simply has no room for anything else. Because joy is an emotion that is outward focused and anger is an emotion that is inward focused, they are incompatible. A persistent, deep-seated anger must be addressed and mitigated before you will have the ability to experience true joy.

You may be able to experience joy in events concerning other people but are unable to experience joy when it relates to your own life. The obstacle here is shame. For some reason, you may believe you are unworthy of experiencing joy for yourself. You allow yourself to experience feelings of joy through other people but deflect any feelings of personal joy over yourself, your situation, or your accomplishments. You are uncomfortable accepting a compliment. Any good thing that happens to you feels wrong and could only have happened because those involved don't really know you. When pressed to accept the good thing, you can become angry because others naturally expect you to feel a joy you do not. This disconnect may cause you to self-sabotage times of celebration through excuses, other commitments, or illness. You're the first one to give accolades to others but the very last to accept it for yourself. There is no joy in these situations, only a reminder of how unworthy you are to experience them.

Any of these conditions—perfectionism, fear, anger, or shame—can cause you to miss out on experiencing joy in life's naturally happy circumstances and situations. These are the "easy" circumstances for joy. If it's difficult for you to experience joy in these instances, imagine how difficult it's going to be for you to experience true joy in the midst of more challenging circumstances. Before you start taking on the distance of that kind, you're going to need to clear your path of obstacles.

I'd like you to think back over your life and write down significant events that most people would consider ones of celebration and joy. These could be births, weddings, graduations, promotions, birthdays, family reunions, first job, first apartment, first house, etc. Write down what most people would typically consider a happy occasion, even if you don't necessarily feel that way about it yourself. I've put down space for five, but go ahead and use a separate piece of paper, if necessary, to write down as many as you can remember.

"Happy" Occasions

1. _____

2. _____

3. _____

4. _____

5. _____

Now, ask yourself the following questions about each:

1. Did you experience joy at this event?

2. Did you experience other emotions as well? If so, what were they?

3. Looking at the list of any other emotions, what category could you put them into:

    *   Perfectionism

    *   Fear

    *   Anger

    *   Shame

4. As you think of each event, which emotion is forefront in your mind?

5. Have you ever been surprised at your reaction to one of these events? Did you expect to be influenced by perfectionism or feel fear, anger, or shame but actually felt more joy than you thought?

6. Can you pinpoint what might have been different about this event that allowed you to feel more joy than you anticipated?

7. How has your ability to experience joy changed over the years? Is it becoming easier or harder? Why do you suppose that is?

I'd like you to do this for all of the events you wrote down. What I'd like you to do is look for an obstacle pattern. What is the shape of your obstacle? What is its name? Once you've determined its shape, it's time to determine where it came from.

Do you recognize the shape of your obstacle as being similar to the obstacles you perceive in others you know, such as others in your family? If so, you may be mirroring someone else's inability to experience joy. This response to life is often learned, due to family patterns or familiarity. If this is the case, it's time for you to disengage from that other person's way of thinking. Stop looking to him or her as the arbiter of your response, and start looking to yourself and the joy you can receive from God.

This obstacle is a point of view, a way of looking at life. I want you to name the point of view, using the name of the person you associate it with. Whenever you feel this way, call it what it is, using the name. Disown it for yourself. Remind yourself, it doesn't have to be yours. Instead, take owner-ship of your point of view and choose joy. Be like Pollyanna and play the "glad game."

If you find your ability to experience joy has grown easier over the years or was easier for a specific situation, this is definitely worth exploring! Work to identify what it is about this change or that specific situation that made it easier for you to experience joy. You will want to support and strengthen these elements in your life. It may be a positive person you've met or a loving relationship that has allowed you to see yourself in a better light. It may be a growing dependence on God and His Word. It may be the birth of a child or another significant event that has colored how you view your-self and the world. It may even be personal work you've done with a thera-pist or other counseling professional. Celebrate your personal growth and commit yourself to continuing along the path of growth.

These are resources you want to utilize now and have available to you when the inevitable happens. Jesus said you will have trouble (John 16:33). He didn't say *if*, or *maybe*, or *might*; He said *will*. These resources can be of great assistance to you when these troubles come, to allow you to transcend them and find God's joy within them. Start using your baby steps on the "easy" circumstances, strengthening yourself and your optimism, hope, and joy for the long run.

Your greatest resource, of course, is a deep and personal relationship with God. He is the reason for lasting optimism, hope, and joy in this world. This attitude isn't something you can manufacture and maintain on your own; it is a gift of God. This gift is one available to you through His Spirit and one He desires for you to have. You don't have to earn it, just accept it and reach for it. Then, having obtained it, use it to your heart's content and God's glory.

THE ROAD LESS TRAVELED

I N THIS WORLD OF DIFFICULTY AND DOUBT, OF STRUGGLES AND hardships, of compromises and second choices, of injustice and affliction, each person comes to a crossroads in life. There are two roads with signposts on each that say, "Way to Happiness." On the one hand is the road championed by the world, which promises much and delivers little. This road is taken by a vast array of people who are tricked into believing the billboards along the way. Those inducements, even your own internal dialogue, for taking this road can be compelling because of all of their glitzy promises. Instead of happiness, though, this road can lead to depression, anxiety, and addiction.

There is another choice, another road. However, this road can appear less attractive when compared with the first. Because of this, it is a road less traveled. This is the road of faith, which uses a cross for a talisman. It does not say, "Take this road to avoid your pain." It says, "Take this road because of your pain." The one road promises you'll be in control. The other says you must give it up. The one appears all about pleasure. The other appears all about sacrifice. In the heat of the moment, it can be hard to make the right choice.

American poet Robert Frost, in one of his most popular works, "The Road Not Taken," illustrates the importance of the choices made in life in the last stanza of the poem:

> I shall be telling this with a sigh
> Somewhere ages and ages hence:
> Two roads diverged in a wood, and I—

I took the one less traveled by,
And that has made all the difference.*

In other words, you've come to a fork in the road—two paths promising to lead you to your desired destination. However, the one you choose may not be the most popular, but it may lead you to *true* happiness.

I guess what I want to leave you with is an exhortation to take the road less traveled because it will make all the difference. The world's road eventually leads to a literal dead end. God's road leads to eternity. Because it can be so difficult to choose the road less traveled, here are just a few things to remember as you stand at the crossroads each day:

- Happiness is a response to life that comes from the inside of a person, not from outside circumstances.

- Happiness is a gift from God, based upon His goodness and mercy apart from circumstances.

- Depression isn't something you live with; it's something you get help for.

- Worry and anxiety are a learned response to life that can be acknowledged, understood, and overcome.

- Addictions both mask and amplify pain; they never heal it.

- What you tell yourself becomes who you are, so be careful what you say.

- Relationships are meant to support you, not drag you down.

- Taking care of your body helps you take care of your heart, soul, and mind—all are used to love God.

- Stop trying to control your own life, and start trusting in God to get you where you need to go.

---

* Excerpt from "The Road Not Taken" from *The Poetry of Robert Frost*, edited by Edward Connery Lathem. Copyright 1916, 1969 by Henry Holt and Company. Copyright 1944 by Robert Frost. Reprinted by permission of Henry Holt and Company, LLC.

- An attitude of optimism is a choice.

- Hope is a response based on an expected future, not a reaction to an experienced present.

- Joy is the spark that uses the tinder of optimism to ignite the fuel of hope.

- Even if happiness isn't a path you've taken before or it seems artificial or unfamiliar, go down the path anyway, taking baby steps.

- Each day presents you with a new opportunity to be happy.

- Each failure today points the way to success tomorrow.

- Sometimes the clearest lesson you receive today is confirmation of where you *don't* want to go tomorrow.

- Don't let anything get in the way of getting the help you need. Ask…expect…act.

- Don't wait on others to hand you happiness; take hold of it yourself.

It just didn't seem right to end without giving you one last opportunity for reflection on all you've experienced working through this book. I'd like you to go back through the Rest Stop sections—or even just what comes to mind as you've read over my few concluding statements—and write down at least three of your own to add to the list.

Try to write them down as succinctly as you can. Each of these statements becomes a powerful present you give to yourself. Each takes essential truths and understandings and packages them together into a short sentence or phrase. Just by reading or saying the sentence or phrase, you can unwrap and release the whole meaning in your mind. This is a vital way you provide encouragement, motivation, and comfort to yourself. Memorize them. Put them on sticky notes on your bathroom mirror or refrigerator, on the dashboard of your car. Start each day by reciting them, agreeing all over again that they represent how you choose to live today.

As you embrace this new way of thinking, living, and responding, may you, in the words of Paul, come "to grasp how wide and long and high and deep is the love of Christ, and to know this love that surpasses knowledge—that you may be filled to the measure of all the fullness of God" (Ephesians 3:18–19). May this overpower the strongholds of depression, anxiety, and addictions in your life. May this be a fountain of unending happiness, the reason for your optimism, the source of your hope, and the reservoir of your joy.

> *Father, there is nothing that You cannot do. I ask You to transform and renew each person who reads this book, through the power of Your Spirit. Give each one strength to persevere and courage to continue each day. Help each one to grow and mature in their trust in You. Reveal in each life, in a unique and personal way, the happiness that is the desire of their hearts. Fill them up to the brim with this happiness, and allow them to overflow in joy to those around them. May each become a source of happiness and blessing in this world until He comes.*

Resource List

Below are other books I've written, some of which were referenced in this book, along with some other helpful resources. For more information about my work and The Center for Counseling and Health Resources, please go to www.aplaceofhope.com or give us a call at 888-771-5166.

Other books by Dr. Gregory L. Jantz

The Body God Designed: How to Love the Body You've Got While You Get the Body You Want. Lake Mary, FL: Siloam, 2007.

God Can Help You Heal. Lincolnwood, IL: Publications International, Ltd., 2006.

Healing the Scars of Emotional Abuse. Grand Rapids, MI: Fleming H. Revell, 2003.

Healthy Habits, Happy Kids: A Practical Plan to Help Your Family. Grand Rapids, MI: Fleming H. Revell, 2005.

Hope, Help, and Healing for Eating Disorders. Colorado Springs, CO: Waterbrook Press, 2002.

The Molding of a Champion: Helping Your Child Shape a Winning Destiny. Green Forest, AR: New Leaf Press, 2006.

Moving Beyond Depression: A Whole-Person Approach to Healing. Colorado Springs, CO: Waterbrook Press, 2003.

Thin Over 40: The Simple 12-Week Plan. New York, NY: New American Library, 2004.

Too Close to the Flame: Recognizing and Avoiding Sexualized Relationships. West Monroe, LA: Howard Publishing Co., Inc., 1999.

The Total Temple Makeover: How to Turn Your Body Into a Temple You Can Rejoice In. West Monroe, LA: Howard Publishing Co., 2005.

Turning the Tables on Gambling: Hope and Help for an Addictive Behavior. Colorado Springs, CO: Waterbrook Press, 2001.

Other resources for *Happy for the Rest of Your Life*

Bellezzo, Jeanne, ed. *Dance Until It Rains: Inspiring Stories of Everyday Persistence.* Melrose, FL: No Dream Too Big Publishing, 2007.

Cloud, Henry. *9 Things You Simply Must Do to Succeed in Love and Life: A Psychologist Probes the Mystery of Why Some Lives Really Work and Others Don't.* Nashville, TN: Integrity Publishers, 2004.

Hawkins, David. *Dealing With the CrazyMakers in Your Life: Setting Boundaries on Unhealthy Relationships.* Eugene, OR: Harvest House Publishers, 2007.

Hansen, Mark Victor, and Art Linkletter. *How to Make the Rest of Your Life the Best of Your Life.* Nashville, TN: Thomas Nelson, Inc., 2006.

Luciani, Joseph J. *Self-Coaching: How to Heal Anxiety and Depression.* Hoboken, NJ: John Wiley & Sons, Inc., 2001.

McWilliams, Peter, and John Roger. *You Can't Afford the Luxury of a Negative Thought: A Book for People With Any Life-Threatening Illness—Including Life.* Los Angeles, CA: Prelude Press, 1989.

Myers, David G. *The Pursuit of Happiness: Who is Happy— and Why.* New York: William Morrow and Company, Inc., 1992.

Shimoff, Marci, with Carol Kline. *Happy for No Reason: 7 Steps to Being Happy From the Inside Out.* New York: Free Press, 2008.

Tracy, Brian. *Focal Point: A Proven System to Simplify Your Life, Double Your Productivity, and Achieve All Your Goals.* New York: Amacom, 2002.

Treat, Casey. *How to Be Your Best When You Feel Your Worst.* New York: Berkley Praise, 2008.

Notes

Chapter 1—Detours on the Road to Happiness

1. "Seattle Residents Among Nation's Most Educated," May 10, 2004, U.S. Census Bureau, http://www.census.gov/Press-Release/www/releases/archives/american_community_survey_acs/001802.html (accessed August 25, 2008).

2. *Merriam-Webster's Collegiate Dictionary*, 11th ed., s.v. "job."

3. Ibid., s.v. "career."

4. Rick Warren, *What on Earth Am I Here For?* from *The Purpose-Driven Life*, (Grand Rapids, MI: Zondervan, 2004), 5. Also available at http://pddocs .purposedriven.com:8088/docs/pdl/samplechapters/woeaihf.pdf.

5. *Merriam-Webster's Collegiate Dictionary*, 11th ed., s.v. "ubiquitous."

Chapter 2—Make Sure to Use MapQuest

1. *Merriam-Webster's Collegiate Dictionary*, 11th ed., s.v. "happiness."

2. Ibid., s.v. "well-being."

3. Benjamin Franklin, *Poor Richard's Almanac* (White Plains, NY: Peter Pauper Press, Inc., 1986), 45.

4. Robert Young, LL. D., Wm B., *Analytical Concordance to the Bible* (Grand Rapids, MI: Eerdman's Publishing Company, 1964), 98.

5. *Merriam-Webster's Collegiate Dictionary*, 11th ed., s.v. "meek."

Chapter 3—The Detour of Depression

1. World Wide Words, "Waiting for the Other Shoe to Drop," http://www .worldwidewords.org/qa/qa-wai1.htm (accessed September 18, 2008).

Chapter 4—The Detour of Worry and Anxiety

1. The Word Detective, "Worry Wart," August 2007, http://www.word -detective.com/2007/07/31/worry-wart/ (accessed September 19, 2008).

2. *Merriam-Webster's Collegiate Dictionary*, 11th ed., s.v. "worrywart."

3. Ibid., s.v. "worry."

4. Ibid., s.v. "anxiety."

5. National Institute of Mental Health, "Generalized Anxiety Disorder (GAD)," http://www.nimh.nih.gov/health/publications/anxiety-disorders/generalized-anxiety-disorder-gad.shtml (accessed September 19, 2008).

6. National Institute of Mental Health, "Panic Disorder," http://www.nimh.nih.gov/health/publications/anxiety-disorders/panic-disorder.shtml (accessed September 19, 2008).

7. National Institute of Mental Health, "Social Phobia (Social Anxiety Disorder)," http://www.nimh.nih.gov/health/publications/anxiety-disorders/social-phobia-social-anxiety-disorder.shtml (accessed September 22, 2008).

Chapter 5—The Dead End of Addictions

1. National Institute on Alcohol Abuse and Alcoholism, "FAQ for the General Public," http://www.niaaa.nih.gov/FAQs/General-English/default.htm#experience (accessed September 22, 2008).

2. Ibid.

3. Ibid.

4. Ibid.

5. Peyton Whitely and Sharon Pian Chan, "Blood-Alcohol Level of Woodinville Driver Breaks State Record," *Seattle Times*, April 19, 2007, http://seattletimes.nwsource.com/html/localnews/2003672880_webalcohol19m.html (accessed September 22, 2008).

6. Peyton Whitely, "Ex-Detective Pleads Guilty to Two DUI Charges," *Seattle Times*, April 18, 2008, http://seattletimes.nwsource.com/html/localnews/2004357402_jarrett18e.html (accessed September 22, 2008).

7. National Institute on Alcohol Abuse and Alcoholism, "News and Events," http://www.niaaa.nih.gov/NewsEvents/NewsReleases/NESARCNews.htm#chart (accessed September 22, 2008).

8. National Institute on Drug Abuse, "Marijuana," http://www.drugabuse.gov/DrugPages/Marijuana.html (accessed September 22, 2008).

9. Ibid.

10. National Institute on Drug Abuse, "Cocaine," http://www.drugabuse.gov/DrugPages/Cocaine.html (accessed September 22, 2008).

11. National Institute on Drug Abuse, "Heroin," http://www.drugabuse.gov/DrugPages/Heroin.html (accessed September 22, 2008).

12. National Institute on Drug Abuse, "Prescription Medications," http://www.drugabuse.gov/drugpages/prescription.html (accessed September 22, 2008).

13. Ibid.

14. Sam Skolnik, "Problem Gamblers Abandoned," *Seattle Post-Intelligencer*, February 25, 2004, http://seattlepi.nwsource.com/local/161939_gambling25.html (accessed September 22, 2008).

15. Focus on the Family, Gene McConnell and Keith Campbell, "Pornography," http://www.family.org/lifechallenges/A000000208.cfm (accessed September 22, 2008).

16. Ibid.

17. National Institute on Alcohol Abuse and Alcoholism, "FAQ for the General Public," http://www.niaaa.nih.gov/FAQs/General-English/default .htm#whatis (accessed September 22, 2008).

Chapter 6—Choose Your Station Wisely (Emotional)

1. Christine Clarridge, "Kent Teen Who Died Apparently Didn't Hear Sound of Oncoming Train," *Seattle Times*, April 23, 2008, http://seattletimes.nwsource .com/html/localnews/2004367164_train23m.html (accessed September 22, 2008).

2. Ibid.

Chapter 8—Make Sure to See Your Mechanic (Physical)

1. Mike Strobbe, "Too Much, Too Little Sleep Tied to Ill Health in CDC Study," *Seattle Times*, May 9, 2008, http://seattletimes.nwsource.com/html/ health/2004397675_apsleepobesity.html (accessed September 23, 2008).

2. Jeffrey M. Ellenbogen, "Cognitive Benefits of Sleep and Their Loss Due to Sleep Deprivation," American Academy of Neurology, http://www.neurology.org/ cgi/content/full/64/7/E25 (accessed September 23, 2008).

3. MedicineNet.com, "Dehydration," http://www.medicinenet.com/ dehydration/article.htm (accessed September 23, 2008).

Chapter 9—God as Your Navigator (Spiritual)

1. *Merriam-Webster's Collegiate Dictionary*, 11th ed., s.v. "trust."

2. J. Hampton Keathley, "The Names of God," Bible.org, http://www.bible.org/ page.php?page_id=220 (accessed September 25, 2008).

3. *Merriam-Webster's Collegiate Dictionary*, 11th ed., s.v. "trust."

Chapter 10—The Role of Optimism in Being Happy

1. *Merriam-Webster's Collegiate Dictionary*, 11th ed., s.v. "Pollyanna."

Chapter 11—The Role of Hope in Being Happy

1. *Merriam-Webster's Collegiate Dictionary*, 11th ed., s.v. "hope."

Chapter 12—The Role of Joy in Being Happy

1. *Merriam-Webster's Collegiate Dictionary*, 11th ed., s.v. "joy."

Index

agoraphobia 84, 89

alcohol abuse 92

alcohol dependence 92, 107

alcoholic 92

alprazolam (Xanax) 94

American Academy of Neurology 163

American Association of Christian Counselors 136

American Medical Association (AMA) 161, 162

anorexia, anorexic 15, 103–104, 117

Beatitudes, the, beatitude 38–39, 48

bulimia, bulimic 103–104, 117

Centers for Disease Control (CDC) 163

cocaine 94, 108

compulsive shopping 90, 102, 115

detox programs 108

dextroamphetamine (Dexedrine) 94

DHA (docosahexamoic acid) 162–163, 170

diazepam (Valium) 94

diphenoxylate (Lomotil) 94

driving under the influence of alcohol (DUI) 23, 26, 92–93

drug abuse 76, 93–94, 113

dysthymia 50

eating disorders 36, 40, 90, 93, 103–104, 117

EPA 162–163, 170

Focus on the Family 100

food pyramid 158

Franklin, Benjamin 29

Frost, Robert 232–233

Gamblers Anonymous 113

gambling 79, 90, 96–97, 106, 109–113

generalized anxiety disorder (GAD) 80–81, 88

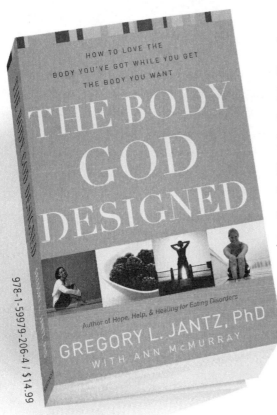

— ANDREA —

You are such a beautiful
soul and it was a blessed
opportunity to have met
you at this point in your
life. Continue to be who
you are and remember
you are well equipped for
this life. Stay you!

A. Tierra